ANIMALS IN PERIL

HOW "SUSTAINABLE USE" IS WIPING OUT THE WORLD'S WILDLIFE

ANIMALS IN PERIL

HOW "SUSTAINABLE USE" IS WIPING OUT THE WORLD'S WILDLIFE

JOHN A. HOYT

Avery Publishing Group

Garden City Park, New York

Cover design: William Gonzalez
Typesetter: Bonnie Freid
Printer: Paragon Press, Honesdale, PA

Photographs: Leonard Lee Rue, Jr. (pages 4 and 194); Leonard Lee Rue, III (opposite title page and pages xii and 82); Dick Randall (pages 178 and 226); and Teresa Telecky (page 128). Used by permission.

Cataloging-in-Publication Data

Hoyt, John A., 1932–
    Animals in peril : how sustainable use is wiping out the world's
wildlife / John A. Hoyt
    p. cm.
    Includes bibliographical references.
    ISBN 0-89529-648-9
    1. Wildlife conservation. 2. Endangered species. 3.
Sustainable development—Environmental aspects. 4. Economic
development—Environmental aspects. 5. Man—Influence on nature.
6. Wildlife management. I. Title
QL81.7.H69 1994   333.95'16
                                      QBI94-1875

Printed in the United States of America.

10   9   8   7   6   5   4   3   2   1

Contents

Acknowledgments,   *vii*

Foreword,   *ix*

Introduction,   1

Part I   The Myth of Sustainable Use

Introduction,   7

1. Sustainable Use of Wildlife—Utopian Dream, or Unrealistic Nightmare?   9

2. Case Studies of Sustainable Use,   39

Part II   The Fight to Save the Elephants

Introduction,   85

3. America's Chance to Save Africa's Elephants,   89

4. The Poaching Explosion of the 1980s: Wiping Out Half of Africa's Elephants,   95

5. How to Stop the Poaching: Ban the Ivory Trade, or Keep It Going?   109

6. The Poachers' Last Stand at Lausanne,   115

7. The Move to Lift the Ivory Ban,   129

8. The Debate Over Culling—Conservation or Commerce?   149

Part III How to Save the World's Wildlife—
   Humane Sustainable Development

Introduction,   181

9. The World Bank: Subsidizing Destruction
   as Development,   183

10. Ecotourism: True Sustainable Use,   195

11. Appreciating Animals for Their Own Intrinsic
    Value,   215

Conclusion,   227

Notes,   229

Index,   247

This book is dedicated to all who respect the place of animals on this planet and understand the value of life.

CREDITS

Excerpts on pages 7–8, 25, 28–29, and 63 are from "The Limits to Caring: Sustainable Living and the Loss of Biodiversity," by John G. Robinson, which appeared in the March 1993 issue of *Conservation Biology*. Used by permission of Blackwell Scientific Publicatons, Inc.

Excerpts on pages 9, 12, and 139 are from "Wildlife's Last Chance," by Michael Satchell, which appeared in the November 15, 1993, issue of *U.S. News & World Report*. Copyright © 1993 by U.S. News & World Report. Used by permission.

Excerpts on pages 14 and 63 are from "Biologists Fear Sustainable Use Is Unsustainable Idea," by William K. Stevens, which appeared in the April 20, 1992, edition of *The New York Times*. Used by permission.

Excerpts on pages 14, 24, 25, and 26–27 are from *Caring for the Earth*, published in 1991 by the United Nations Environment Program. Used by permission.

Excerpts on pages 29–30 and 63 are from "Uncertainty, Resource Exploitation, and Conservation: Lessons From History," by Donald Ludwig, Ray Hilborn, and Carl Walters, which appeared in *Science* Vol. 260 (1993). Copyright © 1993 by the American Association for the Advancement of Science. Used by permission.

Excerpts on pages 34 and 35 are from "Wildlife Conservation as Wealth," by Valerius Geist. Reprinted by permission from the April 7, 1994, issue of *Nature*, copyright © 1994 by Macmillan Magazines Limited.

Excerpts on pages 44–45 and 46 are from "Can Parrots Be Conserved Through Sustainable Harvesting?" by Steven R. Beissinger and Enrique H. Bucher, which appeared in the March 1992 issue of *BioScience*. Used by permission.

Excerpts on pages 57 and 61 are from "U.S. Fishing Fleet Traveling Coastal Water Without Fish," by Timothy Egan, which appeared in the March 7, 1994, edition of *The New York Times*. Used by permission.

Excerpts on page 58 are from "The Cod Shortage," by Tom Knudsen, which appeared in the March 22, 1994, issue of the *Wall Street Journal*. Reprinted by permission of the Wall Street Journal © 1994 Dow Jones & Company, Inc. All rights reserved worldwide.

Excerpts on pages 77 and 211–212 are from "A Conservationist Argument for Hunting," by Raymond Bonner, which appeared in the May 14, 1993, issue of the *Wall Street Journal*. Reprinted by permission of the Wall Street Journal © 1993 Dow Jones & Company, Inc. All rights reserved worldwide.

Excerpts on pages 74–75 are from "$100,000 to Kill a Doddering Rhino?" by Bill Keller, which appeared in the December 27, 1992, edition of *The New York Times*. Used by permission.

Excerpts on pages 91, 118, 119, 120, 125, 129, 145, 149, 152, 157, 160–161, and 175 are from *Battle for the Elephants* by Iain and Oria Douglas-Hamilton © 1992 by Iain Douglas-Hamilton. Used by permission of Viking Penguin, a division of Penguin Books USA Inc.

Excerpts on pages 98, 99, 101–102, 131, 146–147, 156, and 164–165 are from *Under Fire: Elephants in the Front Line* published by the Environmental Investigation Agency, Washington, D.C., April 1992. Used by permission.

Excerpts on pages 122, 125, 134, 135, 137, 149, 151, 153, and 155–156 are from *At the Hand of Man* © 1993 by Raymond Bonner. Used by permission of Alfred A. Knopf Inc.

Acknowledgments

There are several people and organizations whom I wish to thank for their help on this book, which was the result of a real team effort by several colleagues, friends, and staff members of The Humane Society of the United States (HSUS).

HSUS President Paul G. Irwin oversaw and guided the book through a maze of obstacles and details, and his support and encouragement were crucial to its completion.

The idea for the book was originally conceived of and initiated by HSUS vice president for investigations David Wills, whose on-the-scene investigation of the plight of Africa's endangered elephants and rhinos forms part of the basis of the book. Mr. Wills also serves as executive director of Humane Society International.

I relied heavily on the expertise of HSUS's Dr. John W. Grandy and Dr. Teresa Telecky, whose extensive knowledge of the wildlife trade made an invaluable contribution to the book's substance.

Other HSUS staffers and consultants who provided extremely helpful guidance and materials are executive vice president Patricia Forkan; Kitty Block; April Adams; Michael O'Sullivan; Wayne Pacelle; Naomi Rose; Michael Winikoff; Allen Rutberg; Susan Hagood; Nancy Waterman; Debra Firmani; and Jean Redzikowski, whose tireless work researching and providing material for the book were indispensable.

I am also most grateful for the very valuable material and data provided by my distinguished colleagues from other organizations, including Christine Stevens, president of the Animal Welfare Institute; Allan Thornton and Dave Currey of the Environmental Investigation Agency; and Heidi Prescott of the Fund for Animals. I am also grateful for the assistance provided by Constance Flindt, Emilie Posner, and Patricia Olvera, who expertly typed the manuscript.

I wish to express special appreciation to Lewis G. Regenstein, who organized, researched, and compiled most of the data and material used in this book. And finally, I am grateful to my executive assistant Janet Frake, without whose assistance and support most of my efforts, including this book, would not have been possible.

John A. Hoyt
Chief Executive, The Humane Society
    of the United States
President, Humane Society International

Foreword

The twentieth century will be known as the era when the foundation was laid either for the conservation of the world's wildlife or for its destruction. The decisions we will be making in the next few years will be crucial in deciding which outcome will characterize our century.

For much of this period, wildlife conservation meant protecting animals and their habitats. Much of the progress that has been made in protecting wildlife has consisted of the enactment of laws banning the killing, capture, and trade in certain animals, and the setting up of preserves where they and their habitats would be safe from human disturbance.

But there is a new wind blowing through the conservation movement, especially in Africa. We are now being told, by those said to be the "experts," that the old strategies are outmoded and out of date. Modern conservationists, it is said, realize that the best way to save animals is to give them economic value, having them "pay their own way" through international trade in live bodies or dead parts.

Once called "consumptive management" of wildlife, the principle now goes by the much gentler and more scientific-sounding name of "sustainable use." And the term has become the rallying cry of a new generation of big game hunters, traffickers in wildlife—and even some powerful conservation organizations.

The concept of sustainable use seems almost too good to be true—a way to have your cake and eat it, too. It is invariably portrayed as a sort of conservation panacea, a strategy to meet the needs of people, industry, the environment, and even the animals themselves.

But like King Solomon's proposal to divide in half the baby claimed by two mothers, sustainable use has turned out to be provocative in theory but unworkable in application. Dividing up wildlife among various groups of "users" works no better than cutting babies in two.

Indeed, an examination of the species and populations of creatures that have been subjected to consumptive "sustainable" use shows that, almost without exception, they have been decimated, depleted, and destroyed. As a 1993 report by the U.S. Marine Mammal Commission observes, "virtually all species and stocks of wild living resources . . . which are being harvested commercially are being depleted."

Elephants represent the classic case of the supposedly sustainable use of a species. During the 1980s, when wildlife protectionists were trying to stem the massive slaughter of elephants by banning the ivory trade, we were repeatedly assured by governments and certain conservation groups that the industry was not the culprit, and even that ivory trading was a beneficial form of "sustainable use."

As is documented in the pages that follow, the orgy of poaching only ceased when the ivory trade was finally banned in late 1989, after more than half of Africa's elephants had been killed. But the sustainable use lobby is *still* working to reinstate international trade in ivory and other elephant products. Similarly, as the international commerce in parrots has pushed species after species of these beautiful, intelligent birds to the brink of extinction, the pet industry and its allies have continued to defend this exploitation as a viable form of sustainable use.

The list of "utilized"—and ultimately devastated—species goes on and on. Indeed, virtually all animal-exploiters and nature-rapers have begun to justify their destruction of wildlife and the environment as a form of "sustainable use" or "sustainable development." Even when these terms are used to refer to the most blatant, uncontrolled exploitation, they are now widely accepted and popular with governments, development agencies, and, most distressingly, many conservation organizations.

This book is the first to expose the myth of sustainable use and to document its almost unbroken record of failure. Sustainable use has been used as a cover to justify the exploitation, and ultimately the devastation, of elephants, parrots, whales, seals, ocean fish, and numerous other animal species. Unless the concept as currently employed can be discredited and abandoned, many other now-protected and abundant animals will be subjected to unsustainable destruction under the pretext of sustainable use.

There is, of course, such a thing as true sustainable use—humane sustainable use, as I call it. Ecotourism is one example. But true sustainable use is controversial too, for it threatens the profits of certain industries and governments that benefit from the slaughter and suffering of wild animals. Where it falls short, to many of its critics, is in failing to provide elephant tusks to ivory merchants, animal skins to the fur industry, parrots to the wild bird pet trade, and so on.

Because it leaves animals alive, humane sustainable use will always be opposed or belittled by those individuals and industries that rely on the consumptive exploitation of wildlife, as well as by their allies in the conservation movement, such as the World Wildlife Fund and the International Union for the Conservation of Nature.

Only when we learn to appreciate animals for their own intrinsic value will their future be secure. Their lives and their being must have value in and of themselves. Until recognition of that value becomes the norm, the fight over how to "sustainably use" wildlife will continue to be the conservation struggle of the decade. Its outcome could well determine which species will survive the newest justification and rationale for the ongoing exploitation and persecution of wildlife.

Paul G. Irwin
President, The Humane Society
  of the United States
Washington, D.C.

Introduction

If we want to protect bald eagles, should we open up a hunting season on them? In order to ensure the conservation of dolphins and whales, is it necessary to "utilize" them commercially? If we want to save wildlife in our national parks and preserves, should we open them up to hunting and trapping, so as to give the animals economic value?

While such propositions may sound absurd, they are logical extensions of the rapidly spreading philosophy of wildlife management called "sustainable use." According to this concept, in order for wildlife to survive, it must "pay its own way" by being "utilized" to produce economic benefits.

Adopting this principle—which governments around the world, including our own, have done—could eventually mean removing protection from numerous vulnerable and even endangered species. It could require the amendment of the U.S. Marine Mammal Protection Act to allow renewed commercial killing of whales, seals, porpoises, dolphins, sea otters, polar bears, sea lions, walruses, and other ocean mammals. It could mean changing the U.S. Endangered Species Act to permit commercial exploitation of many now-protected imperiled species.

If this sounds alarmist and unrealistic, consider the fact that efforts are now underway to change certain rules governing the Convention on International Trade in Endangered Species of Wild Fauna and Flora (CITES, the 122-nation group that is supposed to protect imperiled wildlife from excessive commerical trade), so that the killing of and commercial trade in various endangered creatures—including humpback whales, chimpanzees, Asian and African elephants, cheetahs, and other internationally protected species—may be permitted.

Indeed, the principle of sustainable use is being used to help promote the lifting of the current ban on international trade in ivory and other elephant products, and to justify the "sport" hunting and commercial killing of these magnificent creatures. And the International Whaling Commission, with the support of the U.S. government, has a adopted a "revised management scheme" to manage the commercial killing of whales, if and when the current moratorium on commercial whaling is overturned.

If the concept of sustainable use is put into widespread practice, it will necessitate a radical and dangerous restructuring of U.S. and international wildlife protection laws, regulations, and strategies. With sustainable use, wildlife would be managed—under the guise of conservation—in such a way as to maximize its commercial value as a source of ivory, fur, hides, trophies, pets, and other such "products."

These abrupt changes in current conservation policy by those responsible for protecting the world's wildlife are being undertaken quietly, behind the scenes, largely without the knowledge or consent of the general public. The only thing preventing the universal application of the concept of sustainable use has been strong and effective opposition from wildlife protection and preservation groups. But many tough battles lie ahead, and the outcome may well depend on how vocal the public is on these issues.

The growing acceptance of the doctrine of sustainable use by governments and certain "conservation" organizations is one of the biggest dangers wildlife has ever faced. Unlike other more obvious threats, such as the fur and ivory industries, sustainable use hides its commercially exploitative orientation under the guise of conservation. It speaks not of shooting, trapping, killing, or capturing animals, but rather of "utilizing wildlife resources" for their own well-being.

If you doubt that such things could be happening, read on. The pages that follow describe and document in detail the threats that so-called sustainable use poses to wild animals across the globe. This book recounts how consumptive sustainable use, when applied to such creatures as elephants and parrots, has resulted in the decimation of the species involved. It describes the plans of governments and wildlife officials throughout the world to apply this misguided and unworkable principle to many other species. It identifies the organizations advocating sustainable use and footing the bill for such projects, and what the alternatives are to consumptive sustainable use. And it tells us what we can do—and must do—to protect our vanishing wildlife from disappearing into the abyss of "sustainable utilization."

If we allow our precious wildlife heritage to be turned into a commercial resource, to be killed and traded for profit, we and our children will forever regret it. For we will not only have betrayed the efforts of many people over the decades to protect wildlife, but we will also have denied future generations the opportunity to share this wondrous planet with marvelous creatures that add great beauty, diversity, and pleasure to our lives. In short, promoting destructive sustainable use of wildlife is as ethically bankrupt as it is politically and economically unworkable.

I believe that most people—indeed, the overwhelming majority—are willing to protect eagles, whales, whooping cranes, and other wild animals, even if we cannot make any money from them. But unless enough people speak out and take action to stop the sustainable use behemoth that is bulldozing its way through the world's conservation community, wild animals will soon become just another commodity to be bought, sold, traded, and finally used up, when, inevitably, the demand exceeds the supply.

I hope that this book will help educate and inform people about what is happening before it is too late. Otherwise, we will one day awaken to find that our wildlife heritage has been stolen from us by those who know the price of every creature, but the value of none.

PART I
The Myth of Sustainable Use

Introduction

... there is virtually unanimous concern for the future of living resources throughout the world . . . Virtually all species and stocks of wild living resources . . . which are being harvested commercially are being depleted . . . Throughout most of the world, species and stocks of wildlife are declining, often rapidly.

U.S. Marine Mammal Commission
1993[1]

S ustainable use of wildlife: It has become the buzzword of the 1990s, the mantra of a generation of conservationists, and the wildlife battle of the decade. But it may also have become, as many fear, the justification for the destruction of much of the world's vanishing wildlife.

There are many threats to the survival of wildlife, with habitat destruction heading most lists. But for many imperiled species, the international commercial trade in wild animals and their products has emerged as the primary threat to their survival. However, under the banner of "sustainable use," various governments, conservation groups, and wildlife agencies are promoting such trade as a conservation tool. This has given cover to such groups as the ivory merchants and those in the wild bird pet industry, who now justify their excessive "harvesting" of wildlife and the economic exploitation of rare and endangered species as a tool of "conservation."

Many scientists and wildlife experts are coming to realize the folly of sustainable use, and some—who do not work for governments or industry and are free to speak out—have begun to express their views. John G. Robinson, head of the international program of the Wildlife Conservation Society, wrote in the March 1993 issue of *Conservation Biology* that "the goals of sustainable use and sustainable development, as defined by 'Caring for the Earth' [the most influential document

7

devoted to the concept] will lead irrevocably to the loss of diversity."[2] In a recent article in *Science* magazine, three highly respected biologists observed that "many plans for sustainable use . . . reflect ignorance of the history of resource exploitation," which has been that "resources are inevitably overexploited, often to the point of collapse or extinction."[3] And a 1993 study by the U.S. Marine Mammal Commission warns that "virtually all species and stocks of wild living resources . . . which are being harvested commercially are being depleted." The report questions "whether it is possible to achieve sustainable management of most living resources."[4]

When one examines the guiding principle of so-called sustainable use, it becomes obvious that the theory cannot effectively be applied to real world conditions. The supposed sustainable use of such species as whales, parrots, and ocean fish—to name just a few of those that will be discussed later in this book—has resulted in their drastic depletion or severe endangerment. As the sustainable use lobby seeks to subject even more species to such "utilization," we should keep in mind the long and consistent history of failure of such efforts.

CHAPTER 1

Sustainable Use of Wildlife– Utopian Dream, or Unrealistic Nightmare?

Within the global conservation community, sustainable use is shaping up as the most volatile and divisive issue of the decade.

U.S. News & World Report
November 15, 1993[1]

The term "sustainable use" has a warm, reassuring tone to it, seeming to combine wise development, sound conservation, and careful concern for future generations. Its application has been less benign, involving lots of "use" but not much "sustainability."

Sustainable use can be either consumptive or non-consumptive. Consumptive use involves the killing, trapping, and/or capturing of wild animals for commerce (fur, ivory, the pet trade) or recreation (sport hunting). Non-consumptive use of wildlife refers to activity that generates income without harming animals or removing them from their habitats. This category includes such activities as ecotourism and viewing, photographing, and otherwise enjoying wildlife in a benign way. Non-consumptive use is generally supported by virtually all conservation groups—although some of the more zealous advocates of consumptive use have attacked it, unfairly, as more damaging than safari hunting.

It is the consumptive economic use of wildlife, which usually involves international trade in animals or their products and is often referred to as "sustainable use," that is mainly at issue in this book.

The biggest problem with consumptive sustainable use, simply put, is that it is not sustainable—after a while, you begin to run out of animals to "use." In short, sustainable use is defensible only in theory; it is unworkable in application, and tragic in effect. It generally results in the overexploitation and decimation of the species involved.

Depletion of the species utilized is almost a foregone conclusion because of several factors, including the short-term financial interests of the users, our inadequate scientific knowledge about wildlife populations, and our inability to predict the outcome of our attempts to manage wild animals with any degree of accuracy. Such factors and results have, almost without exception, characterized past efforts at consumptive management and the commercial use of wildlife populations and species.

It may even be inevitable that utilization of wildlife can be profitable only when it is conducted *un*sustainably. If users were forced to conduct the necessary scientific studies to ensure that "harvest" levels were sustainable; if proper enforcement controls and population monitoring were in place; and if it were required that the animals involved be treated humanely—all of this would drive up the cost of use so exorbitantly that it would no longer be economically attractive.[2]

And there is something else fundamentally wrong with the concept, as Paul Irwin, president of The Humane Society of the United States (HSUS) points out: Even in theory, "sustainable use" is unacceptable to many people because it absolutely ignores the interests of the "used" animals. The concept sets up a relationship between humans and animals wherein animals are "resources" to be "harvested"—their value is judged mainly in financial terms, and a large degree of individual animal suffering is permitted for the financial benefit of humans.[3] This conflicts with the growing sentiment that animals should be treated with at least some degree of compassion and humaneness.

There is nothing really new about having an attitude of respect for animals. Historically, many nations (even poor ones) have recognized the value of pure preservation of animals. That is one reason why real preserves—areas where animals are not "utilized" in any way—can be found in most countries.

Now, however, the new philosophy of sustainable use is replacing the preservation methods that often worked quite well in protecting animals. Poor countries are being told that they have a valuable and marketable commodity in their preserves that can be used and exploited to the benefit of the people, the wildlife, and the environment. This is a very radical and largely untested departure from traditional conservation initiatives, and will result in the utilization and devastation of many now-protected wildlife populations. It can also be seen as a way for the rich industrialized nations, which are promoting "sustainable use," to continue the exploitation of the "resources" of poorer developing countries.[4]

In recent years, the term "sustainable use" has been widely used by many conservation leaders and government officials to refer to the killing of endangered elephants for their ivory tusks; the hunting of endangered rhinoceroses; and the massive commercial trade in parrots, which has brought most of the exploited species of these birds to the verge of extinction.

Yet despite these repeated failures, "sustainable use" has been adopted as official policy by governments, wildlife departments, international environmental agencies, and conservation groups from one end of the globe to the other. It has been endorsed by the United States and most other countries, the 1992 Earth Summit in Rio, the Convention on International Trade in Endangered Species, agencies of the United Nations, the World Bank, and numerous other powerful groups and institutions that set and carry out policy on wildlife.

It would seem that the equivalent of entire forests have been cut to supply the tons of paper that have been used to analyze, describe, and justify arguments and projects for the sustainable use of wildlife. And many of the schemes can be made to appear quite feasible on paper. A few may even work over the short term, particularly if they are highly localized and heavily subsidized. But the vast majority simply cannot, will not, and do not produce the intended results under real world conditions, particularly if they involve the international sale of wild animals or their products.

Unless the world conservation community awakens to the impracticality of applying the theory of sustainable use, much of our wildlife is doomed to be subjected to unsustainable destruction. This will occur at the hands of government wildlife managers, international conservation organizations, and commercial traders. This is what the current controversy is all about, and its outcome will determine the fate of much of the world's wildlife.

THE BATTLE OF THE DECADE

In the last quarter-century, tremendous progress has been made in educating the public about and stimulating interest in wildlife across the globe. The days are gone, or nearly so, when governments, developers, and industries could thoughtlessly wipe out entire species of wildlife with little public protest. Today, most people agree that wildlife is worth saving and that, whenever possible, development and commerce should be conducted in such a way as to avoid or at least minimize the wanton destruction of wild animals.

Now, a different battle of words is being waged, this one for the hearts and minds of the public and various governments on the issue of how best to *save* the world's vanishing wildlife.

The focus of the controversy has been on Africa's wildlife, especially such economically valuable but endangered animals as elephants, rhinos, cheetahs, and leopards. But ultimately at stake is the fate of all of the world's wildlife. The controversy that has developed is over the best way to prevent the disappearance of these species—sustainable use or general protection.

A six-page-long article in the November 15, 1993 issue of *U.S. News & World Report* summarized the conflict, saying that "sustainable use is shaping up as the most volatile and divisive conservation issue of the decade":

> Growing numbers of conservationists reluctantly conclude that protecting the world's most popular and threatened big game species for their tourism value, or for their intrinsic worth, has failed. Without a radical new approach to conservation, some of these species have little hope of surviving longer than a few more decades in the wild . . . Proponents say it may offer the last, best chance for some species on the brink of extinction.

But animal protectionists realize that the continued killing of rare animals cannot save them, as *U.S. News & World Report* points out:

> Some conservationists scorn sustainable use as unworkable and abhor the killing of threatened animals for profit . . . Foes of sustainable use regard it as nothing more than a synonym for exploitation . . . Creating markets for and making profits from wildlife, they feel, inevitably lead to greed, over-exploitation, corruption, and ultimate disaster. Says Allan Thornton of the Environmental Investigation Agency, "Sustainable use doesn't work because it requires rigorous scientific research, management controls and enforcement, and a high degree of political will. None of these exist." To diehard protectionists, killing animals to ensure their survival smacks of the same twisted logic that saw GIs destroying villages to "save" them during the Vietnam War.[5]

Yes, animal protectionists—based on what they have learned from decades of destruction of wildlife populations—*do* feel that the continued hunting of threatened animals and the commercial trade in their products, such as elephant ivory and rhino horns, will inevitably lead to further depletion or extinction of these animals. As described later in this book, evidence that this is precisely what has been taking place in Africa is being suppressed and covered up.

Ultimately, the security of wildlife—and of people—in developing nations can be safeguarded only through *humane* sustainable development, operating with precaution in cases of uncertainty instead of allowing traders and developers to exploit humans and wildlife without restraint. Humane sustainable development must include protecting indigenous peoples and the lands and forests on which they and wildlife depend, plus the development of carefully controlled ecotourism.

This fight is being called the "conservation battle of the decade." The stakes are no less than survival or extinction for many of the world's wild creatures and the well-being of literally billions of people dependent on the protection of their nations' wildlife and natural resources.

CODE WORDS FOR KILLING

The sustainable use debate can be confusing to an outsider. It is full of code words and arcane terms whose actual meaning is apparent only to those involved in and familiar with the controversy.

As the term is usually employed, "sustainable use"—at least in theory—means managing wildlife populations, even endangered species, in such a way as to permit the regulated capture and killing of a limited number of animals. The revenues from the sale of hunting permits and of such wildlife products as horns, ivory tusks, meat, skins, and fur would be utilized to fund habitat protection and acquisition, anti-poaching patrols, park rangers, and improvements to local villages, as well as to provide jobs, local development, and other economic incentives for poor nations to conserve these resources, which, if managed properly, are renewable.

But however well such a strategy might work on paper, in the real world (with a few notable exceptions) it has largely failed to have a beneficial impact. Indeed, the major impact of creating markets for wild creatures and their products is the encouragement of continued and non-renewable exploitation and slaughter of animals, no matter how endangered they may be.

The term "sustainable use" is used so widely and by such a variety of interest groups—including governments, international commissions, conservationists, and exploiters of wildlife and other "natural resources"—that it has now lost much of whatever real meaning it might have once had. The term now means, in effect, whatever the user wants it to. Indeed, it has essentially been appropriated by the consumptive use lobby, and more often than not it is used as a justification for killing, trapping, and trading in wildlife.

Detroit College of Law dean David S. Favre, who has worked on and written extensively about wildlife law, observes that many promoters of sustainable use come out of the old wildlife management tradition of the last half-century, which considers wildlife a "crop" to be "harvested": "The killing of whales and elephants is not viewed any differently than cutting a field of wheat."[6]

To further confuse matters, sustainable use is an integral part of the new "sustainability" movement, a way of approaching international development that includes concepts called "sustainable growth," "sustainable development," "sustainable natural resources management," "sustainable economy," "sustainable society," and "living sustainably." (The broader issue of "sustainable development" and all of its incarnations will be discussed in Chapter 9.)

One problem with the "sustainability" debate is that we are dealing here not so much with a concept as with a religion. As science reporter William K. Stevens writes in *The New York Times*, "The concept of sustainability . . . has become something of a mantra among environmentalists."[7]

The champions of sustainability are found at the prestigious World Conservation Union (formerly called the International Union for the Conservation of Nature and Natural Resources), or IUCN. The bible of the sustainability movement is IUCN's 1991 publication *Caring for the Earth*, which says, "If an activity is sustainable, for all practical purposes it can continue forever."[8] It characterizes "sustainable development" as "improving the quality of human life while living within the carrying capacity of supporting ecosystems" and defines "sustainable use" as "using renewable resources at rates within their capacity for renewal." IUCN says that it "has promoted sustainable use of wild species since 1980, in the belief that by providing people with incentives, they will invest in the conservation of the resource."[9]

From a purely conservation standpoint, who could object to any of these concepts? Indeed, sustainable use is endorsed and promoted by some very distinguished people and organizations. But it has, unfortunately, also been adopted by the rape-ruin-and-run crowd—the despoilers of Western rangelands, the ivory dealers, and the big game hunters, as well as the fur trade, the wildlife pet industry, and the tropical timber industry. Sometimes it is called "wise use"; at other times it is called "sustainable utilization," "intensive management, or "sustained yield." But whatever name it goes by, it is often used as a motto and a cover to justify the business-as-usual, get-it-while-you-can overexploitation and destruction of natural resources, be they public lands, forests, fisheries, or wildlife. And all too often, international conservation groups and agencies—including IUCN and the Convention on International Trade in Endangered Species (CITES), the 122-nation group set up to protect imperiled wildlife from excessive commercial trade—have sided with these destructive interests.

A good summary of the differences between the various groups fighting over sustainable use comes from HSUS associate director for wildlife Dr. Teresa Telecky, who points out that the term is often abused by those who want to justify commercial exploitation of wildlife:

> All groups would say that *if* species are to be used, *then* they should be used sustainably. Otherwise, the use would drive species to extinction.
>
> The difference among the groups would be the *promotion of consumptive use* for international trade purposes. No animal protection groups that I know of support this.

Telecky observes that the foundation of the sustainable use philosophy is based on an invalid premise—that local support for wildlife can protect it from poaching or other destruction:

> The major (most influential in the international arena) groups that promote consumptive use for international trade are IUCN, the World Wildlife Fund (WWF), and its affiliate, TRAFFIC, which are peddling the philosophy that consumptive use for international trade can supply local people with much-needed income and engender a protective attitude toward wildlife because of its value.
>
> Many conservation groups and all animal protection groups recognize the flaw in this philosophy—that international trade in lucrative wildlife is uncontrollable. No matter how much the "locals" value their wildlife, they are no match for poachers with automatic rifles. In other words, interesting theory, but completely unrealistic. The ivory trade proved this.[10]

Telecky explains another reason why the theory of consumptive sustainable use becomes unrealistic in practice: It sets up a situation in which there are tremendous short-term financial rewards to be gained by killing or trapping large numbers of wildlife now, rather than resorting to the slow and careful removal of a limited number of individual animals. Human behavior is biased toward taking the short-term benefits and running.

In addition, humans have far from perfect knowledge about the factors that regulate wild populations of animals, and are incapable of accurately predicting the long-term consequences of removing large numbers of animals from the population. The result, in case after case over the years, has been overexploitation, which is often not recognized until it is too late to save the species.[11]

This, then, is what the controversy is all about: Should we try to provide necessary protection for rare and endangered species, or should we allow them (or their parts) to be sold in international trade in the hope that local people will protect (or be able to protect) wildlife, and that our management plans will ensure the long-term survival of the animal population?

Clearly, for vulnerable species of wildlife, sustainable use—despite the mystical, magical, almost holy reverence with which it is regarded—is an idea whose time has come—and gone. When it has involved commercial trade of wildlife, it has failed over and over again.

Where the concept *can* be, and often is, applied is in "greenwashing" numerous development and revenue-producing projects by conveying the *appearance* of sustainability. And by giving respectability to ecologically devastating programs, "sustainable use" defeats its own purpose. As David Favre writes:

> A primary concern is that like the wolf in sheep's clothing, the concept of sustainable use will be a ruse for exploiters to continue their exploitation of wildlife, and that by the time it becomes clear that the wildlife are not being protected, it may be too late for many species. What is the penalty for mistakes, ignorance and corruption? . . . In a world where many states violate human rights on a regular basis, there is little reason to think the interests of wildlife or future human generations will constrain present economic exploitation of wildlife that is both unsustainable and unethical.[12]

THE FALLACY OF SUSTAINABLE USE

The killing and trapping of animals "for their own good" has long been justified by sustainable use enthusiasts as the best, and sometimes the only, way to conserve wildlife, and this concept has become one of the most revered of the so-called sound principles of wildlife management. But, as some scientists are now pointing out, such policies have almost always produced the same result: the extermination or depletion of the animals being so managed.

Maximum sustainable yield (MSY), supposedly using the best available scientific data, was once the foundation of wildlife management. It managed to reduce many species of once-abundant creatures to severe depletion or near extinction.

Whales were supposedly sustainably exploited for decades under the careful scientific management regime of the International Whaling Commission (IWC)—until all eight species of great whales were pronounced endangered by the U.S. government and placed on its list of endangered species in 1970.

Nor has sustained yield management worked for such depleted North

American "resources" as grizzly bears, ducks, California sardines, ancient forests, or just about anything else that has supposedly been managed, conserved, exploited, utilized, or harvested on a sustained yield basis. Not even white-tailed deer, which have thrived, can be considered an unmitigated management success. Creating and maintaining a "harvestable surplus" of deer has adversely affected other species, and has been achieved in large part by the removal of old-growth forests and predators.

MSY has now been largely discredited and replaced with the somewhat less exploitative concept of sustainable use. Indeed, the rationale for continuing to kill, trap, and maim wildlife, to cut forests, and to exploit natural areas now goes by this term, which is solemnly invoked by everyone from Vice President Al Gore to the United Nations Environment Programme, and by numerous environmental organizations and agencies in the U.S. and abroad.

But it has become increasingly obvious that even in this new and improved wrapper, this form of wildlife management, as taught at dozens of schools and universities across the country and as practiced by wildlife and natural resource agencies in many countries, is failing. It cannot adequately protect the creatures it is designed to conserve, and in many areas is actually causing their demise.

Many people assume that the uncontrolled elimination of wildlife is a thing of the distant past—the extermination of the buffalo in the 1800s through the 1880s; the extinction of the passenger pigeon in the early 1900s; the destruction of one species of great whale after another in the 1950s and 1960s.

But sustained use concepts are allowing the massive slaughter of wildlife to continue. Indeed, it is in the last decade or two that such "natural resources" as tropical and ancient forests, elephants, ducks, parrots, and ocean fish stocks have been massively exploited and drastically depleted (as will be described later in this book). And all the while, many responsible scientists and wildlife officials spoke reassuringly about scientific resource management, sustainable utilization, strictly enforced quotas, extensive scientific data, and controls designed to assure the perpetuation of these "renewable" resources.

The same pattern is being repeated today—except that we are rapidly running out of creatures to subject to such "sustainable" slaughter.

BLAME IT ON THE URBAN PRESERVATIONISTS

Proponents of sustainable use overlook its history and the fact that it has almost never been made to work. Instead, they psychoanalyze, belittle, and scorn its opponents as emotional, uninformed, and unreasonable. This attitude is exemplified by a 1993 essay, "Using Wildlife Sustainably," by Dr. Martin Holdgate, former director general of IUCN. (Holdgate chaired the debate on the African elephant at the March 10, 1992 CITES meeting in Kyoto, Japan.) In this essay, after discussing the valuable benefits of utilizing wildlife, Holdgate virtually ignores the arguments against sustainable use, and he paints opponents as out-of-touch elitists who simply do not understand how nature works. "Why," he asks, "is there such controversy today over sustainable wildlife use?" and then suggests that this controversy "has two principal roots, one practical and one ethical."

Holdgate first dismisses "the practical point . . . that unsustainable use of wildlife has done unquestioned damage to the balance of many ecosystems and contributed to environmental degradation and human misery." (He does not mention that such utilization was often endorsed and portrayed at the time as being sustainable by eminent scientists, experts, and government officials, including IUCN.) "The fact that misuse of such resources is not new . . . is neither here nor there," he writes.

Holdgate then goes on to discuss the "more difficult" ethical part of the controversy, in the process misinterpreting the views and psychological orientation of preservationists:

> As people have moved away from their rural roots, and become both urbanized and relatively wealthy, attitudes to wildlife have diverged. While indigenous peoples and many other hunters have respected wild animals and supported conservation, many urban people who also delight in the beauty of wildlife relish the fact that they no longer have to kill it to live. They find hunting of wild animals for pleasure repugnant, and are unhappy about any commercial use of wild species.

Again, Holdgate conveniently ignores the real reason that these supposed wealthy, urban elitists are "unhappy" about the commercial use of wildlife: because it so often leads to their massive killing, suffering, and eventual near or actual extinction. He even expresses contempt for the wildlife protection laws in the United States and other developed nations, implying that they are ill-suited for the rest of the world:

> . . . those who want to see *no* consumption of wild species . . . have a right to their views. Where they are a majority, as they may be in some countries where wildlife (apart from fish) is no longer exploited for essential food, they may indeed secure protection for their national

mammals and birds, perhaps even including so-called "pests" of agriculture. But over much of the world, wildlife use is an essential foundation for the welfare of communities already suffering from poverty.[13]

Sustainable use proponents do not seem to understand why people would want to give complete protection to animals—even species that are national symbols, such as eagles. They consider compassion and appreciation for wildlife to be a sort of indulgence of the rich, who can afford such a luxury. They appear to believe that animals can have value to people only if they are "utilized"—that is, killed, trapped, or sold. It is this mindset that is responsible for the demise of so much of our wildlife, and it is still attempting to justify continued devastating commercial trade in animals, no matter how endangered—including elephants and rhinos.

PROMOTING TRADE IN ENDANGERED SPECIES

Advocates of sustainable use are so zealously committed to this concept that they insist it can potentially be applied to virtually any species, no matter how rare or endangered. It is as if excluding a species from utilization might discredit the theory by demonstrating that complete protection could be desirable or effective. The sustainable use lobby well understands that successful, non-consumptive wildlife preservation programs threaten its "use-it-or-lose-it" philosophy.

Thus, the mantras of "sustainability" and "regulated trade" are still often solemnly invoked, even when the concept behind them is being rejected. At the October 1989 CITES meeting in Lausanne, Switzerland, a U.S. delegate explained the American vote in favor of a ban on international trade in elephant ivory and other products almost apologetically:

> Mr. Chairman, the whole world is watching us. Although the U.S. strongly supports the concept of sustainable management of wildlife, in the case of the African elephant, forces beyond the control of any one nation are conspiring to make any regulation of the ivory trade impossible.[14]

Within CITES, there is strong pressure to emphasize "economic utilization" of wildlife. This comes in large part from the IUCN Species Survival Commission subgroup called the IUCN/SSC Specialist Group on Sustainable Use of Wild Species—often referred to as the Sustainable Use Committee. This group produced a draft report in July 1992 stating, "The social and economic benefits from sustainable use can provide a powerful incentive to conserve wild species and their supporting ecosystems, provided the people most likely to have an impact on the species and ecosystems concerned receive an adequate share of these benefits."[15]

In response to this effort to further commercialize CITES' orientation, Dr. Teresa Telecky of The HSUS wrote to the committee objecting to the way its report linked social and economic benefits from sustainable use with the conservation of wild species and their supporting ecosystems:

> In reality, such a linkage has rarely if ever been demonstrated; indeed, the relationship between these two factors is merely theoretical . . . Simply stated, the link between conservation and use, particularly consumptive use, of wild species is weak, untested, and should not be promoted as though it is fact. To do so is irresponsible and not in the best interest of conservation of wild species.[16]

Environmental law expert and professor David S. Favre calls the IUCN document "an example of how a logical proposition can be twisted when policies are adopted," and argues that "it is unwise to implement a policy fostering economic utilization of wildlife":

> The creation and fostering of international economic markets for wildlife products may create demands, legal and illegal, which are not predictable, and put species at higher risk. One clear lesson from the history of the ivory trade is that if a legal market exists, it is easier for the illegal market to exist and sometimes overwhelm the legal one . . . There is inadequate scientific data and enforcement resources to adopt this approach as an organizing principle.[17]

Sometimes it seems that CITES is run in part not just by those who favor commercial trade in imperiled wildlife, but by people who are participants in the trade. For example, at the 1992 CITES meeting in Kyoto, thirteen members of the Indonesian delegation were dealers in wildlife and their products. One was a man whom a 1991 British Broadcasting Company (BBC) documentary had exposed as one of the biggest traffickers in endangered species, including animals whose trade was banned by CITES.[18]

Writing of the 1992 meeting, author Conger Beasley, Jr., described "the prevalence of a pro-market mentality that seemed more suitable to a band of rabbit breeders than a distinguished body of professional scientists and administrators that had convened to discuss the plight of the world's plants and animals."[19]

A rather shocking example of the sustained use mindset can be seen in a recently proposed change in rules that are used to determine which animals are eligible for protection under CITES. Wildlife protectionists fear that the proposed change could result in now-protected endangered species being drastically reduced in number.

In fact, some charge that in preparing a new study on listing criteria for CITES, IUCN "has placed its safety net [at] the very edge of the cliff of extinction."[20] In an earlier version (which has since been amended), among the suggested criteria to make a species eligible for listing on Appendix I, CITES' most endangered category, were a population of fewer than 250 mature individuals, and a range of less than 500 square kilometers (195 square miles)! The species that could be denied Appendix I protection include such spotted cats as cheetahs and snow and clouded leopards; great apes such as chimpanzees and gorillas; and blue and bowhead whales.[21]

Izgrev Topkov, secretary general of CITES, has endorsed these proposed listing criteria, and wrote a letter dated February 25, 1994 in which he defended the possibility of commercial exploitation of species that are almost extinct:

> For certain species of animals, even from a small population producing, say, 20 offspring a year, it is possible, under the right circumstances, to allow one or two in trade without any harm to the population. In fact the conservation of the species can be enhanced if the animals are sold at a high price to support the work of the conservation authorities. There is an increasing realization by States that this approach can be beneficial to wildlife.[22]

Topkov goes on to reveal, surely inadvertently, that all of the language of the sustained use lobby can be, and often is, used to block efforts to protect imperiled wildlife and to justify their continued commercial trade, all in the name of "conservation":

> A number of people and organizations have indeed espoused and promoted a protectionist ethic, but many conservationists have a very different perspective. For many years, the conservation literature has been thick with papers discussing ways in which wildlife can be sustainably used within the framework of management for conservation . . . .

Indeed, he writes, utilizing wildlife commercially is what CITES is all about:

> . . . the objective of the convention, clear for anyone to see, is not to stop the exploitation of wildlife, but to ensure that it is limited to avoid harm to wild populations. This may not be protectionism, but it is conservation.

The CITES Parties, at their last meeting, reinforced this conservation principle by unanimously adopting a Resolution recognizing that "commercial trade may be beneficial to the conservation of species and ecosystems and/or to the development of local people when carried out at levels that are not detrimental to the survival of the species in question."[23]

What Topkov does not say is that this resolution is a considerably watered-down fourth version of what the sustainable use lobby within CITES wanted to have adopted. Favre describes the language of this version of the resolution as "meaningless," and he points out that this "defanged" version was the result of opposition from states that were "concerned that consumptive sustainable use not become the underlying policy of CITES."[24] (The preamble to CITES states, "International cooperation is essential for the protection of certain species of wild fauna and flora against overutilization through international trade.") Keep in mind that all this language could have been used to endorse trade in an animal population so small it produces only twenty offspring a year, according to the head of CITES.

By the spring of 1994, the proposed new listing criteria had been somewhat improved, with those for eligibility for Appendix I including a population of less than 5,000 mature individuals and a range of under 10,000 square kilometers (3,900 square miles). Still, such seriously endangered animals as chimpanzees, cheetahs, Asian and African elephants, humpback whales, olive ridley sea turtles, and many others would not meet these criteria and could be subjected to international trade. The proposed new listing criteria would also eliminate the current protective requirement that in order for a species to be down-listed from Appendix I to Appendix II, or to be de-listed entirely, there must be scientific evidence that the down-listing or de-listing will not have a detrimental impact on the species.

Topkov defends the weakening of CITES' listing criteria, acknowledging that the purpose of the revision process is to make it easier to trade in certain species of wildlife:

The aim . . . is simply to inject more science into the decision-making process and to make it consistent with modern conservation. But it is wrong to imply that conservation means not exploiting wildlife. Some organizations oppose the use of wildlife, and their position is legitimate and ethical, but it is not conservation.[25]

But Dr. Ronald Orenstein, director of the International Wildlife Coalition in Toronto, contends that it is the new CITES rules that are not conservation, and that many distinguished scientists are appalled by the new proposals:

> The U.K. supports the new rules. So do Zimbabwe, China, Norway, Canada, South Korea, and Japan, all countries that want to see CITES' restrictions on wildlife trade reduced. Japan, which funded IUCN's efforts, is now rumored to be threatening other Asian countries with economic consequences if they oppose them. So much for objectivity.

Orenstein concludes:

> "The new rules represent a disaster for CITES. If they are not rejected [at the November 1994 meeting in Fort Lauderdale, Florida], CITES' ability to protect the growing number of species under threat from international trade will be tragically reduced."[26]

THE HISTORY OF "SUSTAINABILITY"

Until the environmental movement attained national prominence and widespread public support in the early 1970s, little attention was given to conservation concerns by most government agencies and international organizations. Industrialization and development were the economic buzzwords of the 1950s and 1960s; the poorer countries of the Southern Hemisphere were inevitably referred to as "underdeveloped."

The solution of the day, of course, was to try to raise the living standards of people around the globe by boosting the economic growth and the gross national product (GNP) of nations, particularly the so-called underdeveloped ones. This was to be accomplished in large part by increasing the exploitation, consumption, and international trade in "renewable natural resources"—many of which, such as fish, wildlife, and tropical forests, turned out to be non-renewable if "harvested" too intensively.

By the early 1970s, it had become apparent that the uncontrolled and rapacious exploitation of natural resources was creating serious environmental, social, agricultural, and economic problems, and often having the opposite result of what was intended. In many areas of the world, the loss of fisheries and other wildlife, deforestation, desertification, pollution, and general environmental degradation were having profound and serious impacts on people, and creating growing public concern about such problems.

In the 1970s, conservation and animal protection groups proliferated, growing in number, influence, and membership. A plethora of books, newspaper and magazine articles, and television programs on wildlife and the environment began to appear, increasing public interest in and concern about these issues still further. As a result, governments and international agencies were forced, often reluctantly, to begin to address environmental problems—or at least to be seen as doing so.

Over the years, there have been several attempts by various organizations to reconcile and integrate development with conservation. Some of these attempts received widespread attention and publicity and were able to have a significant impact on policy makers and public opinion.

In 1972, the Club of Rome published *The Limits of Growth*—widely seen at the time as overly alarmist—which warned of the dangers to humanity of the world population explosion, the overexploitation of natural resources, increasing pollution, and limited food production potential. That same year, the United Nations Conference on the Human Environment took place in Stockholm, resulting in the U.N. Environment Programme (UNEP) being set up to address such issues.

In 1980, under the auspices of IUCN and the World Wildlife Fund (WWF; also called the World Wide Fund for Nature in some countries), *The World Conservation Strategy* was published. It laid out for the first time a well-reasoned, scientifically based blueprint for "sustainable development." As its authorizing organizations described the document:

> It stated a new message: that conservation is *not* the opposite of development. It emphasized that conservation includes both protection and the rational use of natural resources and is essential if people are to achieve a life of dignity and if the welfare of present and future generations is to be assured . . .
>
> It emphasized that humanity, which exists as part of nature, has no future unless nature and natural resources are conserved. It asserted that conservation cannot be achieved without development to alleviate the poverty and misery of hundreds of millions of people.[27]

The report sought to incorporate conservation principles into global development programs in order to make the projects "sustainable" and avoid the destruction of natural systems and biological diversity. But the document also made it clear that development and conservation are often incompatible and irreconcilable, and that preservation, restoration, and enhancement of the natural environment have to be part of any effective strategy to attain truly "sustainable development." The emphasis was on conserving nature, recognizing that humans depend for their survival and welfare on the maintenance of a healthy environment.[28]

In 1987, a seemingly similar report on sustainable development was issued by the World Commission on Environment and Development—frequently referred to as the Brundtland Commission—which was chaired by Gro Harlem Brundtland, the Prime Minister of Norway. A socialist, Brundtland is often called "the Mother of the Environment," although she supports her government's policy of engaging in commercial hunting of protected whales in violation of international rules and regulations. The commission's report, entitled *Our Common Future*, decried the growing pollution and environmental degradation engulfing the planet. But it focused on the effects *on humans* and life forms useful to them—specifically "the impact of ecological stress . . . upon our economic prospects."[29]

One finding of the commission that was not widely publicized was its call for the world's economy to grow to five to ten times its current size, giving all the world's people the same standard of living (in terms of per-person resource consumption) as Americans have today. Even if such economic expansion were possible (which probably it is not) such growth would surely wreak catastrophic environmental havoc.

As Herman E. Daly, a senior economist with the World Bank, points out:

> . . . even expansion by a factor of four is impossible if experts are correct in their calculations that the human economy currently uses one-fourth of the global net primary product of photosynthesis (NPP). Since land-based ecosystems are the more relevant to humans, and we preempt 40 percent of land-based NPP, even the factor of four is an overestimate.[30]

In other words, since humans are already consuming almost half of the terrestrial plant material (crops, trees, and forest products, for example) that the world produces each year for food, clothing, building material, and other uses, our ability to expand the economy is quite limited.

The latest, and most influential, blueprint for saving the planet while developing it is entitled *Caring for the Earth: A Strategy for Sustainable Living*, released in October 1991. This document was authored and published by three of the world's most influential conservation groups and agencies: UNEP, WWF, and IUCN.

The document has been quite important in influencing the policies of governments around the world. Indeed, its introduction states that "*Caring for the Earth* is intended to be used by those who shape policy and make decisions that affect the course of development and the condition of our environment."[31]

Caring for the Earth has a significantly different focus than does the *World Conservation Strategy* in that it strongly promotes development (in a "sustainable" way) and assumes that conservation will be a compatible, inevitable, and even essential part of such development.[32] (These assumptions, as we shall see, ignore history, human nature, and common sense.)

Most of all, the document overlooks the limitations of human intelligence and knowledge. Humans do not know everything about the factors that regulate natural wild populations. It is thus impossible for us accurately to predict how much "harvesting" can take place while ensuring sustainability.[33]

CARING FOR THE EARTH—OR DEVASTATING IT?

In many ways, *Caring for the Earth* forcefully and accurately describes the environmental crisis we face and tells what we must do to address these problems. The document begins by warning that humans are "gambling with survival":

> Because we have been failing to care for the Earth properly and living unsustainably . . . we are now gambling with the survival of civilization . . .
>
> Our civilizations are at risk because we are misusing natural resources and disturbing natural systems. We are pressing the Earth to the limits of its capacity . . . The capacity of the Earth to support human and other life has been significantly diminished.[34]

The document goes on to emphasize the necessity of preserving the biosphere in its entirety:

> Biological diversity should be conserved as a matter of principle, because all species deserve respect regardless of their use to humanity, and because they are all components of our life support system. Biological diversity also provides us with economic benefits and adds greatly to the quality of our lives . . .
>
> The diversity of nature is a source of beauty, enjoyment, understanding and knowledge—a foundation for human creativity and a subject for study. It is the source of all biological wealth—supplying all of our food, much of our raw materials, . . . and genetic materials for agriculture, medicine, and industry worth many billions of dollars per year.[35]

In its "elements of a world ethic for living sustainably," *Caring for the Earth* even recognizes the innate integrity and worth of other creatures irrespective of their economic value to humans, and urges that they not be treated inhumanely:

Every life form warrants respect independently of its worth to people. Human development should not threaten the integrity of nature or the survival of other species. People should treat all creatures decently, and protect them from cruelty, avoidable suffering, and unnecessary killing.[36]

Such humane considerations are unprecedented for a document of this type, and constitute an endorsement of principles that most wildlife officials would consider a threat to the "proper management" of "living resources." Indeed, one can argue that all killing for international trade purposes is "unnecessary."

But on the next page, the document seems to backtrack from this ethical principle, even implicitly endorsing commercial trade in fur and elephant ivory, both of which certainly involve unnecessary killing:

The obligation to protect all creatures from cruelty, avoidable suffering, and unnecessary killing can also conflict with the requirement that no people should be deprived of its means of subsistence. The campaign against the fur trade has deprived indigenous peoples of Greenland and northern Canada of a major source (and for some communities, the only source) of income, even though they were harvesting those resources sustainably. Elephant conservation may have been made more difficult in several southern African countries because they can no longer obtain a financial return from the animals they have to cull. The ban under CITES of trade in elephant products could thus reduce the perceived value of elephants to communities that are well aware of the damage that other species can cause.[37]

This endorsement of the fur and ivory trades (apparently inserted at the insistence of IUCN) undermines the credibility of the document and reveals its pro-commercial bias. Indeed, these sweeping statements—suggesting that natives killing seals, wolves, and depleted or endangered fur-bearing animals in Canada and Greenland were "harvesting resources sustainably," and that banning international trade in ivory *harms* elephant conservation—are demonstrably false. They show that when it comes to wildlife, "sustainable use" can be used to justify the commercial killing of almost any species, no matter how vulnerable or threatened, as long as humans are financially benefitting from the "harvesting."

THE DEMISE OF BIOLOGICAL DIVERSITY

Many scientists, conservationists, and wildlife experts believe that "sustainable use" as promoted by IUCN is a prescription for disaster.

John G. Robinson, director of the International Program of the Wild-life Conservation Society (WCS; formerly called the New York Zoological Society) in the Bronx, New York, writes that "the goals of sustainable use and sustainable development, as defined in *Caring for the Earth*, will lead irrevocably to the loss of biological diversity." In warning that sustainable use will cause the disappearance of species, Robinson uses language and demonstrates courage about as strong as you will ever see from a senior establishment conservation official of his stature.

Writing in the March 1993 issue of *Conservation Biology*, Robinson calls "the sustainable society" as envisioned in *Caring for the Earth* "an unattainable utopia," and he points out that the document's failing is that it never acknowledges that the goals of development and conservation are fundamentally different:

> *Caring for the Earth* does not recognize that while improving the quality of human life, we will inevitably decrease the diversity of life. If we do not acknowledge the contradictions, we will smugly preside over the demise of biological diversity while waving the banner of conservation.

Robinson makes the point that rather than effectively limiting or improving development projects, the publication may be used to endorse them, because it "emphasizes traditional development at the expense of the conservation of natural resources and biodiversity":

> . . . human development can lead to species extinction, and conservation can limit development. *Caring for the Earth* does not recognize this incompatibility . . . Indeed, it does not appear to deviate from the traditional development formulae of the 1950s and 1960s, and a continuation of such policies will surely decrease biological diversity . . . [I have not discussed the] danger that advocating sustainable use will give a green light to nonsustainable exploitative use. Resource extraction schemes are proliferating everywhere, and most advertise themselves— without justification—as sustainable . . . *Caring for the Earth* places no limits on the loss of biodiversity that is acceptable . . . .

Robinson believes that *Caring for the Earth* is fatally flawed, because it focuses almost exclusively on human beings:

> It is concerned with improving the quality of life for people. This is a worthy goal, but it is not the same goal as conserving the full spectrum of biological diversity. Because of this anthropocentric orientation, *Caring for the Earth* emphasizes sustainable use of natural resources as the only approach to conserving natural systems . . . Many species

and biological systems will be lost unless they are protected and managed with the express goal of their conservation. Sustainable use . . . will almost always lower biological diversity, whether one considers individual species or entire biological communities. . . If sustainable use is our only goal, our world will be the poorer for it.[38]

DISTRUST CLAIMS OF SUSTAINABILITY

A growing number of scientists are now realizing and speaking out about the fact that human efforts to "manage" the exploitation of wildlife and natural resources have, over the centuries, been a dismal failure. "There is remarkable consistency in the history of resource exploitation: resources are inevitably overexploited, often to the point of collapse or extinction," write three such scientists in the April 2, 1993 issue of *Science*.[39] According to Donald Ludwig of the Department of Mathematics and Zoology at the University of British Columbia, Ray Hilborn of the School of Fisheries at the University of Washington, and Carl Walters of the Department of Zoology at the University of British Columbia, we are making the same mistakes today as we did thousands of years ago.

The authors cite many practices that continue today despite "abundant scientific evidence that they are ultimately destructive." Among these are widespread attempts to irrigate arid, desert-like areas and make them fertile. Some 3,000 years ago in the ancient Mesopotamian country of Sumer, the once-abundant wheat crop had to be abandoned because efforts to irrigate the land had made the soil too salty. Similarly, in 1899, E.W. Hilgard warned that efforts to irrigate arid areas in California would have similar results. But his writings were ignored, and the predicted effects—as well as other environmental disasters— have indeed ensued.

Citing further examples, such as the overfishing and collapse of California sardine and Peruvian anchovy populations, Ludwig, Hilborn, and Walters conclude that even thousands of years of experience and a good scientific understanding of various environmental disasters, the things that caused them, and how they might have been prevented are apparently not enough to prevent the misuse and destruction of resources. They note that there are many similar plans today for sustainable use or sustainable development projects, supposedly based on sound and widely accepted scientific information and principles, and they bluntly observe:

Such ideas reflect ignorance of the history of resource exploitation, and misunderstanding of the possibility of achieving scientific consensus concerning resources and the environment . . . Initial overexploitation is not detectable until it is severe and often irreversible. In such circumstances, assigning causes to past events is problematical, future events cannot be predicted, and even well-meaning attempts to exploit responsibly may lead to disastrous consequences.

The three scientists discuss how the prospect of economic gain can often overwhelm common sense and scientific evidence:

> . . . the larger and the more immediate are prospects for gain, the greater the political power that is used to facilitate unlimited exploitation . . . Forests throughout the world have been destroyed by wasteful and short-sighted forestry practices. In many cases, governments eventually subsidize the export of forest products in order to delay the unemployment that results when local timber supplies run out . . . the long-term outcome is a heavily subsidized industry that overharvests the resource.

Ludwig, Hilborn, and Walters assign much of the blame for this situation to political leaders, who "base their policies upon a misguided view of the dynamics of resource exploitation" and to the scientific community, which "has helped to perpetuate the illusion of sustainable development . . . Scientists have been active in pointing out environmental degradation and consequent hazards to human life, and possibly to life as we know it on Earth. But by and large, the scientific community has helped to perpetuate the illusion of sustainable development through scientific and technological progress." They argue that "our lack of understanding and inability to predict mandate a much more cautious approach to resource exploitation," and they offer several "Principles of Effective Management," including the following:

- The shortsightedness and greed of humans underlie difficulties in management of resources;
- Act before scientific consensus is achieved . . . calls for additional research may be mere delaying tactics;
- Scientists and their judgments are subject to political pressure;
- Distrust claims of sustainability . . . past resource exploitation has seldom been sustainable.

IS SUSTAINABLE MANAGEMENT POSSIBLE?

More scientists are also coming to realize the special difficulties involved in managing wildlife on a sustainable basis. This is made clear in a September 1993 "preliminary report" by the U.S. Marine Mammal Commission entitled "Principles for Living Resource Conservation," authored by Dr. Lee M. Talbot.[40] The study was supported by the U.S. Department of State, the National Marine Fisheries Service, and the U.S. Fish and Wildlife Service, and should be studied carefully by the officials of these agencies responsible for wildlife conservation. They would learn much that is valuable about how they have been mismanaging wildlife from this report, which questions the ability of humans to manage *any* wildlife on a sustainable use basis.

The draft report clearly warns that the world's wildlife is in serious trouble:

> Among those consulted, there is virtually unanimous concern for the future of living resources throughout the world . . . Virtually all species and stocks of wild living resources . . . which are being harvested commercially are being depleted. While habitat change is often a contributing factor, the harvest itself is the principal cause of depletion . . . Throughout most of the world, species and stocks of wildlife are declining, often rapidly. The greatest losses are in the developing world, particularly in Africa. Many feel that African wildlife is "in a crisis situation."[41]

Nor are we managing forests much better than wildlife. As the report observes:

> We do not have sufficient knowledge of the ecological basis to enable us to manage harvests sustainably in most forests, especially tropical ones. In practical terms, no tropical moist forest is being harvested on a sustainable basis, and there is real question as to whether truly sustainable harvest is possible in tropical forests in conditions other than plantations.[42]

The report comes to a remarkably strong conclusion for a government document, saying:

> . . . many have questioned whether it is possible to achieve sustainable management of most living resources, at least in terms of economically viable commercial harvest, but also in many cases in terms of other consumptive and non-consumptive conservation objectives ranging from sport hunting and fishing to preservation.[43]

In other words, humans are simply unable to sustainably manage wildlife effectively, especially when it involves large-scale killing of animals.

And while some scientists are profoundly changing their perspectives on ecosystems, the study emphasizes that the facts have been known by some scientists and managers for many years, yet only relatively recently has this knowledge been recognized and accepted more widely. Indeed, some scientists have, for decades, questioned the validity of applying sustained yield management principles to commercial harvests:

> . . . as Colin Clark wrote in the mid-1970s, the free exercise of traditional economics can (and in most fisheries situations, will) lead to overharvest, mining the resource for maximum benefit at the expense of possible future benefit. This truth is recognized by few scientists or managers, and even fewer have sought to come to grips with it. However, many of those consulted in this project questioned whether the market economy ever serves to support sustainable commercial use of living resources, because it is so often more economically beneficial in the short run to mine the resource and move on to something else . . . .[44]

The report's epilogue stresses that attempts to manage wildlife are always fraught with peril and unpredictability:

> Finally, it is important to understand that the unpredictability of recruitment fluctuations makes fisheries management an exercise in gambling . . . The ultimate joint responsibility of scientists and managers is to ensure that this gambling is carried out intelligently. Butterworth et al. emphasized this principle for marine fisheries, but to a greater or lesser degree applies to management of all living resources.[45]

The study recommends that wildlife utilization programs adopt a "new principle of uncertainty":

> . . . an ecosystem is characterized by uncertainty rather than the opposite, and therefore . . . management must recognize uncertainty as an overriding factor . . . Management decisions should include a safety factor to allow for the fact that knowledge is limited . . . In practice, our knowledge is often seriously inadequate, and predictions are uncertain. Uncertainty may arise from ignorance of such things as biological growth rates, interactions with other species, effects of the species on its habitat, and unpredictable environmental events.

Unfortunately, the report notes, uncertainty is considered inadequately (if at all) in most projects that seek to "manage" wildlife, and many managers and scientists simply do not acknowledge that it exists at all. Yet, the report says, it is imperative that we learn to recognize our limitations and the limitations of science:[46]

> For example, in the tuna–dolphin situation in the Pacific there has been a five year period of abundant research and monitoring with budget of millions and two research ships surveying an area of 5.5 million square miles. In spite of good background data and favorable conditions for good results, they found they couldn't detect even a 40 percent change in the population.[47]

The Talbot report acknowledges what wildlife protectionists have always known: Scientists are often in error, but seldom in doubt:

> "People's expectation of what science can do is greatly overrated. Many of those consulted also spoke of the arrogance of scientists, mostly fisheries biologists, as being a major obstacle to moving forward."[48]

THE SORCERER'S APPRENTICE

Warnings about the fallibility of sustainable utilization programs are more relevant than ever in our modern, highly technical society. It is becoming increasingly clear that sustainable use is particularly unworkable when it involves valuable commodities in international trade. If governments cannot control the drug trade, which causes so much harm to society, how can we expect them to stem the lucrative trade in illicit wildlife products, which causes much less apparent damage to humans?

After a quarter-century of studying and writing about the wildlife trade, Dr. John Grandy, HSUS vice president for wildlife, has observed, "The history of wildlife exploitation in developing countries proves that, no matter how well-meaning the justification, trade in wildlife and its parts and products leads not to conservation but rather to decimation."[49]

Today, because of new technologies and the burgeoning human population, introducing species into, or maintaining their availability in, international trade is more dangerous than ever before. It is usually a recipe for disaster, not a conservation tool. For example, describing how the demand for tiger bones and rhino horns has driven these creatures to the brink of extinction, *New York Times* reporter Thomas L. Friedman writes:

... as trade grows more global and as barriers between countries come down, the environmental consequences can be enormous. When advances in hunting techniques are combined with lower trade barriers and rapidly growing [human] populations that demand medicines made from exotic wildlife, an entire species can be wiped out in one generation.[50]

Indeed, "wildlife conservation is incompatible with global markets or private ownership," according to Valerius Geist of the University of Calgary in Calgary, Alberta, Canada. Geist is a well-known, highly respected mammalogist whose work on wild sheep is considered authoritative.

Writing in the April 7, 1994 issue of *Nature,* Geist calls the creation of a global luxury market in wildlife products a "bad initiative," saying:

> ... this approach to sustainability is invariably ineffective, with devastating consequences for conservation and detrimental effects to agriculture and public health ... The important lesson is to keep wildlife out of the marketplace, and thus out of private hands, while encouraging its diverse use under close scrutiny ... a global luxury market in wildlife is compatible with neither conservation nor good economics. Markets in dead wildlife reward its killing, foster its private ownership and manipulation, spawn disease, and are open to corruption.[51]

Though Geist recognizes the danger of commercializing wildlife, he is no wildlife protectionist or animal rights advocate. In fact, he offers as the alternative "the 70-year-old North American system of wildlife management," which relies in large part, he says, on such consumptive activities as hunting and fishing (on a restricted basis). But, he writes, this system, "although deliberately kept outside a global community market, generates both wealth and employment and is a proven conservation success, a model example of sustainable ecological development." Geist estimates that the system has created a manufacturing and service industry worth over $70 billion a year in the United States and Canada, compared with the legal and illegal *global* market in wildlife products of just $8 billion.[52]

If American-style wildlife management works at all, it is because it largely prohibits consumptive commercial use of wildlife. Thus, most legal killing of wildlife takes place within a heavily subsidized system based on recreational hunting. Although this has a very damaging impact on many animals and their ecosystems, the inherent uncontrollability of commercial consumptive use, which Geist recognizes, is largely minimized or avoided in the United States and Canada, in contrast to the much less restrictive situation that prevails in developing countries.[53]

Although Geist gives far too much credit to hunting as a conservation tool, he recognizes the overriding dangers of the *commercial* trade in wildlife:

... in the face of high market demands, illegal killing and selling of public wildlife is both lucrative and reasonably safe, and an industry in wildlife products remorselessly pits wealthy private interests, backed by powerful agricultural bureaucracies, against public conservation interests ...

Private interest in tropical forests and ocean fish, and the market price on them, have surely been powerful factors in the demise of these resources. So why place this price on dead wildlife too?[54]

Geist is especially alarmed by recent efforts by the IUCN and other proponents of sustainable use to cripple what limited effectiveness CITES has enjoyed:

The IUCN's approval of global trade in wildlife, and the weakening of CITES control of trade in endangered species, would make the IUCN a sorcerer's apprentice. Uncontrollable forces of wildlife destruction would be unleashed. ...

Geist concludes by asking: "When will politically powerful conservation organizations learn from the experience of others and stop endorsing a global luxury market in wildlife products?"[55]

WIPING OUT TIGERS AND RHINOS

When luxury products from wildlife are legally traded in international commerce, the economic incentives for killing such animals are overwhelming. This is what almost wiped out the spotted cats, and they were saved only when the United States banned their import and campaigns by animal protectionists made wearing their fur unfashionable in Europe and America. But between 1968 and 1970, the American fur industry imported the raw pelts of 18,456 leopards; 31,105 jaguars; 349,680 ocelots; and 3,100 cheetahs.[56] When the U.S. Department of the Interior finally placed these cats on its endangered list in 1972, it estimated that just 2,000 cheetahs remained in all the parks of Africa—a third less than the number killed in just a three-year period for the U.S. market![57]

Current examples of the difficulty of controlling trade in wildlife parts when illicit markets for them exist are the critically endangered tiger and rhino, particularly the black rhinoceros. These species are being hunted into extinction for their body parts. The worldwide tiger population has fallen from 100,000 at the turn of the century to less than 6,000 today.[58] Black rhinos have declined from about 65,000 in 1970 to around 2,300 now.[59]

Most of the illegal rhino horns and tiger parts are smuggled into Taiwan, China, and South Korea, in violation of CITES. Bones from tigers and horns from rhinos are ground up and used in Asia in traditional medicines and aphrodisiacs, which are prescribed by doctors in China, South Korea, and Taiwan for such ailments as arthritis, fever, and impotence. In 1993 alone, China exported to South Korea one and one-half tons of tiger bones, representing 200 dead tigers, although China had previously officially banned such exports.[60]

U.S. President Bill Clinton at first refused to invoke trade sanctions against these nations, as he is authorized to do under U.S. law—legislation known as the Pelly Amendment to the Fishermen's Protective Act allows the United States to impose economic sanctions against nations that undermine international conservation agreements it has signed.[61] But pressure from animal protectionists and conservationists—including a 1993 consumer boycott of Taiwan launched by The HSUS and other organizations—finally forced him to act.

On November 3, 1993, Dr. Teresa Telecky of The HSUS testified before a congressional hearing that "at the present rate of decline, there will be no rhinos left in the wild in two and a half years, and no tigers in less than five." She pointed out, "The U.S. could use its considerable diplomatic, political, and economic power and leadership to halt this decline, but it has failed to do so."[62]

Finally, on April 11, 1994, President Clinton announced that the U.S. would impose trade sanctions on Taiwan, but not on China or South Korea. In doing so, he said, "This is the first time any country has acted on the international call for trade sanctions to protect endangered species, but if the illegal trade in rhinos and tigers is not eliminated, these species could be extinct in five years."[63]

The trade penalties invoked against Taiwan were relatively modest, amounting to less than one tenth of 1 percent of the country's $25.1 billion in exports to the United States. Still, the potential ban on imports of all wildlife products from Taiwan could affect some $25 million in trade in such things as crocodile, lizard, and snake skin items and coral and mollusk-shell jewelry. China was not sanctioned, ostensibly because it had taken a few modest steps to discourage the illegal trade (although actually for political reasons).[64] China remains one of the largest traders in endangered wildlife products. South Korea was also spared sanctions.

And incredibly, although the species in question are on the verge of extinction, some governments (such as those of China and Zimbabwe) and "conservation" groups are pushing for their "sustainable use"—tigers through captive breeding, and rhinos through the sale of horns removed during de-horning operations.

THE DANGERS OF WILDLIFE "FARMING"

Some sustainable use schemes involve the captive breeding of rare animals. Advocates claim that this reduces pressure on wild populations by satisfying the commercial market for wildlife products. The international sale of "specimens" or products from certain farming or ranching operations are, as usual, to be addressed at the November 1994 CITES meeting.

The main problem with wildlife or "game" farming (besides the cruel and inhumane conditions under which the animals are usually kept) is that it tends to stimulate and perpetuate the market for such products, thus *increasing*, or at least maintaining, the poaching pressure on wild populations.

China, for example, has established the first tiger farm at Hengdaohezi, where endangered Siberian tigers are being raised, and expects to have a "crop" of some 600 adults by the turn of the century. The Chinese government claims that it intends to reintroduce tigers into the wild, but it also is seeking CITES approval to sell in international commerce tiger bones, blood, and genitalia to Asian merchants, who employ these products in tonics, medicines, and food items, used in a practice called *jinbu*, that are thought to increase strength and sexual prowess.[65]

Michael Day of the United Kingdom's Tiger Trust points out that "farming tigers encourages poaching," and that wild tigers will always be more in demand than farm-raised cats: "What would you rather have for a *jinbu*: a factory-farmed pussycat fed on rotten chicken and old fish heads, or the real thing? Perception is everything."[66]

China is also farming endangered bears, and has a reported 8,000 to 10,000 in captivity at some four dozen bear farms. Some of the bears spend their entire lives immobilized in small, cramped cages, and are "milked" daily for their bile (used in medicine) through tubes implanted in their gallbladders. The demand in Asia for bear parts such as gallbladders, paws, and meat has endangered bear species throughout Asia and even caused widespread poaching of black bears in the United States, whose gallbladders now sell for up to $5,000 apiece.[67] The unrestricted international trade in bear parts has increased the demand for and poaching of bears throughout the world.

Canadian biologist Valerius Geist has expressed alarm about the spread of "game farming" in North America, observing that it relies on the killing of local predators, spreads diseases (such as bovine tuberculosis) to livestock, causes the "genetic pollution of wild stocks" (as happened when "mongrel escapees from deer farms" bred with giant deer or wapiti), and displaces native species (when ranched animals escape from captivity and reproduce in the wild). Game farming can even endanger human health; "mad cow disease" (spongiform encephalopathy) is now found in at least three species of free-roaming deer that are used as stock for deer farms.[68]

DEVELOPING THE PLANET

It is thus clear that sustainable use of wildlife is a dead-end street. And not just because urbanites and animal protectionists think so—this is the published conclusion of some of the most respected and knowledgeable scientists. And it is the opinion of many more, who work for governments and wildlife agencies and are not at liberty to speak out.

CHAPTER 2

Case Studies
of Sustainable Use

. . . large parrots in the Amazon . . . cannot withstand any
harvest whatsoever for the pet trade without declining to local
and then global extinction.

Dr. Charles A. Munn
Wildlife Conservation International[1]

Virtually all stocks of Marine living resources, which are or have
been commercially exploited, are being or have been depleted.

U.S. Marine Mammal Commission
preliminary report
September 1993[2]

I am calling for a national hunting ban . . . the land can no longer
sustain its impact. Hunting in its various forms has been the prime
reason for making large portions of Botswana devoid of wildlife.

Dereck Joubert
filmmaker and wildlife photographer
1993[3]

I n looking at sustainable use—and sustained yield management, and
the other euphemisms for the consumptive commercial utilization
of wildlife—we must ultimately ask the question, "Does it work?"
Let us therefore examine some case studies of creatures that have been
subjected to sustainable use in the past.

In fact, the concept of sustainable use and variations of it have been
tried and tested on various species and situations over recent decades,
and the result has almost always been the depletion of the "utilized"
species. The pages that follow describe how parrots, whales, fish, and
animals "managed" by sport hunting have been devastated by consumptive use, which was always portrayed as being "sustainable."

There are important lessons to be learned from these well-documented case studies. They will show the inability of consumptive use programs to manage wildlife without destroying much of it.

PARROTS: ON THE VERGE OF EXTINCTION

Millions of parrots are captured from the wild each year to supply the international pet trade. As a result, many species have been devastated for the sake of the commerical pet trade and are on the verge of extinction. The answer to this problem, some now say, is to perpetuate the international trade through "sustainable harvest" of parrots from the wild. But stimulation of this trade under the guise of sustainability is likely to result in further depletion of parrot populations.

Loving Parrots to Death

A trip to any pet store will testify to human fascination with the rare and beautiful jewels of the forest called parrots. Numbering over 300 species, parrots have for centuries been coveted for their beauty, intelligence, ability to "talk," and, ironically, their representation of freedom ("free as a bird").

Centuries ago, Alexander the Great brought rose-ringed parakeets from India back to Greece. Roman emperors surrounded themselves with birds. In recent decades, with the development and expansion of international airline services, hundreds of thousands of parrots captured from far-flung countries around the world have been, and still are being, transported to consumers in Europe, North America, and Japan every year. Expanding markets, along with the destruction of nesting trees and habitat, have devastated populations of these birds throughout the tropical and subtropical regions where they live.

About 30 million birds are captured from the wild each year to supply the international pet trade.[4] Because of grossly inhumane capture techniques, injuries, inadequate care, and trauma sustained during capture, up to 80 percent of these birds may die before they reach the final markets.[5] More than 7 million birds were imported into the United States alone over a recent ten-year period.[6] Over 1.2 million died during transport or during the mandatory quarantine period upon arrival.[7]

The horrid conditions under which parrots are so often shipped violate the transport standards adopted under the Convention on International Trade in Endangered Species of Wild Fauna and Flora (CITES), but enforcement of these standards is rare. For example, in April 1994, the West African airline Air Afrique was fined $17,500 for shipping approximately 10,000 African grey parrots to the United States under inhumane conditions.[8] However, since only about 25 percent of all live wildlife shipments entering the United States are inspected by enforcement officers, it is likely that most cases of inhumane treatment go undetected.

The Uncontrollable Parrot Trade

About one third of the 140 species of parrots native to the Western Hemisphere are threatened with extinction, and populations of many others are declining.[9] The large-scale capture of parrots for the legal and illegal pet trade has been one of the biggest causes of the disappearance or decline of these beautiful birds. CITES has listed all but three species of parrots on its appendices of species imperiled by trade. Many species of macaws and cockatoos are listed on Appendix I, the most endangered category, and their international trade is legally banned. The remainder are listed on Appendix II, and their legal trade is supposedly regulated.

Despite CITES requirements, the capture of parrots for international trade continues to drive populations to extinction because the trade is characterized by a lack of control and enforcement of regulations. Under CITES, in order to receive approval for the export of parrots, countries that are parties to the treaty are supposed to ensure that the birds are "so prepared and shipped as to minimize the risk of injury, damage to health or cruel treatment." It is further mandated that "such export will not be detrimental to the survival of the species," so that the species will be maintained "throughout its range at a level consistent with its role in the ecosystems in which it occurs and well above the level at which that species might become eligible for inclusion in Appendix I."[10] However, many countries allow the collection and export of parrots without implementing these provisions of the treaty.

For example, the single largest source of wild birds for the pet trade is Senegal, which annually exports anywhere from one to ten million birds. Two thirds of the revenues from this trade come from just one species, the African grey parrot—a bird that does not even live in Senegal![11] An American man was recently indicted for smuggling nearly 2,000 African grey parrots into the United States. The parrots were collected illegally in Zaire, where such trapping is banned, and smuggled to Guinea, the Ivory Coast, and Senegal, where false CITES export documents were supplied.[12]

Another example is the gray-cheeked parakeet, which has a very small range that straddles the border between southwestern Ecuador and northwestern Peru. This bird is rare, and declining, due to habitat destruction and the trade. Ecuador has banned the export of this species, but Peru continues to allow it. Approximately 90,000 gray-cheeked parakeets were imported into the United States alone between 1980 and 1989; 79 percent of them were captured illegally in Ecuador and exported from Peru, which granted CITES export permits for the poached birds.[13]

The American pet trade is primarily responsible for the decimation of several species of parrots, including the Moluccan cockatoo. This once-common Indonesian parrot was upgraded from Appendix II to Appendix I of CITES in 1989. But during the three years prior to this, 15,749 of the birds are known to have been imported into the United States. Indeed, just before the trade ban took effect, Indonesia tripled its capture quota to 3,000 birds to help dealers dispose of the huge number that had been stockpiled in anticipation of the listing.[14]

Perhaps the most endangered wild bird is the Spix's macaw, which has been driven to the very edge of extinction by trapping for the pet trade. Individual birds were worth tens of thousands of dollars, and now only a single bird is known to remain in the wild, somewhere in northeastern Brazil, under heavy guard against poachers.[15]

Ironically, as parrots become increasingly rare or endangered, they become more valuable and sought after. Some of them have brought over $10,000 apiece. Shortly before President Bill Clinton named him Secretary of the Interior, former Arizona Governor Bruce Babbitt, in a keynote address to the annual meeting of The Humane Society of the United States (HSUS) in October 1992, expressed dismay at "the looming extinction" and cruel exploitation of South American parrots and macaws:

> These birds are captured for buyers in the United States who will pay up to $30,000 for a hyacinth macaw. You can stand on docks outside of Manaus, Brazil, and other towns in the Amazon and see confiscated crates with blue and yellow macaws, their feet taped, their beaks wired, stacked up like cordwood in boxes. They have a fatality rate of 50 percent by the time they're smuggled into Miami. [16]

Due to the lax implementation and enforcement of CITES, conservationists and animal protectionists have for years fought to ban or restrict the trade in wild birds by other means. Efforts to close down the largest market for birds, the United States, have been led by The HSUS, the Animal Welfare Institute, Defenders of Wildlife (DOW), and the Environmental Investigation Agency, all based in Washington, D.C. The strongest opposition to such efforts has come from the Pet Industry Joint Advisory Council (PIJAC), which has repeatedly stymied efforts to control the trade.

Finally, after years of work, animal protection and conservation groups have made some important progress in restricting the trade in parrots. Over 100 airlines have agreed to stop transporting wild birds destined for the pet trade. And the U.S. Wild Bird Conservation Act of 1992 banned importation of all parrots and other birds listed on the CITES appendixes. This law puts the burden of proof that these species can withstand trade, and that the captured birds will be treated humanely, on the exploiters, thus reinforcing CITES' requirements for export. Under the act, countries that are not implementing CITES are not able to export parrots to the United States.

Unfortunately, after the Wild Bird Conservation Act was passed, the U.S. Department of the Interior failed to regulate the import into the United States of wild birds as the law intended, continuing to allow the importation of over 100 species of wild-caught birds listed on CITES' Appendix III. This violated the section of the act stating that effective October 23, 1993, "the importation of any exotic bird of a species that is listed in any Appendix to CITES is prohibited." Appendix III is the portion of CITES that allows a nation to protect its own wildlife; species a country chooses to list on it are protected from international trade and require a permit for export.[17]

Through the volunteer work of the prestigious Washington, D.C., law firm of Howrey and Simon, The HSUS and DOW filed a lawsuit to force the Interior Department to ban the import of all birds listed on any CITES appendix. The result was a stunning victory for wild birds.

On April 4, 1994, a U.S. District Court ruled in favor of The HSUS and DOW, extending protection to the 117 species of wild birds commonly imported into the United States. The decision meant that some 100,000 birds—including finches, wild canaries, hill mynas, and ring-necked parakeets—then coming into the United States each year, plus several hundred thousand that die during capture and transport, will instead be flying free.[18] Some of the affected species had had a 90-percent mortality rate.

Meanwhile, the pet industry—including PIJAC and the American Federation of Aviculture—has been pressuring Congress and the Interior Department's Fish and Wildlife Service to weaken the regulations implementing the Wild Bird Conservation Act so that the United States could again become the number-one importer of wild birds instead of the world leader in protecting them.[19]

In any event, the remaining legal and illegal trade in some species of these birds abroad, especially the substantial markets in Europe and Japan, will continue to threaten the survival of parrots. In 1992, CITES began to examine the implementation of the treaty with respect to the trade in species listed on Appendix II, including parrots. To date, the international trade in certain species of parrots from several countries (including Indonesia, Peru, and Tanzania) that have failed to implement the treaty has been suspended by the CITES Standing Committee (CITES' governing body).[20]

Can Parrots Be Saved Through "Sustainable Harvesting"?

Because of restrictions on the trade in wild birds, such as the Wild Bird Conservation Act, there is now strong interest in reviving the trade through "sustainable use" projects. An article in the March 1992 issue of *BioScience*, "Can Parrots Be Conserved through Sustainable Harvesting?" concludes that they can—someday, perhaps, but not now. The study, by Steven R. Beissinger, an associate professor of ecology and conservation biology at Yale University, and Enrique H. Bucher, director of the Center for Applied Zoology at the University of Cordoba, in Argentina, presents what it calls a model for sustainable harvesting regimes for parrot nestlings.[21]

The authors warn:

"Neotropical birds have become one of the most threatened groups of birds in the world, primarily as a result of habitat destruction and international trade. . . An immediate halt to the international trade of parrots is urgently needed to reverse the declines of many species, but habitat conservation is also required. Sustainable management could potentially achieve both.

In theory, controlled, sustainable harvest of nestlings could provide important benefits in helping to conserve parrot habitat. As Beissinger and Bucher observe:

Severe nesting habitat destruction is caused by local *campesinos* who destroy the nest cavity or even cut the tree to gain access to nestlings—if parrots can be sustainably harvested from tropical rain forests, this commodity might help to make extractive reserves more economically valuable than forest land cleared for timber harvest or cattle production.

But while advocating sustainable use of parrots in theory, particularly the "harvesting" of young parrots, Beissinger and Bucher candidly point out that this cannot realistically be achieved at the present time. They suggest that while the concept may work on paper, in practice we are still a long way away.

For example, they contend that there are six areas of biological knowledge that are needed to "harvest" any type of species sustainably. But, they write, "the population biology of all parrots is too poorly known to calculate yields for even a single species. In fact, few parrots have received enough study to satisfy the requirements of any one of the six necessary areas." In addition, Beissinger and Bucher state:

> . . . substantial social, political, and economic difficulties still lie in the way of implementing sustainable harvest schemes with parrots. . . it will always be cheaper and easier to take birds from the wild in an unsustainable manner and sell them through legal or illegal channels than to harvest them sustainably. Implementing successful sustained-harvest operations may require both the passage of legislation to control the parrot trade and truly effective control over illegal harvests.[22]

One of the biggest obstacles, the authors point out, is enforcement of regulations:

> Even if unlicensed commercial operations are outlawed, we expect regulatory problems to persist because maintaining a market for parrots may encourage the harvest of birds from outside the managed population. It will be especially difficult and important to protect the highly endangered, valuable Amazons and macaws from illegal trade. Determining the source of nestlings is difficult, and cheating may be hard to detect. . . The maintenance of a market for parrots may also encourage the poaching of birds from sustained-harvest programs, if they can be sold on the black market.[23]

Beissinger and Bucher conclude:

> Realizing many of the benefits from sustained harvesting will require a degree of control over trade that currently is difficult, if not impossible, to achieve. . . In the absence of effective controls, attempts at sustained harvesting could exacerbate the conservation problems. Because of the urgency of the situation, there is no rational choice but to halt the international trade in parrots until evidence can be presented that such trade in any species can be constituted in a sustainable manner.[24]

I question the authors' belief that parrots cannot be preserved with preservation strategies alone, that sustainable use could play an important role, and that "legislative initiatives should encourage a future for sustainable harvesting of parrots." But the authors acknowledge that the best immediate approach towards protecting parrots is *not* a sustainable use program, but rather a moratorium on trade in the birds:

We recommend that importing countries and CITES adopt an immediate moratorium on the importation of parrots for a fixed time period, such as five years. The American Ornithologists' Union recently made a similar recommendation for the importation of all wild-caught birds into the United States.[25]

In reality, using wild birds for international trade in a sustainable manner would be both technically difficult and labor-intensive and, as a result, generally not financially profitable. In order to ensure that use is sustainable, technical experts would be required to collect extensive baseline information on the biology of the species involved and their interactions with their habitats and ecosystems, and to continually monitor the effect of "use" on the population. Additional personnel would be required to guard the management area from poachers; to enforce national laws to prevent illegally taken wildlife from being funnelled into the trade; and to provide sanitary and humane care for animals in the live trade. This is why consumptive use is so rarely demonstrated to be sustainable; it is easier and more profitable to use species in an unsustainable manner.[26]

An exhaustive and extensively researched 1992 report on the wild bird trade documents the futility of trying to conserve parrots through sustainable use. The study, done by the Animal Welfare Institute and the Environmental Investigation Agency, demonstrates conclusively that only an end to the trade in birds can save them from actual or near extinction:

> Some conservationists, as well as some traders, are to blame for serious errors of judgment and a blind wish to prove that the bird trade can be "sustainable"—despite there being no documented cases, but a wealth of scientific evidence proving that the opposite is true. . . The bird trade has been studied very closely, and if nothing else, the last 16 years should have taught us that no amount of tinkering with the regulations will improve the situation. . . It is the responsibility of the international community to admit to its failures and end the wild bird trade without delay.[27]

Dr. Charles Munn, a wild bird expert and senior research biologist with Wildlife Conservation International (WCI), wrote in 1991, "In my research on the reproduction and demography of . . . large parrots in the Amazon, my colleagues and I have shown that these birds . . . cannot withstand any harvest whatsoever for the pet trade without declining to local and then global extinction."[28]

True Sustainable Use of Parrots

There are, of course, ways to generate revenue "sustainably" from parrots without removing them from the wild. In 1992, in southeastern Peru's Manu region, WCI worked out an arrangement with the village of Tayakome that protects parrots and macaws while providing valuable data to scientists and financial benefits to the villagers. In return for the payment of $500 a year, the local people provide WCI with information on the birds, plus the types of trees and vegetation that furnish food for twenty-three species of parrots.[29]

According to Munn, who has worked in Manu for seventeen years, ecotourism is helping macaw conservation to pay for itself, and at the same time increasing awareness about these birds:

> The national park in Tambopata has been planned with a farsighted balance of Peru's conservation and economic needs. . . . The country will also benefit from tourists drawn to the rich wildlife in a 1.8 million acre park that will protect the world's largest known macaw clay lick. (These salt licks are riverbank clays that are high in mineral salts and draw large numbers of birds and animals.)[30]

The area's 7,000-square-mile Manu National Park and Biosphere Reserve, one of the biggest rain forest preserves on earth, provides sanctuary not just for parrots and macaws but for many other species as well. Among the rare creatures that can regularly be seen are jaguars, pumas, giant river otters, harpy eagles, spectacled bears, and several species of monkey.

But it is the birds that are the main attraction at Manu. According to ecology professor Charles H. Janson, over 1,000 species of birds live in this bird-watcher's paradise, and more than 560 different species have been seen and recorded in one area comprising a five-mile circle.[31]

Indeed, as Janson says: "For seeing the rainforest in all its splendor, Manu has no rival. . . It is one of the few places on Earth so untouched that you can see a tropical rainforest essentially the way it was on the day Columbus first set foot in the New World." Experienced bird-watchers can observe over 300 species in a single day, including "the kaleidoscope spectacle of hundreds of brilliantly colored but highly endangered macaw sitting nearly shoulder to shoulder along the water's edge."[32]

And this natural paradise is more secure because it enjoys strong local support and participation. As Munn observes:

> Eleven years of thoughtful, conservation-oriented development of locally-owned lodges in Manu has paid off by enriching local people

while raising their conservation awareness. Manu's regional ecotourism companies are excellent models of how ecotourism can and should produce political support by indigenous people for key wilderness parks.[33]

This, then, represents a truly humane and sustainable use of parrots: using these spectacularly beautiful birds to attract tourists into an area in a project that will provide major benefits to the local people, the environment, and, of course, the parrots themselves.

THE GREAT WHALES—WILL THEY EVER RECOVER FROM "SUSTAINED YIELD MANAGEMENT"?

The "conservation," management, and destruction of the great whales provides an instructive example of how commercially valuable wildlife species have been subjected to "sustainable use," supposedly using the most up-to-date scientific data and principles, over recent decades.

Throughout the years of large-scale whaling, the world was assured that the hunting was always carried out on a "sustained yield" basis, with strict quotas based on good science. The slaughter continued until there were relatively few great whales left to hunt economically. The result of this exploitation was that in June 1970, stocks of the great whales were so depleted that the U.S. Department of the Interior was forced to place all eight species of them on its list of endangered species: the blue, the humpback, the right, the sei, the fin (or finback), the sperm, the bowhead, and the gray. Of these, only the California gray whales have verifiably experienced any significant recovery, and they have been downgraded to "threatened" status. Experts doubt the others will ever come back in viable numbers, and some may disappear completely.

Ironically, whales are worth much more alive than dead. In 1992, tourists spent over $317 million on whale-watching expeditions, without a single whale being killed (see Chapter 10).[34]

The Largest Animals Ever to Live

Whales once commonly lived throughout the world's oceans and coastal areas, and they became part of the culture and folklore of many areas. The Bible refers to whales on several occasions, with the tale of Jonah being the best known story. Early paintings and depictions of ships often show the vessels amidst groups of frolicking, curious whales.

Whales are by far the most massive animals ever to have lived on the earth. The blue whale is bigger than thirty elephants combined, or three of the largest dinosaurs. When a blue whale calf is nursing, it takes in up to 1,000 pounds of milk a day![35]

Whales are warm-blooded, air-breathing mammals that are long-lived, slow-reproducing, and far-ranging animals. They show remarkable concern and affection for each other, and often refuse to leave a member of the pod, or family, that has been beached, wounded, or—in the case of mothers with calves—harpooned. Whales have been known to follow or wait for days, or even weeks, for a mate or family member that has been captured or harpooned and taken to shore.

Whalers operating from shore stations have long been well aware of the whales' loyalty to each other, and would often harpoon a baby whale, tow it into shore, and then kill the mother or even the entire pod that followed it in.

Yet despite the decades of virtually unrestrained slaughter of whales, these gentle giants still seem well-disposed towards humans, often allowing divers and photographers to approach them closely. Attacks on humans and their boats are amazingly rare, except in cases when whales are defending themselves against whalers.

The Destruction of the Great Whales

By the early 1970s, over 2 million whales had been killed, with some 40,000 a year being added to the toll. About 67,000 whales were "taken" in the peak hunting year of 1962.[36]

The collapse of whale populations worldwide and the success of the "save-the-whales" movement have resulted in drastically reduced whale hunting. Today, most of the whaling is done by Japan and Norway, each of which reports killing about 300 minke whales a year.[37] In addition, pirate whalers kill an unknown number of whales to supply Japan's whale meat market.

The protection belatedly accorded the great whales came too late to help the Atlantic gray whale, which is now extinct, or the Asiatic gray whale, which is virtually so. Among the most severely depleted and critically endangered of the whales is the mighty blue, the largest creature ever to inhabit the earth. The worldwide population of blues may once have numbered over 600,000, with at least 200,000 in the Antarctic alone. Today, according to most estimates, the blue has been reduced by at least 97 percent, to just 5,000 to 15,000—possibly even fewer.[38] Indeed, when the Interior Department listed the blue as endangered in 1970, it estimated the entire worldwide population of blue whales at only 600 to 3,000. Data presented at the May 1994 meeting of the International Whaling Commission (IWC) indicated a population of just 460 blue whales in the entire Southern Hemisphere.[39]

Data and statistics gathered and maintained by IWC—the international organization with responsibility for managing and regulating whaling—document the carefully controlled destruction of the blue whale. The peak year for killing blue whales was the 1930–1931 winter whaling season, when 29,410 were killed in the Antarctic over a four- to five-month period. Thereafter, the blue whale "catch"—and the whales themselves—experienced a steady decline.[40]

By 1945–1946, fewer than 10,000 blues were being killed; the average take in the late 1950s dropped to less than 1,500 a year. By the 1962–1963 season, only 944 blues could be found and killed. The following year, the take fell to just 112, and by 1964–1965, only 20 blues were caught. Later in 1965, after the whaling nations (mainly Japan, the Soviet Union, and Norway) could not locate enough blue whales to set quotas for the next whaling season, IWC finally declared the Antarctic whales to be protected, and their killing was banned. In earlier years, IWC had continued to insist that the blue whale kill was not exceeding "maximum sustainable yield."[41]

But between 1900 and 1965, when international protection was nominally given to blue whales, over 325,000 were killed, and the stocks were clearly on the verge of collapse.[42]

Dr. Ronald Nowak, a biologist and endangered species specialist with the U.S. Fish and Wildlife Service, writes that the whales, like elephants, "are good examples of large animals that could supposedly sustain international exploitation and commerce." He summarizes the systematic destruction of whales under international sustained yield management as follows:

> For decades the argument was made that a total ban on whaling was undesirable and that limited controls, together with the whaling industry's own claimed interest in conserving the resource, would maintain large stocks of whales. The result was the near destruction of all major populations of great whales. Year after year the killing and commerce continued; all sorts of limits and regulations were set up, but never the final total ban. Remarkably, this process went on right up to the times of modern conservation, through the 1960s and even into the 1970s and to some extent until the present.
>
> Only within the last few years has it become fully apparent how severe the losses were, and there now is fear that the blue, fin, humpback, and right whales may have been reduced to such an extent that they have permanently lost the viability needed for recovery.[43]

Commercial Whaling Finally Banned

In 1982, over a decade of pressure by wildlife protectionists finally came to fruition, when a ban on commercial whaling was agreed on by IWC, to be phased in by 1986.

But even though the "legal" hunting of whales has been drastically reduced, these animals are still seriously endangered from a variety of threats, including pirate whaling, pollution, drowning in fishing nets, the decimation of fish stocks worldwide, and the depletion of the atmosphere's protective ozone layer, which imperils the survival of whales and the creatures on which they feed, such as Antarctic krill.

Today, with the larger whales largely gone, the whalers have shifted to smaller species, especially the thirty-foot-long minke whale. Minke whales are curious creatures and are said to often swim over to boats to observe and "check them out." Indeed, traditional Norwegian whale hunting relies on the technique of sitting in a boat in an area where the whales gather to feed or through which they migrate, and shooting whales when they approach the boat.[44]

Since 1986, when the whaling ban went into effect, several countries have continued to hunt whales under the pretext of "scientific research." Japanese whalers kill some 300 minkes a year in the Antarctic, ostensibly to gather information about whale populations, but the meat from these whales is sold commercially and consumed in Japan.[45]

In 1993, Norway openly defied IWC by also killing some 300 minkes, and it even tried to smuggle several tons of whale meat out of Norway in violation of the ban on international sales of whale products. In 1993, three-and-a-half tons of frozen whale meat were discovered at Oslo Airport, labeled as shrimp and destined for Japan via South Korea.[46]

In 1993, The HSUS called for an economic boycott of Norway, including avoiding both travel to the country and the purchase of Norwegian products such as cheeses, sardines, salmon, and other fish. In September 1993, General Motors announced that it would no longer purchase products from Raufoss A/S, a Norwegian firm that produced whaling harpoon grenades for the government.[47] Later, Raufoss announced that it had no plans to manufacture the harpoon grenades in the future, but by that time the whalers had already stockpiled a large supply of them.[48] The HSUS plans to continue the boycott for as long as Norway continues to kill whales for profit in violation of the international moratorium on commercial whaling.

Japan and Norway are two of the wealthiest nations on earth, and hardly need the income or meat from whales for their populations. Indeed, Japan's "scientific" whaling is clearly a ploy to continue commercial hunting. In recent years, the IWC has urged Japan to cease its legal "research," pointing out that the data gathered were not relevant. The 1994 IWC resolution states that Japan's proposed kill of minke whales in the Southern Hemisphere (the Antarctic) and in the North Pacific "does not fully satisfy [existing] criteria . . . in that the proposed research is not structured so as to contribute information presently required for the management of whaling in these areas for this species . . ." The resolution goes on to recommend that Japan "restructure its research program concerning minke whales . . . in such a manner that the research interests can be adequately addressed with non-lethal methods."[49]

Will Whaling Be Legalized?

The latest ploys under which the pro-whaling nations want to again "sustainably harvest" whales are called the "Revised Management Scheme" (RMS) and the "Revised Management Procedure" (RMP), which is a mathematical model for setting quotas to be incorporated into the overall RMS. It is anticipated that these schemes will be used to organize commercial whaling if the present indefinite moratorium is overturned, which would require a three-fourths vote by IWC member nations.

The RMP and RMS are backed by the United States and most European countries, which have endorsed the principle of allowing 46 percent of a species' original population to be removed before intervention is required. After that, the whaling would be required to be "sustainable," with the number of kills not exceeding the number of births.[50]

As Ian Stewart, New Zealand's Commissioner to the IWC, warned at the summer 1991 meeting, "No matter how scientifically sensible such a management procedure may seem, it will appear to the people of New Zealand that we are repeating past mistakes all over again."[51]

Indeed, at the 1994 IWC meeting, U.S. Whaling Commissioner James Baker endorsed a resolution in favor of the IWC Scientific Committee's work on the RMP. But he pointed out that several important issues had not yet been addressed by the resolution, which, he said, "does not seek to resolve questions about unauthorized whaling, . . . illicit trade in whale products, . . . underreporting catch data, . . . [or] the concerns of a number of countries about humane killing methods, . . . [and] it does not imply that the effects of environmental degradation are understood."[52]

The U.S. Sellout of the Whales

For over two decades, the United States has opposed commercial whaling and often has led the fight against it. The Marine Mammal Protection

Act of 1972 established such a policy, which has frequently been reiterated by Congress. In 1993, both the U.S. Senate and House of Representatives passed *unanimous* resolutions calling for the United States to oppose any IWC management scheme that included commercial whale hunting.[53]

The high hopes many environmentalists held for the Clinton-Gore administration were shattered when the administration reversed two decades of U.S. anti-whaling policy and secretly agreed to help Norway cripple the ban on commercial whaling.

In August 1993, the U.S. Department of Commerce determined that Norway's resumption of whaling in defiance of IWC's ban had "diminished the effectiveness" of an international conservation agreement, and that Norway was thus subject to economic sanctions. But in October of that year, President Clinton announced that rather than imposing sanctions and limiting the imports of fishing products from Norway, he would try to persuade the country to "follow agreed conservation measures." Instead, the Clinton administration has supported Norway's pro-whaling policies.[54]

The reasons for this turnabout in U.S. policy became clear in May 1994, when whale protectionists received a leaked transcript of a September 29, 1993 meeting between Vice President Al Gore and Norwegian Prime Minister Gro Brundtland. The text of the confidential "Memorandum of Conservation" quotes Gore as assuring Brundtland that the U.S. administration would support the RMS being promoted by Norway and Japan.[55]

At one point in the meeting, Gore seemed to imply that the administration will say one thing publicly while working behind the scenes on an opposite policy. He said to Brundtland, "While the U.S. will continue to oppose commercial whaling as a national policy, we are willing to join you in working in good faith within IWC to complete all aspects of the Revised Management Scheme in 1994, and present a scientifically based, observable regimen to the body. Do you feel that's a reachable goal?"[56]

In arguing for a resumption of legal hunting of minke whales, Brundtland often employs the usual language of sustainable use, saying, "We would never have a policy which is not long-term sustainable development."[57] But it is neither her data nor her charm that is responsible for Norway's ability to reverse American policy. There are other reasons why Norway was able to persuade the United States to support its effort to renew commercial whaling. Christine Stevens, as president of the Animal Welfare Institute, has been leading the fight against whaling since the early 1970s. She observes:

Norway has pumped more than $1 million to Washington lobbyists over the past two years to subvert the long-standing U.S. policy against commercial whaling. . . The Norwegian Foreign Ministry hired the powerful, influence-peddling law firm of Akin, Gump, Strauss, Hauer and Feld to open doors at the White House, National Security Council, and Commerce and State Departments.[58]

Stevens reveals that over $50,000 a month was paid to the firm to lobby the administration and to "massage Congress and public opinion." The firm's senior partners are powerful and influential Washington insiders, including Robert Strauss, former head of the Democratic National Committee and adviser to presidents; Vernon Jordan, who headed up Bill Clinton's transition team; and Joel Jankowsky, who Stevens says is known on Capitol Hill as the "Wizard of Oz" for his skill at covert manipulations. "Norway has hired a team of fixers to override the U.S. policy against commercial whaling," Stevens observes, "and now, Vice President Gore is repeating the propaganda of Brundtland and her high-paid lobbyists."[59]

Gore's reference to a "scientifically based" policy is especially ominous, because the history of whale hunting has been characterized by inflated, fabricated data. This is a ploy that could—and probably will—be repeated by future whalers. In late 1993 and early 1994, investigators in Moscow discovered that for the past thirty years, Soviet whaling fleets illegally and secretly killed tens of thousands of whales, including critically endangered blue, humpback, and right whales.

In a letter published in the January 13, 1994 edition of *Nature*, Alexey V. Yablokov, Special Adviser to the President of Russia for Ecology and Health, discussed the lack of validity of catch data from commercial whaling operations. Referring to "actual Soviet catch data on right, humpback, and blue whales from the 1960's . . . from one of four factory ships that operated in the Southern Hemisphere," he states, "These numbers are much higher than were previously reported to the IWC"— in some cases, ten to fifteen times higher. Specifically, catches for blue whales were reported as 156, while 1,433 were actually killed. Similarly, 152 humpbacks were reported, but in fact 7,207 were landed.

Yablokov also refers to "a Soviet factory ship [that] illegally operated for a couple of weeks in Sea of Okhotsk and caught several hundred right whales." He writes that "it was also well known in the Soviet Union that blue whales continued to be killed after they were protected by the IWC." It can be assumed that other Soviet whaling fleets cheated in a similar manner.[60]

And Russian official Ernst Cherny has reported, "We have discovered the hunting of protected species, whaling at prohibited times in prohibited areas, extermination of entire herds and even populations— all were commonplace." Reportedly, the KGB threatened death to any-one who revealed the illegal overhunting of whales.[61]

And there is still concern that illegal and "pirate" whaling may be continuing on a larger scale than has been thought. At the May 1994 annual IWC meeting, held in Puerto Vallarta, Mexico, the New Zealand delegation presented evidence that some of the most critically endan-gered species, as well as other legally protected whales, are still being commercially hunted. Whale meat purchased in 1994 from stores in Japan was subjected to DNA analysis and found to be from such species as fins, North Atlantic minkes, North Pacific humpbacks, and other types that could not be identified.[62]

HSUS executive vice president Patricia Forkan, who has attended every IWC meeting since 1973, points out, "Such illegal practices flour-ish today. Regardless of whether whales are killed under the banner of 'sustainable use' or the guise of 'scientific whaling,' there is no way to know what rare and special species are being served up as delicacies on someone's table."[63]

Fortunately, at its 1994 meeting, IWC, with the strong support of the United States, voted to create a vast 8 million square mile whale sanctuary in the waters of Antarctica, where whales are found in greater numbers than anywhere in the world. The measure, which covers the feeding grounds of 90 percent of the world's potentially huntable whales (under the RMS), was strongly opposed by Japan and Norway, but will continue to allow Japan to hunt minke whales for "scientific" purposes and to sell the meat for domestic consump-tion.[64]

The sanctuary does provide effective protection against a future resumption of large-scale whaling in that region. But left unaffected by the sanctuary are the highly vulnerable populations of whales in other oceans of the world. Especially at risk are coastal stocks that are subject to hunting from shore-based boats and harm from pollution—includ-ing, hypothetically, the California gray whales. However, although they have been removed from the federal endangered species list, these whales remain completely protected by the U.S. Marine Mammal Pro-tection Act, and should be safe from hunting at least while migrating along the U.S. coast.

In any event, some species of nominally protected whales (such as the blue, fin, sei, humpback, and right) remain severely depleted. There is serious doubt they will ever be able to recover from the carefully controlled, scientifically based sustained yield management that has brought them to the brink of extinction.

But perhaps the greatest flaw in the theory of sustainable use is the one fundamental fact it ignores: There is simply no way to humanely kill a whale. As HSUS's Patricia Forkan observes, "Every whale killed, regardless of its rarity or its comparative value in the marketplace, is a sensitive creature that dies a painful and needless death, often leaving behind a disrupted family and social fabric. Even if there are theoretically enough of a certain species to kill some without endangering them all, it is ethically unacceptable to a growing number of people to kill any whales for the sake of greed and commerce."[65]

THE DESTRUCTION OF OCEAN FISHERIES

One would think that if sustainable use could be made to work anywhere, it would be with schools of deep-water fish. Those sought by commercial fishermen were once enormously abundant, capable of reproducing rapidly, closely monitored, and scientifically managed—so much so that it was thought mistakes in overfishing could be corrected before any permanent damage was done to population stocks.

Indeed, few natural resources have been as closely studied, monitored, regulated, and discussed as have the ocean's fisheries. In the United States, an entire federal agency—the National Marine Fisheries Service (NMFS)—has for decades regulated ocean fishing, as have dozens of state, foreign and international commissions, councils, and agencies. But political pressure and economic considerations have prevented any real conservation from resulting from this extensive regulation, and today most major commercial fish stocks and fisheries are seriously depleted or near collapse.

In May 1993, the United Nations Food and Agriculture Organization (FAO) warned that virtually every commercially utilized species of ocean fish worldwide was either "depleted," "fully exploited," or "overexploited." FAO says that of the world's seventeen major deep-sea fisheries, thirteen—three quarters of them—are depleted or in steep decline.[66]

Yet even now, with the evidence at hand that some species should be protected, the overfishing continues, with full knowledge that recovery for some stocks and species might be impossible. And as the fish disappear, they are lost not only to future generations of humans, but also to other creatures that depend on fish for survival, including sea birds and marine mammals such as dolphins, porpoises, seals, sea lions, and some species of whales.

The Collapse of Coastal Fisheries

Belatedly, the destruction of fish populations—long a concern mainly of conservationists and a few fisheries scientists—has now become a national scandal, a disaster for entire communities and regions, and the subject of major stories in the national media. Indeed, the situation made headlines on March 21, 1994, when President Bill Clinton said that fishing in New England is in "virtual collapse," offered the industry there $30 million in federal aid, and promised to ask Congress for $50 million more.[67]

The near-destruction of deep-sea fish stocks off the U.S. coast was aptly summarized in a March 7, 1994, front-page story by Timothy Egan in *The New York Times*, whose headline described the "U.S. Fishing Fleet Traveling Coastal Water Without Fish":[68]

> The surging Pacific salmon and steelhead are gone. . . across the country, in Gloucester and New Bedford, Massachusetts, the story is the same. After 350 years, the oldest American fishing area is largely barren of the great swarms of haddock, cod, and flounder that sustained more than 10 generations of New Englanders and became millions of fish sticks.
>
> From Chesapeake Bay, where oystermen are fading like fog in the afternoon sun, to the Gulf of Mexico, where grouper and red snapper are mostly a memory, people who pull fish from the sea for a living are singing the same sad song.

Indeed, the loss of fisheries is pervasive. As Egan observes:

> Government officials say most of the major commercial fishing areas in this country outside Alaska are in trouble. . . As for salmon in the Pacific Northwest and three main commercial salmon species in New England, the decline is catastrophic—threatening to wipe out not only whole industries but also cultures and communities . . . For the first time, there may be no ocean salmon fishing on the West Coast this year, a situation roughly akin to Georgia not producing any peaches.

In the North Atlantic's Grand Banks, once one of the world's richest fisheries, northern cod have declined by some 95 percent in recent years, and are now considered "commercially extinct." This belatedly prompted the Canadian government in early 1994 to ban cod fishing indefinitely, throwing 30,000 fishermen and processors out of work in Newfoundland and Labrador. In the next few years, an additional 25,000 fishing-related jobs are expected to be lost in these areas.[69]

On March 22, 1994, a front-page story in the *Wall Street Journal*— whose editorial page writers regularly bash environmental groups, leaders, and regulations—described how the overfishing and depletion of North Atlantic cod may soon make Boston, "the home of the bean and the cod [into] just the home of the bean":

> Years of overfishing and mismanagement have drastically reduced the cod population in local waters . . . And New England consumers— steeped in a cod-eating tradition that predates the first Thanksgiving—are reeling from higher prices . . .
>
> When the explorer John Cabot reached North America in 1497, cod were so thick his crew caught them with baskets. For centuries, the bottom-feeding cod fed New England, helped fuel its economy, and framed its regional identity. Generations grew up salting cod, eating codfish cakes—and swallowing cod-liver oil. . . cod was the economic building block of the region. . .[70]

But the once seemingly inexhaustible stocks of cod have been so overexploited that they are now in jeopardy:

> Today, the beloved cod is in deep trouble. Spawning stocks are at historic lows across one of the most fabled fishing grounds in North America, stretching from the Georges Banks off Massachusetts, through the Gulf of Maine, to the Grand Banks of Newfoundland. . . The catch is expected to decline further, fisheries scientists say.[71]

And haddock, another staple of New Englanders, is in even worse shape. It was once one of the most abundant fish caught off the coasts of New England and Canada, but now it is almost gone. On January 1, 1994, NMFS took emergency action to close down the haddock fisheries on George's Bank and the Gulf of Maine for four months. The latter population was considered "commercially extinct."[72]

Also in January 1994, NMFS warned that New England's stocks of yellowtail flounder had collapsed, and estimated that 92 percent of the yellowtails alive in 1994 would not survive until the next year. NMFS advised that it might have to ban fishing for yellowtail, but meanwhile, the population continued to be overfished and devastated.[73]

Almost all tuna stocks worldwide are in peril, with Atlantic bluefin tuna declining 90 percent in the last two decades, from 225,000 in 1970 to only 22,000 in 1990. These magnificent fish can grow to be twelve feet long and weigh 1,500 pounds, and can swim at speeds up to fifty miles per hour. They are in great demand in Japan, mainly for sushi, and can bring as much as $30,000 wholesale.[74]

Attempts to secure protection of bluefin tuna under CITES have been rebuffed. Here is how the TRAFFIC bulletin described the last such effort, at the Kyoto meeting in 1992 (which was introduced, "debated," and dismissed in under five minutes):[75]

> ... official discussion over the merits of a proposal to list the western Atlantic population of the northern bluefin tuna on Appendix I never even took place, due to backroom politicking and deal-cutting domi-nated by the powerful tuna industry and the three countries trading in the endangered western Atlantic tuna: Canada, Japan, and the United States. In a well-orchestrated presentation designed to fore-close any open debate, proponent country Sweden, under extreme pressure from the three detracting countries, withdrew its proposal before any views could be heard. A loose pledge made by Canada, Japan, Morocco, and the United States during the session to seek a 50 percent reduction in catch of western Atlantic bluefin tuna under another treaty, the International Commission for the Conservation of Atlantic Tunas (ICCAT), was all but denied during a press conference held by these countries only minutes after the CITES staging.[76]

Kenya proposed to place the northern and southern Atlantic bluefin tuna on CITES Appendix II for the 1994 CITES meeting. But Japanese pressure forced Kenya to withdraw its proposal four months prior to the meeting.

Although conservationists have repeatedly urged that the catch be lowered, regulators have allowed the near-destruction of these tuna stocks. As the National Audubon Society points out, "The ICCAT, which regulates the tuna fishery, has bowed repeatedly to the commer-cial fishing industry and failed to significantly reduce the tuna catch, despite continued warnings from its own scientists." In November 1993, the twenty-two-nation commission finally announced that it would phase in a 50-percent catch reduction over a two-year period for west-ern Atlantic bluefins. But this action, adamantly fought by the tuna industry, may be too late and too modest to allow the tuna stocks to recover. Indeed, the commission's own scientists calculate that the 50-percent reduction will only stabilize the population at its present, highly depleted level.[77]

Swordfish, which are long-lived and slow to mature and reproduce, are especially vulnerable to overfishing. Stocks of these fish are often described as being near collapse; in the north Atlantic, the population has dropped by half since 1978.[78]

Even sharks are being massively overfished—for meat; for their fins, used by Asians in soup; and for their cartilage, promoted as an anti-cancer agent. Several dozen shark species appear to be seriously depleted and rapidly declining. And with populations along the U.S. East Coast devastated, pressure is now shifting to stocks off of California. No one knows precisely how the elimination of these predators, which play an important role in marine ecology, will affect the chain of life in the seas.[79]

In the Southeast, off the coasts of Florida, Georgia, and the Carolinas, a dozen species of fish are in serious trouble, including the popular red snapper and grouper. The federal South Atlantic Fishery Management Council warns that these dozen species have been so overfished that unless action is taken to conserve them, they may not be able to reproduce in future years.[80]

America's last great fishery, the North Pacific off Alaska, is under assault from huge factory trawlers. According to Fish Forever, a national coalition of conservationists and commercial fishermen, "time is running out," in large part because of the massive and wasteful incidental killing of non-target species:

> Factory trawlers haul up tens of thousands of fish in one pull, keeping the most profitable ones and dumping the rest, dead or dying, back into the ocean. Catch limits don't matter when fish too small, too big, or out of season are killed rather than conserved.
>
> These bulldozers of the sea drag their heavy nets over the sea floor. They destroy marine habitat and kill everything in their path. Keeping only high-profit species, factory trawlers dump half a billion pounds of dead or dying fish overboard each year. And it's all legal!
>
> Each year, 20 million crabs are killed in Alaska by trawlers going after other species. . . Sea birds, sea lions, and other animals that live on fish have been devastated by fish shortages.
>
> The fishing season for halibut is down to two days a year . . . but for every halibut caught in season, 15 more are snagged and dumped by factory trawlers at other times of the year.[81]

The Politics of Overfishing

Although pollution, destruction of wetlands and estuaries, the construction of dams, and other factors have taken a heavy toll, the main reason that fisheries around the world are drying up is a simple one: overfishing. As put succinctly by Dick Schaefer, the conservation director of NMFS, "You can boil it all down to the fact that there are far too many fishermen and not enough fish."[82]

The world's oceans are fished by over one million large fishing ships and two million smaller ones. Across the world, some 12.5 million people make their living catching fish, and another 150 million people are employed in on-shore operations or processing the fish.[83]

And as with so many other situations involving the exploitation of natural resources, the foxes are guarding the chickens. As Timothy Egan wrote in *The New York Times:*

> The system set up to regulate these public resources is awash with conflicts of interest. Fishing in United States waters is regulated by eight regional councils, which themselves are dominated by the fishing industry. In most cases, the councils have been unwilling or unable to set fishing limits for themselves.[84]

And the government, instead of enacting and enforcing effective measures to prevent the loss of important fisheries, has actually helped make the situation worse in some instances by encouraging and subsidizing overfishing. In 1976, when the United States extended its coastal economic zone from 3 miles offshore to 200 miles, effectively barring unregulated fishing by foreign fleets, this was hailed as a major victory for conservation. But the federal government guaranteed and helped make available low-interest loans to American fishermen to enable them to expand their fleets and purchase large ocean-going vessels. These are equipped with sophisticated technology that can quickly and efficiently fish out the richest of fishing grounds.

In this way, a vicious cycle is created, wherein fishermen must continue to intensively exploit a limited and diminishing resource in order to be able to meet payment schedules on boat mortgages and equipment loans. Thus, even though the fishermen realize that they are exhausting the source of their livelihood, they cannot get off the treadmill and practice conservation without losing their boats.[85]

Moreover, the massive overexploitation of commercial fisheries is extremely wasteful and destructive of other species, and has caused widespread plundering of the "resource." Large, highly mechanized fleets using enormous nets bring in entire schools of fish, up to 80 percent of which are unwanted and are thrown back dead or dying.[86] In the Gulf of Mexico, it is estimated that shrimp fishermen kill ten to twenty-two pounds of fish for every pound of shrimp they catch. Shrimpers off the southern coast of the United States catch some 48,000 endangered sea turtles every year, almost a quarter of which are killed.[87] Drift nets in the North Pacific are thought to have killed some 750,000 sea birds annually, before their use was restricted.[88]

And the easy availability of cheap and abundant fish has not always led to better nutrition for humans. For decades, through the 1980s, two thirds of the fish caught in U.S. waters were fed not to humans, but to farm animals. Indeed, American livestock were consuming more fish than Western Europe and Japan combined![89]

We have thus wasted, squandered, and endangered an invaluable "resource" that now may not survive for future generations of humans. As Steve Cusick of the National Audubon Society observes:

> Once thought to offer a limitless supply of fish to the growing mass of humanity, the oceans are only now being recognized as complex ecosystems that are overfished and underprotected, particularly in the biologically rich coastal waters. This decline could have far-reaching consequences not only for the fragile marine ecosystems, but also for future world food supplies and the world economy.[90]

Why Sustainable Yield Does Not Work

There is nothing new about fishermen destroying or depleting their fisheries; indeed, that has been the history of the industry.

One of the best known examples is that of the Pacific sardine, which was fished into commercial extinction decades ago. This happened because the fishing industry was able to evade catch quotas by having its own scientists argue that it was almost impossible to overfish an ocean species. In the 1936–1937 season, over 790,000 tons of sardines were landed on the West Coast; by 1968, the fishery was gone.[91]

According to NMFS, among the lessons to be learned from the collapse of this fishery are that "development-oriented government agencies can contribute toward delayed and ineffective fisheries management," and that "fisheries management can behave like a subsidy because it encourages investment if its perceived presence engenders optimism or decreases the expectation of risk."[92]

The Peruvian anchovy was heavily exploited as a source of fish meal for cattle, and it went from yielding 12.4 million metric tons a year in 1970 to almost zero in a few years.[93] But even today, the industry denies that overfishing was the cause of the fishery's collapse, instead blaming almost exclusively the weather and oceanographic phenomenon known as El Niño, which brings warm water toward Peru.[94]

The tragic and irreversible loss of much of the world's commercial fisheries is yet another example of the inability of humans to manage wildlife on a sustainable use basis, a fact that is now being recognized by many scientists and experts in the field. In an essay in the March 1, 1993 edition of *Conservation Biology*, Dr. John G. Robinson of the Wildlife Conservation Society (WCS; formerly called the New York Zoological

Society), discusses the difficulty of sustainably managing natural resources:

> The history of natural resource use in modern times bears witness to the frequency that resource potential and human needs are incompatible. Even systems like marine fisheries, which are highly productive and heavily managed, have been consistently exploited, and stocks of many economically important species are today highly precarious.[95]

These points are reinforced in an article by three experts in zoology and fisheries—Donald Ludwig, Ray Hilborn, and Carl Walters—that appeared in the April 2, 1993 issue of *Science*. They conclude that:

> . . .the impossibility of estimating the sustained yield without reducing fishing effort can be demonstrated from statistical arguments. These results suggest that sustainable exploitation cannot be achieved without first overexploiting the resource. . . For some years, the concept of maximum sustained yield (MSY) guided efforts at fisheries management. There is now widespread agreement that this concept was unfortunate. P. Larkin concluded that fisheries scientists have been unable to control the technique, distribution, and amount of fishing effort. The consequence has been the elimination of some substocks, such as herring, cod, ocean perch, salmon, and lake trout. He concluded that a MSY based upon the analysis of the historic statistics of a fishery is not attainable on a sustainable basis . . .[96]

One reason that it is so difficult to manage fisheries and other resources is that setting limits and quotas depends on yield calculations by scientists, who are not only fallible but also usually subject to political and financial pressure. In any event, scientists still are unable to anticipate or predict the natural fluctuation of fish populations under changing ecological conditions, yet they continue to set fishing quotas as if the "resource" were stable. Dr. Walters cites as an example of scientific ineptitude the "huge disaster" that has befallen Canada's cod fishery: "That's a really good instance where the scientists were trusted to produce answers . . . They were way overestimating how many fish were left in the ocean . . . The net result of putting trust in scientists was to put 20,000 people out of work" (as of mid-1993, when the cod population collapsed).[97]

A September 1993 publication of the U.S. Marine Mammal Commission—a preliminary report entitled "Principles for Living Resource Conservation," authored by Dr. Lee M. Talbot—emphasizes that "virtually all stocks of marine living resources which are or have been commercially exploited are being or have been depleted." The report describes how this happened, and why it was inevitable:

> The well-documented progression is that a new fishery (or new technology or methodology) is discovered; the fishery is developed rapidly by the industry on the basis of market demand but with no other regulation; industry efforts lead to overcapitalization and the capacity for fishing rapidly exceeds the potential of the stocks to sustain it; the fishery is depleted and harvests decline, while fishing effort increases to offset the decline in catch and amortize the investments, thus accelerating the depletion of the resource . . . and finally, with the stocks depleted below economic levels, industry abandons the fishery and moves to new stocks on which to follow the same process.

The result of this progression has been that stocks of one species after another have been lost:

> . . . with the most economically valuable species (i.e., those which bring the highest prices, are most accessible, or are the easiest to catch) going first, followed by increasingly less valuable ones. With the loss of the initially most valuable species, the "less valuable" ones then become "more valuable," and so on down the line. This generalization applies to all commercially harvested marine living resources, including fin fishes, marine mammals, reptiles, mollusks, crustaceans, and other invertebrates and plants.[98]

But, the publication notes, we seem to have learned very little from our mistakes, for "on a global basis, management is still the exception rather than the rule":

> There have been very few cases where management in the sense of developing regulations, etc., preceded the initiation of a commercial fishery. Most management is attempted after the fishery is well established, overcapitalized, and the resource is depleted . . .
> There is essentially no management of much of the fishing by the distant water fleets, particularly those of Japan, Russia, and eastern Europe . . . , Korea, and Taiwan.[99]

The report concludes that "there is a general belief among the fisheries scientists consulted—and among a surprisingly high percentage of the managers consulted—that there are no examples of managed fisheries which are not depleted," with the possible exception of the North

Pacific halibut. Moreover, the report notes, "the situation with freshwater living resources is very similar to that of marine ones. Whenever there is commercial exploitation, the stocks are nearly always depleted, with or without the benefit of management."[100]

Have We Learned Any Lessons?

With modern fishing fleets using such sophisticated technology as sonar, radar, and even satellite navigation systems, remaining fish stocks hardly stand a chance of surviving the relentless assault. Suggestions that the fleets switch to new areas and species have been compared to rearranging the deck chairs on the *Titanic*.

In their efforts to protect the fishing industry from regulation, politicians have doomed it, along with the fish, to extinction or devastation. But even with vanishing fish stocks and the closing of fisheries in the headlines, it appears that few lessons have been learned.

When Senate Majority Leader George J. Mitchell (D-Maine) announced in early 1994 that he would retire, he boasted that one accomplishment in which he took special pride was his intervention on behalf of the New England fishing industry. He said that he had persuaded Commerce Secretary Ron Brown *not* to implement a proposal by the Commerce Department to reduce catches by placing limits on the number of days fishing boats could stay at sea.[101]

SPORT HUNTING:
SUSTAINABLE USE OR A WAR ON WILDLIFE?

Among the strongest supporters of the sustainable use concept are sport hunters, and their extravagant claims of the benefits of such "utilization" would make one think that a species could hardly survive without being hunted. Indeed, this is exactly the argument made by the gun lobby to justify the hunting of such endangered African wildlife as leopards, elephants, and even rhinos—that unless the money spent by safari hunters gives wild animals an economic value, local people will not have the incentive to tolerate or protect wildlife.

This has long been a fundamental tenet of wildlife management— that sport hunting is beneficial, even essential, to the well-being of wildlife, since it raises money for conservation and removes only surplus animals from the population.

But as we shall see, sport hunting not only fails to benefit wild animals or even to be sustainable, it represents a serious threat to the survival of wildlife populations worldwide—including in Africa.

Strictly speaking, the subject of "sport" hunting, particularly in America, is somewhat removed from the central focus of this book, since it does not constitute commercial sustainable use in the usual sense of the term. Commercial use of wildlife is largely prohibited throughout the United States, except for fur trapping. Indeed, legal hunting in the United States is basically recreational—that is, killing for fun.

Yet it is important to consider, at least superficially, the subject of sport hunting, since it is constantly touted—especially in Africa—as a prime example of how consumptive sustainable use can promote the conservation, recovery, and general welfare of wildlife. In fact, however, the main impact of hunting has been just the opposite.

One of the biggest battles currently being fought is over safari hunting in Africa, especially the issue of shooting threatened and endangered species such as elephants, leopards, and lechwe (a type of antelope), all of which can legally be brought back into the United States as "trophies." And the shooting threatens wildlife not just by killing but also by frightening the animals into unprotected areas, making them vulnerable to poaching, and hurting the tourism potential for the areas where shooting is allowed.

Thus, not only is the hunting not sustainable to the species involved, it disrupts and harms other animals as well.

Sport Hunting in America

In the United States, wildlife managers have traditionally pointed with pride to deer and ducks as successful examples of hunting-based management policies. But now, with many duck populations in North America near a thirty-year low and in precarious condition for several years, hunters have almost run out of species they can allege are being conserved through killing.

Not even the utilization (by hunting) of white-tailed deer in North America can be cited as an unmitigated management success, since deer numbers are generally kept high (sometimes overly so) by habitat manipulation (the bulldozing and clearcutting of forests, for example) and other techniques that are undertaken at the expense of other species. Indeed, the abundance of deer in many areas can be partially attributed to the elimination of old-growth forests and predators such as wolves and cougars. Even today, Alaska is killing wolves to try to increase the number of moose and caribou for out-of-state hunters.

Other successes claimed for American wildlife management—such as increasing the populations of turkey, quail, and some exotic, non-native species such as pheasants, Hungarian partridges, and chukars—are largely illusory. These alleged successes have mainly been the result of small initial populations expanding into suitable habitat, often with the help of "predator control"—the trapping, poisoning, and otherwise killing off of foxes, raccoons, coyotes, and other native predators that might interfere with the propagation of the introduced species.[102]

Sport hunting has traditionally been a threat to the survival of rare and endangered species, and it remains so today. Among the imperiled American animals that have been subjected to legal sport hunting in recent years are the grizzly bear in Montana and the black bear and Sherman's fox squirrel in Florida (although lawsuits brought by protectionists in the early 1990s concerning the grizzly and the black bear forced a closing of the hunting seasons for those animals). Florida also permits large-scale hunting in the Big Cypress National Preserve, the prime habitat for the thirty to fifty remaining Florida panthers (the most critically endangered mammals in North America). Hunters scare off the panthers, damage their habitat, and shoot large numbers of deer and wild hogs, disrupting and depleting the panthers' main prey.

North America's heavily hunted waterfowl population is also in serious trouble, and in 1985 the U.S. Department of the Interior warned in a press release, "The total breeding numbers of ducks this year is the lowest recorded during 31 years of surveys, and includes declines in all but one of the 10 duck species most important to waterfowl hunters."[103]

In recent years, duck populations have remained severely depleted, but the hunting of most of them—including increasingly rare pintails and black ducks—continues. There are only one fifth as many pintails now as there were forty years ago, their numbers having dropped from 9.4 million in 1955 to just over 2 million in 1993. Black duck winter inventories have declined from 761,000 in 1955 to 290,000 today.[104] (On July 22, 1994, Interior announced that its May aerial surveys showed a sharp rebound—up 24 percent from 1993—in breeding populations of ducks, in response to heavy rainfall and better wetland and nesting conditions.)

Moreover, of the funds raised by taxes on gun and ammunition sales—which hunters constantly claim go for "wildlife restoration" and conservation—only a small part is actually spent for habitat acquisition. Most of the rest is spent on population monitoring, enforcement of hunting regulations, and environmentally destructive activities such as building and maintaining roads, fences, trails, buildings, and duck blinds, as well as bulldozing and burning forests, mainly to generate an artificial "surplus" of deer.[105]

How Hunting Affects Evolution

By definition, trophy hunters seek out the largest and strongest animals to kill, but the creature whose trophy will look best on the hunter's wall often plays an important role in the reproduction and social biology of the species. Because of this, hunting can change the character and affect the evolutionary development of a species.

Even where animals are hunted "sustainably," and wildlife remains abundant, it may be irreparably harmed by such "management." By killing off the biggest and the best of the breeding population, be it a bear, an elephant, or a lion, the trophy hunter affects the process of natural selection. It can also be theorized that by eliminating the bravest, largest, and most curious or aggressive animals—the ones the hunter is most likely to encounter or be challenged by—hunters can, over time, help change the nature of a species by selecting in favor of smaller animals that are less able to survive.

This subject has been eloquently addressed by Douglas Chadwick, author of numerous articles in *National Geographic* and of the highly acclaimed 1993 book, *The Fate of the Elephant*.[106] A wildlife biologist and former employee of the Montana Fish and Game Department, he has lived for years in the wilderness and travelled the world carrying out independent research on wildlife. As Chadwick has pointed out:

> Large-scale hunting is a potent agent of biological change. . . Whenever we kill more members of a population than any other single cause, we become the dominant selection force. This means that the animals will begin to evolve largely in response to us.
>
> Prey species evolved under hunting pressure of course, but the furred or feathered predators which hunted them concentrated on the weak, infirm, and unfit. While sustaining themselves, predators helped check population fluctuations among prey at the same time that their hungry jaws pushed the prey onward toward the development of swiftness, strength, and grace. The modern human predator performs somewhat the opposite function. Armed with high-powered rifles and telescopes, we prefer the largest and most superb animals; the healthy dominant creations . . . .[107]

Chadwick describes how hunting, even when "sustainable," can change a wildlife species or population:

> A fully grown bull elk, for example, would be virtually immune to predators until he reached old age; but he is highly vulnerable to man. We prize such mature, vigorous, majestic individuals. The more

boisterous and visible he is, the more likely we are to find him and kill him. Those qualities which grant him success in the natural world and a chance to pass on his genetic traits bring about his death at the hands of man. Many hunters, and trophy hunters as a group, stalk the very special genetic achievements of a population. . . We already know, for example, that heavy hunting pressures on large, palm-antlered moose in Europe led to the appearance of thin cervine, or deer-like, antlers on males within a short time.

Thus, Chadwick observes, even ostensibly successful model hunting programs can have disastrous long-term effects on the species involved:

A game department official once described to me a certain elk herd in which high hunting success went hand in hand with high reproduction and replacement for future harvests: a perfect example of high-yield animal crop production. He mentioned, sort of as an afterthought, that there were scarcely more than a handful of bulls older than two years of age in this herd. There were plenty of young bulls to mate with the cows, but of course the older, large-antlered bulls had been removed by the many successful hunters. What, I wondered, are the genetic consequences of this sort of herd structure? And what becomes of the elaborate social structure? When does an elk herd lose the qualities that make it an elk herd and become something else?

Chadwick concludes that such issues must be addressed:

Even when we preserve high numbers of a hunted animal, we must take care that we are not altering its very character. Regardless of one's position on hunting, we cannot afford to ignore such questions or dismiss them as misguided attacks on the sport.[108]

Promoting Hunting of Endangered Wildlife

In the current debate over sustainable use of wildlife, one of the best funded and organized campaigns is the one being waged to defend and promote sport hunting—even hunting of rare and endangered species. In recent years, the focus of the battle has centered on African wildlife, particularly such imperiled species as elephants and rhinoceroses.

Perhaps the most avid organization involved in this campaign is Safari Club International (SCI), which lobbies on behalf of big game hunters. Its studies, bulletins, press releases, monographs, and other literature are widely circulated, seriously discussed, and effectively used to influence the policies of governments and wildlife officials across the world. Its members include former Vice President Dan Quayle and Montana congressman Ron Marlenee.[109]

The attitude of these big game hunters toward endangered wildlife was demonstrated in August 1978, when SCI applied to the Interior Department for a permit to allow its members to kill and import into the United States *each year* some 1,125 animals from various endangered species. The list of rare creatures to be turned into trophies included, per year: 150 African leopards, 100 cheetahs, 100 mountain zebras, 25 tigers, 10 snow leopards, 5 clouded leopards, 5 gorillas, 5 orangutans, and many other animals from critically endangered species of deer, gazelles, impalas, crocodiles, and others.[110]

While protests from conservation groups and the public forced this permit application to be withdrawn, pressure by SCI and other hunting groups caused the Interior Department, a couple of years later, to downgrade the status of some populations of the African leopard and the lechwe from "endangered" to "threatened." This allows American hunters to import into the United States the "trophies" of leopards and lechwes that they hunt in Africa, thus providing a major incentive for the continued killing of these endangered animals by Americans.

SCI and other hunting groups are still working to have the Interior Department remove other foreign animals from the endangered list so that they may be killed and imported. SCI complained to a congressional subcommittee in late 1993 that government regulations were preventing the hunting of endangered African wildlife. As the group wrote in its newsletter, "SCI told the subcommittee of its concern that restrictive application of the Endangered Species Act and CITES by the U.S. Fish and Wildlife Service was interfering improperly [sic] with the ability of Africans to utilize their own resources."[111] Apparently, one reason SCI wants to loosen the rules on hunting rare wildlife is that several of its members have been apprehended and prosecuted for illegally killing or importing rare and endangered species. This has been widely publicized in newspapers, magazines, and books.[112]

SCI's statement further asserted that in Africa, "tourist sport hunting . . . has virtually a zero biological impact on the wildlife populations, and is easy to regulate. In comparison to other forms of wildlife-related tourism, the impact of sport hunters on the environment is minimal."[113]

In another hearing, SCI defended the hunting of the critically endangered rhinoceros. Testifying in November 1993 before the House Subcommittee on Environment and Natural Resources, SCI representatives displayed various charts showing, in the organization's own words, that "the only population of rhino in the world that is doing well—the southern white rhino—is the subject of 'tourist' hunting." In fact, however, the real reason that the population of 5,800 white rhinos is stable is strict protection from poaching. There is very limited hunting in South Africa—just eight per year in Natal Province, where most of them are found.[114]

While SCI's propaganda may not be accurate, it is effective. It has hoodwinked people not familiar with the issue into supporting trophy hunting. Writer Raymond Bonner has become so enamored of hunting that he even prefers it to tourism as a "conservation" tool. Swallowing SCI's distortions hook, line, and sinker, he writes in the *Wall Street Journal*—apparently with a straight face—that "from a conservation perspective, it can be argued that hunting should be promoted over tourism . . . tourism may even kill more animals than hunters do."[115] (More about this in Chapter 10.)

Shooting Animals to Save Them

SCI has been very active in lobbying to allow continued international movement of elephant "trophies," and was instrumental in pressuring the Interior Department to allow continued imports of trophies when it banned other ivory imports and elephant products in 1989. In pursuit of this, SCI commissioned a 1992 report on the African elephant that has been widely circulated in the U.S. and abroad among government officials, conservation officers, and international agencies such as CITES. It was partially reprinted in the February 1994 edition of *Safari Journal*, the group's publication.[116]

The report, by Dr. William I. Morrill, SCI director of wildlife conservation, portrays big game hunting as a benign, even valuable, activity that benefits wildlife, people, and governments. According to Morrill:

> Tourist safari hunting can be a controversial subject, and that controversy is the result of the misunderstanding of current tourist safari hunting. Tourist safari hunting is low volume and select and not to be confused with the commercial hunters of yesterday.
>
> Among the uninformed, safari hunting is seen as exploitative. . . Modern safari hunting . . . is tightly regulated, and is a major positive influence on conservation in Africa.

Morrill goes on to assure the reader that "modern safari hunting" is guided by ethical behavior:

> Government representatives accompany most hunters and their parties, assuring compliance with regulations, and often gather in man-

agement information. Harvest quotas are set by governments to ensure sustainability . . .

As a wildlife use, tourist safari hunting is strongly regulated,
low volume, select, low impact, and high return to the range state
. . . It extends conservation beyond the protected and general
tourist areas.

Morrill concludes that tourist safari hunting provides an ecologically
correct solution to the problem of providing funding for conservation
efforts:

By giving wildlife an economic value, tourist safari hunting is a vital
tool to be used in wildlife conservation to provide benefits, and
therefore a stake in the resource, to local people.[117]

There is, of course, nothing new or unusual in SCI's mindless, relentless pro-hunting propaganda, which can be found—usually in less
sophisticated language—in countless hunting magazines and "out-
door" columns of newspaper sports sections. What *is* disturbing about
this misinformation is that by using the scholarly, buzzword-filled
language of sustainable use, such "studies" are sometimes able to attain
credibility and be taken seriously by key wildlife officials and agencies
in critical decision-making positions.

To the uninformed, such arguments may seem persuasive. But the
true picture of safari hunting is the one painted by objective on-the-
scene observers and researchers who are in direct contact with the
wildlife and safari hunters. Few of these people will speak up, but many
have seen hunters kill off the animals in area after area, with complete
disregard for any hunting ethics or regulations.

Does Trophy Hunting Help Polar Bears?

Safari Club International and other advocates of sustainable use recently succeeded in having some restrictions lifted on the hunting of
polar bears. With the help of the Congressional Sportsmen's Caucus,
led by Representatives Jack Fields (R-TX) and Don Young (R-AK), SCI
has persuaded Congress to amend the 1972 Marine Mammal Protection
Act to permit the importation into the United States of polar bear
"trophies" from Canada.[118] This will greatly increase the interest of
American "sportsmen" in hunting polar bears in Canada, where U.S.
and German hunters have been paying $15,000 or more each to shoot
the animals. Before the law was amended, American hunters could not
legally bring their trophies back into the United States.

For years, polar bears were heavily hunted in the Arctic, leading many scientists and conservationists to fear for the bears' future. However, the 1972 Marine Mammal Protection Act and an international treaty limited hunting of the bears (except by natives), as well as international transport of their hides and "trophies."

But in early 1994, pressure began to build to allow polar bear hunting again, especially with Russia's new free-market system opening up the largest remaining population of polar bears to "sport" hunting. As usual, the language of sustainable use was invoked to justify putting more polar bears under the gun. As *The New York Times* reported:

> A House of Representatives subcommittee [has] agreed to allow Americans to import polar bear trophies, a step that would encourage American hunters to shoot the bears in Canada or Russia . . . Some conservationists defended the provision, saying it would raise the value of a thriving bear population to Canada's Inuit inhabitants, who could sell their bear-hunting licenses to American trophy buyers.
>
> "Providing ongoing economic value to an animal species is the surest way to guarantee its health and perpetuation," said Joseph P. Kalt, a natural resource economist who is faculty chairman of the environment program at the Kennedy School of Government at Harvard University.[119]

This argument ignores the key fact that giving the bears a monetary value will *increase* the number being killed for "subsistence." Natives frequently do not take their entire allotted quota, but they certainly are more likely to if a bear is worth $15,000, the current going rate.

Unfortunately, Congress did amend the Marine Mammal Protection Act to permit the import of polar bear trophies from Canada, and President Bill Clinton signed the amendments into law on April 30, 1994. As pointed out by HSUS vice president Wayne Pacelle, who led the fight against crippling the act, and who prevented even worse damage from being done to it, "Now that the law has been amended to permit polar bear hunting, the exploitation of all marine mammals could eventually be on the table—including walrus, sea otters, seals, and sea lions—and since hunting is supposedly so good for animals, maybe even whales and dolphins."[120]

Trophy Hunting Doddering Rhinos

Half a dozen times a year, an American or German hunter flies into South Africa's Pilanesburg National Park for the thrill of shooting one of the park's white rhinos—at a cost of $25,000. Hunters will even pay thousands of dollars for the privilege of shooting a tranquilizer dart into a rhino needing to be relocated or de-horned, and posing for pictures with the drugged, immobilized creature. In 1993, park officials even considered allowing a hunter to shoot an old and ailing black rhino, figuring that the chance to shoot one of the last surviving members of this critically endangered species could be worth $100,000 to a sportsman.

The peculiar obsession of trophy hunters with killing large, fearsome-looking animals does, theoretically, have the potential to raise money for parks and wildlife. And it is the possible financial benefits of trophy hunting that are used over and over again to justify the killing of almost any creature, no matter how rare or endangered.

Sustainable use proponents often use extreme, unusual situations on which to base their arguments that the hunting of endangered species is good for the animals. In doing so, they are often able to persuade conservationists and the press that their arguments are valid and to cast doubt on their protectionist opponents. In their arguments, the issue almost always seems to concern some old and crippled animal that would starve to death in a few days if some rich white hunter didn't fly in to pay tens of thousands of dollars to put it out of its misery. The money, of course, is always said to go towards conservation, although in fact little if any of the money raised this way actually ends up going for that purpose. In Zimbabwe, for example, only a small fraction of the cost of a hunting safari is the fee paid to the government, and this money goes to the central treasury, not back into conservation.[121]

A version of this classic and oft-repeated tale appeared in *The New York Times* in 1992 in an article entitled "$100,000 to Kill a Doddering Rhino? Africa Thinks About Making Wildlife Pay for Its Survival." The article, by Bill Keller, begins by describing the "weary meanderings" of an old and scarred rhinoceros in South Africa's Pilanesburg National Park, "past breeding and near death." But there is hope! The rhino "would be a rare trophy for a big game hunter, who might pay $100,000 for the chance to kill one of the planet's 2,000 surviving black rhinos. And $100,000 in the right hands would buy a lot of protection for [the rhino's] endangered kin."

And sure enough, a park biologist is quoted as saying that she supports such a hunt: "Personally I can't understand the desire to hunt animals at all. But I believe that putting a value on animals is one way we can really increase the chances of survival of the animals."

But, alas, Keller writes, the hunt was not to be:

In the end, parks officials here finally decided not to allow the hunt. The reason was not biology but politics—fear of a backlash from abroad, especially by the United States, where anti-hunting and animal-rights sentiments run high. A black rhino hunt, officials here worried, could invite a tourist boycott, or ostracism from the world conservation community.

Never mind that no bleeding-heart animal protectionists are accused of having opposed or even known about this particular proposal—it's still their fault that the "doddering" rhino is allowed to live. According to Keller, many African conservationists see this not as issue concerning rhinos, but as an example of a great cultural gap between the reality they know and the fantasies of American conservationists concerning the way Africa should be:

> Utilization has become the prevailing wisdom in Africa, but the attitude in America is considerably more ambivalent. Raymond Bonner . . . says mainstream American conservation groups understand the virtues of utilization, but have buckled to pressure from animal rights groups on issues like hunting and selling ivory.
> "Their real fear is what the animal rights groups will do to them," Mr. Bonner said. "They use the animal rights group lists for their fund-raising mailings."[122]

But even though elderly rhinos may not soon be dispatched by generous trophy hunters in Pilanesburg, Keller assures us that the park "has a reputation among specialists as an innovative center for a philosophy of wildlife protection called sustainable utilization."

Thus, to the sustainable use advocate, the doddering, suffering rhino joins the supposedly overpopulated, crop-trampling elephant and livestock-killing cheetah or leopard as archetypical animals that need to be "harvested" and "controlled" by wealthy, conservation-minded hunters. These rationalizations are regularly employed to defend the shooting of many wild species. When an elephant is shot, it always seems to be described as an aged, lone bull past his prime, too old to breed, probably in bad health. The same is said of any lion killed—unless it is characterized as a livestock killer, as leopards and cheetahs invariably are.

But the simple truth is that on many, if not most, safaris, the hunter shoots whatever animal he first encounters. In areas where the animals are rare, inaccessible, or have been killed or driven off, it would be a rare hunter or safari guide who would pass up the chance to shoot a trophy animal when one is seen, since it may be the only one the safari comes across. And there is nothing worse for a tour operator than an unhappy client. There is usually no time, opportunity, or way to determine the age, health, sexual prowess, or family status of an elephant, lion, or leopard in the bush, even if a safari guide wanted to do so. It's usually only after the fact that the trophy is declared to have had one foot in the grave before the sportsman put it out of its misery.

Thus, allowing the hunting of endangered species and the importation into the United States of their "trophies" will simply add to the number of these animals being killed anyway by poachers, local hunters, and farmers protecting their crops or livestock.

Selling Off the Wildlife

The argument that hunting brings in revenues for local conservation and development was recently carried to its logical extreme when an entire wildlife area was, in effect, "sold" to a big game hunter.

In late 1993, Tanzania secretly sold exclusive hunting rights for ten years of one of its richest wildlife reserves to Brigadier Mohamed Abdul Rahim Al Ali, Deputy Defense Minister of the United Arab Emirates (U.A.E.). The area involved is the 1,400-square-mile Loliondo Game Controlled Area in north central Tanzania, bordering the famed Serengeti National Park.

According to author Caroline Alexander, who helped publicize the scandal of this sale, previous hunting parties from the U.A.E. freely shot rare and protected species in Tanzania:

> On a trip to Tanzania last March [1993], I interviewed several witnesses who had accompanied previous safaris from the Emirates. One such safari in 1991 was reliably reported to have indiscriminately shot cheetah and wild dogs. Another, in October 1992, illegally shot seven lions and two leopards in Loliondo ... another party [in January 1993], reportedly 60 members strong, swept through the tiny controlled area of Longido and is believed by wildlife officials to have significantly reduced the region's population of gerenuk, a rare antelope.[123]

The brigadier's proposal to Tanzania for the exclusive hunting concession candidly indicates an intention to pursue these rare and endangered species, asking that quotas be waived and fees paid to local officials to allow for the hunting of cheetah, leopards, and lions.

The brigadier has learned to use the language and code words of sustainable development. His proposal is pitched as a program of "wildlife conservation, management, and rural development," with the hunting concession to generate jobs and money for housing, schools, clinics, and the rehabilitation of villages.[124]

Whether or not the wildlife in the area will ever be able to be rehabilitated is another matter.

Safari Hunting as It Really Is

The conduct and impact of safari hunting in Africa varies from place to place. And local conservationists, researchers, and wildlife officials working in the bush are often reluctant to publicly criticize hunters, since they sometimes work with and rely on safari outfitters and hunting guides for assistance, cooperation, and information on animals and poachers. But almost anyone who has worked in Africa on wildlife projects knows how damaging and uncontrolled safari hunting can be.

In his 1991 book *To Save an Elephant*, an undercover investigation of the ivory trade, coauthor Allan Thornton asks a Tanzanian hunter, identified only as "Rex," about illegal elephant hunting, and receives this reply:

> "Do I know anyone killing elephants illegally?" he repeated incredulously. "You'll have to arrest half the foreign diplomats in this country if you want to stop that. They're all doing it, and sending [ivory] home in their luggage because they've got diplomatic immunity." His manner suggested he found this quite amusing. "I've taken guys from embassies out myself to shoot elephants," he admitted. "It costs them ten or twenty bucks to get the ranger to look the other way. But that sort aren't the worst."

Thornton then asks Rex if the rules were obeyed during safari sports hunting:

> "Don't make me laugh," said Rex. "I'll tell you what happens. You get a permit which allows you to shoot an elephant, a leopard, whatever you like. So you shoot the elephant. But it's not a very big one. Your client is a fat old American who has just spent twenty-five thousand dollars on this safari, and he's not happy. He grumbles that the tusks aren't big enough. So what do you do? Another elephant comes along with bigger tusks. There's a ranger with you who's supposed to make sure you keep to the rules, so you give him ten or twenty dollars to look the other way and then you shoot the bigger animal as well. He goes off with the big tusks and you're left with a spare set of tusks to sell. Who's going to find out? Most of the hunting outfits do it. If they don't, they're going to be out of business. None

of their clients will come back again. Sure it's hard on the elephants but . . ." He shrugged. "You have to make a living."[125]

The recent near-destruction by sport hunting of one of the world's richest wildlife sanctuaries has been documented by the highly respected television filmmaker Dereck Joubert. His award-winning wildlife programs, produced for National Geographic and others, have been seen by millions of viewers in the United States and throughout the world.

Joubert and his filmmaking partner and wife, Beverly, have lived, studied, filmed, and counted wildlife in northern Botswana for over a dozen years. They have observed first-hand the disappearance of much of the wildlife from the region, which he describes as "one of the last wilderness areas in Africa today." Joubert notes, "In 1983, when we first visited the area, we were astounded by the abundance of animals. . . Records show that in the late 1970's, numbers of animals were at least 10 times what they are now . . . ." Joubert warned in late 1993 that many of the local species were "on the verge of extermination," and could be "resurrected" only by immediate restrictions on hunting.[126]

Courageously going public in late 1993 with his concerns, Joubert presented extensive and alarming data documenting the depletion of the area's wildlife in the Botswana-based periodical *Wildlife Watch* and in a 25-page report on the situation.[127] His data focused on an area known as the Linyanti Concessions, consisting of Controlled Hunting Areas 5 and 6, located west of Chobe National Park and north of Moremi Wildlife Reserve.

Rather than blaming droughts and poaching—the usual excuses cited by wildlife officials—for the decline in the area's wildlife, Joubert candidly points out that the main culprit is sport hunting. Moreover, he observes that in addition to the overkilling, most of the hunters regularly violate legal and ethical rules and regulations:

> . . . with few exceptions, every hunter who has used this area has broken the law. Men shoot from the back of vehicles into buffalo herds, wounding animals and leaving them to die while they chase after the herd to shoot another. Lions and leopards are sometimes wounded, and when they run into thickets, a fire is set to flush them out.[128]

Joubert would thus hardly recognize the so-called low-volume, select, tightly regulated, and low-impact safari hunting that is described in articles and studies circulated in Congress, in the news media, and at international wildlife meetings.

Wiping Out Wildlife Populations

Joubert's studies and writings are especially remarkable and valuable because instead of repeating undocumented platitudes, as the gun lobby does, he carefully details the specific destruction and depletion of wildlife populations that he has observed for years. And he can hardly be dismissed as some urban elitist who knows little about wildlife. Here are some of his findings:

- **Zebra.** The zebra population has been reduced from "well over 50,000" to between 7,000 and 9,000 at most in 1991, less than 20 percent of their original numbers. Joubert writes that poachers have had very little effect on the zebra population and that the main cause of the decline was overshooting. "Most disturbing was the collective shooting financed by the tanning and taxidermy companies who gathered people together, and financed the safaris to shoot zebras for the skins only." Since zebras are often shot after being chased by vehicles, he notes, "a high proportion of stallions are shot, [since they] always drop back to protect their kinship groups and are then most vulnerable."
- **Buffalo.** Once there were approximately 25,000, Joubert says; today, "if there are 500 in the area it would surprise everyone who knows the area." He blames the decline on overhunting by local people and safari operators: "We estimate the safari companies shoot up to 25% more than their quota by wounding animals and not following up . . . citizen hunters have had a heavy effect. Vehicles loaded with men and weapons have been driving into the herds of buffalo and firing randomly into the herds. By our observations, this type of hunting can easily take more than four times the licensed quota. . . we believe that as many as 10 times the licensed quotas have been removed from the area . . . It is our firm belief that the buffalo of northern Botswana . . . are no longer in viable numbers."
- **Hyenas.** Hunters are indiscriminate in hunting these animals, with potentially disastrous results. "When hunting hyenas as a trophy animal, the hunters simply shoot at any hyena, regardless of whether or not it is a female (possibly with cubs in a den) . . . if the leading female is shot, the clan goes into social disorder, sometimes disbanding and disappearing. The damage of one animal being shot has a ripple effect, easily influencing the lives of up to 40 others."
- **Lions.** Joubert estimates that "at its prime, the Savuti Channel boasted about 120 lions, which we spent years documenting and researching . . . From 1981 until now, hunters have been shooting male lions . . . the total

lions killed is nearly 300—all males . . . it is considered that almost every male lion in the area is shot each year." This results in a rapid depletion of the gene pool and damage to the lion population as a whole. Joubert says that "there is no more supply of male lions of good quality." Since male lions of inferior quality are replacing those that are killed by hunters, and are killing off the prides' cubs as well, Joubert estimates that "in the extreme case, each lion that is shot takes with it a total of 14 other lions, calculated out over the ten years of hunting, this means that anything up to 5,000 have died."

- **Lechwe.** This endangered marsh-dwelling antelope is being killed off in much greater numbers than the official data indicate. Joubert says he believes that the ratio of animals killed to hunting licenses issued must be greater than five to one, because hunters will not pursue wounded animals into the crocodile-infested marshes. Indeed, Joubert writes, "When you take into account the dishonesty level of taking many lechwe on one permit, the rate must match the other animals like impala, zebra, wildebeest, and buffalo at 10:1. In years when 50 permits were issued, 500 lechwe died."

- **Chobe bushbuck.** These animals number only about a dozen. Joubert writes that "almost every individual is known. . . Bushbuck should never be allowed to be hunted."[129]

Other species that are being depleted because of hunting and other factors include sable antelope ("without exception, all the hunters agree that sable should be given protection"); eland ("none of the hunters in this area have encountered an eland to shoot this year. We last saw eland in 1990"); and rhinos ("Today, I doubt very much if there is a single living rhino . . . in the area!").[130] Even legally protected species are adversely affected by the hunting of other creatures, as Joubert points out:

> . . . despite the fact that hunting of elephants was closed in 1983 . . . Gunshots are immediately reacted to by elephants and other animals. We have watched peacefully grazing herds suddenly flee into the forest or reeds at the sound of gunfire over two kilometers (1.2 miles) away . . .[131]

Many of the elephants flee across the river into Namibia, where it is possible that many are immediately shot.

Joubert also points out that if elephant hunting is opened up again, even with extremely small quotas:

no ecological good will come of it . . . It may however have an adverse effect on the distribution of elephants by forcing them to seek refuge in sanctuaries [such as] national parks . . . , where the vegetation damage will increase as a result.[132]

Some species in the area are under pressure not from legal hunting but from poaching. These animals include hippopotamuses, crocodiles, and giraffes. Only impala populations seem to have avoided serious damage over the past decade as a result of of hunting or poaching.[133]

Joubert concludes that only an immediate ban on hunting can prevent the complete disappearance of the area's once-abundant wildlife:

> I am calling for a national hunting ban. Safari hunting is an 80 year old tradition in Botswana, but the land can no longer sustain its impact. Hunting in its various forms has been the prime reason for making large portions of Botswana devoid of wildlife.[134]

Joubert warns that unless hunting is quickly halted or severely limited, the area will soon be so devastated that recovery will be impossible:

> The hunting concession areas #5 and #6 are often deserted of any animals . . . the only way to even attempt a reconstruction of the populations of all species of the northern parts of Botswana is to put into immediate effect a management plan that will limit hunting. I can assure whomever may listen that the area will be devastated past the point of no return within a few more years if this is not done. If this is not the last season of full hunting, the value of the land will be so vastly diminished that no hunting will be available soon. But neither will there be any photographic potential, which is already very difficult. As a wildlife area it will be useless.[135]

The solution, Joubert writes, is to replace hunting with ecotourism:

> The photographic potential in an area like this was amazing and should be able to be reconstructed. Photographic tourism will allow the numbers to build up while still bringing in some good revenues for the land.

Joubert ends by observing that "to witness a land being destroyed by man is a heavy responsibility to bear, because once the animals have gone, the land becomes silent in its sterility, and it is lost forever."[136]

PART II

The Fight to Save
the Elephants

Introduction

The original elephant classification and regulations published by the U.S. Fish and Wildlife Service in 1978 . . . emphasized the idea that the ivory trade was sustainable, socially acceptable, and of value as a conservation mechanism. This line of thinking contributed to the loss of nearly a million elephants in the period that has since passed. Let us learn from this historical experience and not repeat the same mistakes.

Dr. Ronald Nowak
endangered species expert
with the U.S. Fish and Wildlife Service
July 1991[1]

A few short years ago, we came painfully close to losing the fight to save Africa's elephants. In the 1980s, between one half and two thirds of Africa's elephants were killed off, mainly for their ivory tusks.[2] Had the killing gone on a few years longer, there would be few elephants left to worry about today.

The slaughter has now been drastically reduced. But stopping the killing was not just a simple matter of halting the ivory trade. For over a decade, we faced the opposition of numerous prestigious conservation leaders, organizations, agencies, and officials of various governments, including our own, who had the responsibility to protect the elephants, but instead protected the industry that was destroying them.

The African elephant situation warrants detailed discussion because it is *the* best example of how the theory of consumptive sustainable use can go wrong in a big way, with tragic and perhaps irreversible results. It also illustrates how, even when faced with irrefutable facts, some people still promote the consumptive use of elephants.

The fight to save Africa's elephants is a tale of corruption, cowardice, greed, and betrayal by many of the main players in this drama. It tells of heartbreak and hope; of defeat and victory; and most of all, of continuing danger for the elephants.

But it is also a story of incredible courage, persistence, and hard work on the part of a few dedicated wildlife protectionists who refused to consign to extinction the mightiest land animals on earth. In the end, the defenders of the elephants prevailed, and the mighty beasts were given a reprieve for a few more years.

But the fight goes on, between those who would protect the elephants and those who still want them killed for their ivory. And this is more than just a fight over elephants; both sides have long realized that what is also at stake is the sacred and revered concept of "sustainable use."

The pro-ivory bloc perceived that if sustainable use were rejected by the world community as a strategy for conserving elephants, and replaced with a protectionist scheme, this might tend to discredit the utilization concept as applied to numerous other imperiled species. That is one reason why the pro-trade bloc has fought so hard against stopping commerce in elephant products, and was willing even to sacrifice the elephant on the altar of sustainability.

A delegate at the 1992 meeting of the Convention on Trade in Endangered Species of Wild Fauna and Flora (CITES) in Kyoto, Japan, expressed the mentality of the pro-ivory trade bloc this way:

> The issue of ivory is a trivial sideshow. The real issue is sustainable utilization, which countries like South Africa have successfully practiced for 40 years, but which is being willfully undermined by the liberal media and humane society NGO's [representatives of non-governmental organizations] from the developed countries.[3]

What is really of concern to the proponents of sustainable use is that the current protectionist strategy, in which elephants have been given strong and effective protection from international trade, has clearly worked! It has resulted in a drastic and immediate drop in the value of ivory, and in the illegal killing of elephants.

As long as elephants are protected from the commercial market and continue to recover from the devastating slaughter of the 1980s, the fallacy of the sustainable use concept will be apparent. It is now clear that elephants and other threatened wildlife do *not* have to be killed in order to justify their existence.

That is why so many government and conservation officials are fighting so hard to overturn the ivory ban. And it is also why this fight may determine the fate not only of elephants, but of many other creatures as well.

The pages that follow describe how Africa's elephants were almost lost; how they were saved at the last minute; and what must be done to ensure their future survival. It is a story that should be known, retold, and acted upon by anyone interested in the fate of Africa's still endangered elephants.

CHAPTER 3

America's Chance
to Save Africa's Elephants

The U.S. Fish and Wildlife Service has considered the argument that some commercial and sporting take gives an economic incentive for the maintenance of the species. While not yet convinced that such a position is fully valid, the Service is willing to allow the benefit of the doubt. . . .

U.S. Department of the Interior rulemaking
explaining why it is listing the African elephant as "threatened"
but still allowing trade in ivory to continue
May 12, 1978[1]

. . . the elephant was classified as threatened in 1978 when its numbers were estimated at 1,500,000. Total numbers are now little more than a third as great . . . If the elephant was threatened in 1978, it is "endangered" now.

Dr. Ronald Nowak
U.S. Fish and Wildlife Service biologist
and endangered species expert,
author of the 1978 rulemaking
July, 1991[2]

The United States has had several opportunities to help stop the illegal slaughter of elephants, and has forfeited most of them. The result has been the slaughter of over half of Africa's elephants—perhaps 700,000 within just a decade.[3]

By the mid-1970s, it had become apparent that elephants throughout Africa were being massively, and illegally, killed for their ivory, at a rate that would soon devastate the species. Numerous news accounts described the uncontrolled hunting, and reports from African conservationists, such as Iain and Oria Douglas-Hamilton, documented the widespread massacres.

Because of corruption, political instability, civil wars, and a general inability to enforce anti-poaching laws, African governments were unable and/or unwilling to stem the slaughter. Many poachers were armed with submachine guns and other sophisticated weaponry, often supplied by Western or Soviet-bloc nations backing different factions in the numerous civil wars and military conflicts raging throughout the continent. Even in Kenya, once a model of wildlife conservation, numerous government officials, including the wife of then-President Jomo Kenyatta, were known to be deeply involved in ivory trading.

The only hope for the elephant's survival seemed to be for ivory-consuming nations to close their markets to imports of ivory, 80 to 90 percent of which was thought to come from poached elephants.[4]

Wildlife protectionists thus appealed for help in saving the elephant to the administration of President Jimmy Carter, who often spoke of his deep commitment to conservation. On August 18, 1977, the Fund for Animals formally petitioned the Interior Department's Fish and Wildlife Service, under the Endangered Species Act, to list the African elephant as "endangered," thereby banning imports of ivory into the country.[5] The organization pointed out that this would not only remove much of the economic incentive for the killing of elephants, but would also focus international attention on their plight and set an example for other Western nations to follow. It was the only strategy that held any real hope for stemming the uncontrolled elephant slaughter.

The Fund for Animals noted that while the tusks of a large bull elephant could weigh fifty pounds, the average weight of the tusks then being sold was less than twenty pounds, indicating that most of the large elephants had already been killed off. At this time, the price of ivory on the world market was about $30 a pound, a rise of 1,000 percent over the 1969 price of $2.80 per pound. By 1976, the demand from Hong Kong alone was running at almost 2,500 dead elephants a month. Closing off the U.S. market and that of other nations to ivory seemed the first, best hope of saving the elephants.[6]

THE FIGHT TO BAN IVORY PRODUCTS

On January 16, 1978, Interior responded to the petition by publishing for public comment a proposal to list the African elephant not as "endangered" but "threatened"—a less protective designation—and to consider four different options for dealing with ivory imports.[7]

Option 1 consisted of a complete ban on commercial imports into the United States. It was supported by major national animal protection groups; the President's Council on Environmental Quality, the administration's official advisory body on conservation issues; and some eighty-three members of Congress who cosponsored legislation introduced by Congressman Anthony Beilenson (D-CA) calling for such a ban.[8]

Opposing Option 1 were an assortment of hunting, conservation, zoo, and industry groups, including the nation's largest conservation group, the National Wildlife Federation; the National Rifle Association; Safari Club International (SCI), a big game hunters group; the American Hunters' Educational and Legal Protection Fund; the American Ivory Importers Association; the American Association of Zoological Parks and Aquariums (now called the American Zoo and Aquarium Association); several African countries; and even the World Conservation Union (IUCN) Elephant Specialist Group.[9] This faction was represented by the world-renowned Iain Douglas-Hamilton, who, the Interior Department noted, "explained that it would be preferable for the United States to remain involved with the ivory trade, and so have the means of helping to regulate and control such trade." His comments were especially damaging to efforts to enact an import ban, since Interior acknowledged that he was "a highly respected authority on the biology and conservation of the species, and is in continuous contact with numerous other experts . . . The Fish and Wildlife Service considers him to be the best available source for data on the general status of the species."[10]*

Another group endorsing continued trade in ivory (even from certain nations that had no elephant populations of their own) was South Africa's Endangered Wildlife Trust, a conservation group based in Johannesburg, which has raised some $150,000 just from selling wildlife artist David Shepherd's prints of elephants.[12]

Thus, because of the strong opposition from various conservation groups and elephant experts, Option 1, a ban on ivory imports into the United States, was portrayed by its opponents as an emotional, unwork-

---

*A decade and a half later, in an Author's Note to his excellent 1992 book, *Battle for the Elephants*, Douglas-Hamilton would write that in the late 1970s, he and his wife Oria "became aware of a continental threat to the species caused by a burgeoning ivory trade . . . Our life moved from the scientific orbit to campaigning for elephants . . . At first, we were mostly alone, but later the world recognized the threat to the elephants and finally the trade in ivory was banned in 1989." He adds that he agreed with "the belief that all trade in ivory is a pact with the devil, which can never be adequately controlled. . . we fear that any trade in ivory opens a Pandora's box of vested interests and commercial incentives. At best, these exert an insidious pressure towards ever-more interference with Nature, and at worst they give rise to criminal killing of elephants and smuggling of ivory."[11]

able proposal by animal protectionists that would do more harm than good. It never had a chance of being seriously considered by Interior's bureaucrats, much less adopted. And it wasn't.

SELLING OUT THE ELEPHANTS

On May 12, 1978, the U.S. Department of the Interior published a rulemaking listing the African elephant as "threatened" and adopting a version of Option 2. This allowed continued ivory imports from nations that are members of CITES (which the previous year had listed the elephant on its Appendix II). In its rulemaking, the department stated that it had decided to reject Option 1 because "a total ban on international and interstate commercial activity in ivory and other products is not in itself necessary for the conservation of the African elephant."[13] The decision not to ban ivory imports was essentially made by Robert Herbst, Assistant Interior Secretary for Fish, Wildlife, and Parks, and Keith Schreiner, Associate Director of the Fish and Wildlife Service. The result has been the destruction of elephant herds throughout Africa, and the deaths of hundreds of thousands of elephants.

In its *Federal Register* notice, written by the Endangered Species Office's Dr. Ronald Nowak, Interior explained its decision, acknowledging that "problems could develop in verifying" that imported ivory was legal, and that "there may be some basis for the argument that merely allowing the ivory trade to function will encourage some poaching and ill-advised exploitation." However, the department stated that it was giving "the benefit of the doubt" to ivory traders and trophy hunters:

> No substantive basis, however, has been presented to show that such problems . . . would be insurmountable or would result in significant declines of elephant populations. The Service also has considered the argument that some commercial and sporting take gives an economic incentive for the maintenance of the species. While not yet convinced that such a position is fully valid, the Service is willing to allow the benefit of the doubt, within the scope of the regulations now being issued.[14]

The Fund for Animals' response to Interior's sellout was blunt and forthright; it accused then Secretary of the Interior Cecil Andrus and Assistant Secretary Robert Herbst of condemning the African elephant to possible extinction:

> It is obvious that Interior has once again turned its back on the

conservation community and the American public (which over-whelmingly endorsed the ivory ban) . . . in order to placate trophy hunters and commercial interests. This will doom to a cruel and unnecessary death hundreds of thousands more elephants . . .[15]

That is, of course, precisely what happened. And it was to be over a decade before Interior finally agreed to take effective action to protect elephants.

According to Lewis Regenstein, who was then coordinating the project to have the elephants listed and ivory banned, the group wanted to sue Interior to force it to take the appropriate action. But their lawyers advised that they would have little chance of prevailing without the support, testimony, and assistance of the acknowledged experts on elephants and the major international conservation groups who were funding them.[16] But these groups not only refused to support the ivory ban; some—such as the World Wildlife Fund (WWF), IUCN, and the African Wildlife Foundation (AWF)—actively opposed it.[17]

HALF OF AFRICA'S ELEPHANTS KILLED

The Interior Department's decision has, of course, proved tragically wrong. As it stated in its August 1992 rulemaking, which finally banned commercial ivory imports, "One half the elephant population, perhaps 700,000 animals, was lost in the decade 1979–1988."[18] Indeed, one of the endangered species specialists at Interior told Lewis Regenstein in 1988, "It looks like you all were right after all."[19] And Dr. Ronald Nowak, who authored the 1978 rulemaking, wrote in 1991 that its results were "disastrous," with elephant numbers being reduced to a "little more than a third" of those of the 1970s.[20]

Moreover, the loss of so many elephants may not have been completely unanticipated by the Interior Department's bureaucrats. Their inaction violated both the letter and the spirit of the Endangered Species Act, which clearly requires the department to take action to protect imperiled animals while there are enough left to safeguard the species' survival. Indeed, it defines an endangered species as one "in danger of extinction throughout all or a significant portion of its range," a status that certainly applied to the African elephant. But in the environmental impact assessment it prepared for its 1978 rulemaking, Interior made it clear that although the African elephant was extinct or in serious trouble throughout much of its range, the department would not take action to protect elephants until they were even further reduced in numbers. The assessment stated that even though "the African elephant had been eliminated from much of its original range and is subject to severe overexploitation, there still are relatively large populations, some of them stable and well protected. An endangered classification thus would not accurately express the situation of this species."[21]

In other words, Interior seemed to be saying, let's wait until elephants are even more threatened before we decide they qualify for our protection from the commercial interests exploiting them. Interior's policy is nothing new; just more of that old sustainable use theory in action—"conserving" wildlife by giving it economic value. Indeed, what is remarkable is the similarity between the sustainable use arguments being made today and those adopted a decade and a half ago, which led to the killing of over half of Africa's elephants.

CHAPTER 4

The Poaching Explosion of the 1980s: Wiping Out Half of Africa's Elephants

One half of the elephants [in Africa], perhaps 700,000 animals, was lost in the decade of 1979–1988.

U.S. Department of the Interior
Federal Register
August 10, 1992[1]

D uring the height of the elephant poaching, from 1979 through 1989, between one half and two thirds of Africa's elephants were destroyed. The population was cut at least in half, from between 1.2 and 1.5 million to 600,000 at most, according to most estimates.[2] In the late 1980s, an elephant was killed every eight minutes.[3] Today, it is thought that just 400,000 to 600,000 elephants remain on the continent.[4]

Poaching and ivory prices reached their all-time high in the late 1980s, and many elephant herds and populations were destroyed. If the slaughter had continued at that level for a few more years, the elephant would have been eliminated from most of Africa, certainly outside of protected areas. By this time, experts estimated that at least four fifths of the world's ivory trade, perhaps even 90 percent, came from illegally killed elephants.[5]

The data on elephant losses are incredible, but well documented. In Kenya, 90 percent of the elephants were wiped out.[6] In Zambia, 80 percent were slaughtered; in Mozambique, 75 percent.[7] Only a quarter of the estimated 800,000 elephants in Tanzania, Zaire, and Zambia survived— that population was *reduced* by 600,000, about the maximum number of elephants now thought to remain throughout the entire continent.[8]

The massive poaching came to a halt only after trade in ivory was largely banned. But if those trying to lift the trade ban get their way, the uncontrolled killing will soon start all over again.

THE THREAT FROM THE IVORY TRADE

By far, the major threat to elephants has always been the ivory trade. And the campaign to save the elephants has been in large part a fight to control this industry, which more recently kills elephants not in the cause of commerce, but in the name of conservation, wildlife management, and "sustainable use."

Over the centuries, the ivory trade has been responsible for wiping out elephant populations throughout Africa. In its official notice re-enforcing the ban on most ivory imports into the U.S., in August 1992, the Interior Department emphasized that "it is the ivory trade that historically has had the greatest impact on elephants . . . the illegal killing of elephants to satisfy a worldwide demand for ivory severely impacted and endangered many elephant populations."[9]

As early as the era of the Roman Empire, beginning in the first century B.C., elephant populations were depleted by ivory hunters and captured for entertainment and shows in the Roman Coliseum. Ivory hunters eliminated the elephants of North Africa by the early Middle Ages, and by the sixth century A.D., the species was extinct north of the Sahara. In South Africa, massive killing of elephants for ivory decimated the population from 1790 to 1870. By 1920, only about 120 elephants survived in the country. By the late 1800s, ivory hunting had eliminated much of the elephant population of East Africa; and by the early 1900s, it had led to the eradication of most elephant herds in West Africa.[10]

The ivory industry has always operated without conscience or scruples. Dr. Ronald Nowak, an elephant and endangered species specialist with the U.S. Fish and Wildlife Service, has observed:

> The ivory trade has demonstrated for centuries that it is detrimental to the elephants and to many people as well. It formerly was associated closely with the slave trade, with people being collected in the course of ivory-hunting expeditions and being forced to carry tusks until both were sold.[11]

During World War I, both the demand for ivory and ivory prices plummeted. This, along with protective legislation, permitted the partial recovery of elephant populations throughout the continent.[12] But demand for ivory began to grow again in the early 1970s, leading to the return of massive ivory hunting in the 1970s and 1980s, and the subsequent destruction of elephant populations throughout Africa. Particularly hard hit were the elephants of Kenya, Zambia, Mozambique, and Zaire.

Kenya Loses 90 Percent of Its Elephants

According to the Kenya Wildlife Service (KWS), from 1973 to 1989, the country's elephant population was reduced by almost 90 percent, from 167,000 to 16,000.[13] Since then, reduced poaching has allowed the population to recover somewhat, although some experts believe that the new population estimate of 26,000 may be either inflated or simply a result of more accurate counting methods.[14]

As Richard Leakey, then director of KWS, described the situation,

In May, 1989, elephant ivory in Kenya was attracting a price of about $140 per pound. Elephants were being illegally killed at the rate of close to three a day, even though the average tusk size had fallen to about 13 pounds. Each dead elephant could yield about $3,600 for the middleman or final exporter. The average wage at that time for a farmhand, guard, or factory worker was no more than $1,000 a year. Park personnel engaged in protecting elephants were earning even less. Is it any wonder that corruption and dishonesty were rampant?[15]

Indeed, Leaky pointed out, the profits from ivory were so enormous that corruption of public officials was rampant:

Important personalities within the Kenyan government had also become directly or indirectly involved in the trade. Payoffs for turning a blind eye, the use of official transport, protection, and other racketeering activities thrived. The ivory market appeared insatiable, and there was an ever-increasing premium to be paid for the diminishing resource.[16]

What Leakey did not say, but is widely known, is that in the 1970s, the main ivory trader in Kenya was President Jomo Kenyatta's fourth wife, Mama Ngina. Also reportedly involved were one of Kenyatta's daughters, Margaret, then mayor of Nairobi; his foreign minister; and other officials throughout all levels of government.[17] Such corruption continued throughout the 1980s—a bit more discreetly, to be sure, but no less pervasively.

80 Percent of Zambia's Elephants Killed

In Zambia, the elephant population has been decimated by poaching. In the mid-1970s, Zambia is thought to have had well over 100,000 elephants and 8,000 black rhinoceroses. The heart of elephant country was the Luangwa Valley, once known as "the last Kingdom of the Elephant." But in the 1980s, massive poaching and corruption stimulated by foreign demand for ivory and rhino horns turned the Luangwa into a kingdom of carcasses.[18]

Today, the rhinos are gone, or almost so. And so are some 80 percent of the elephants, which have been reduced to an estimated 20,000 to 32,000.[19] In 1987, wildlife warden Caleb Nkonga warned that "the rhino population in Zambia is now so low that the poachers operate principally for ivory, and regard rhino horn simply as a welcome but incidental bonus. The odds are still heavily on the side of the poacher, and we need to be much more effective in the next few years, or we will be left with literally nothing to save." Zambian poachers have thus resorted to invading neighboring countries, particularly Zimbabwe, to hunt elephants and rhinos, and some have been caught in Hwange National Park, 120 miles inside Zimbabwe.[20]

By the late 1980s, Zambia had become a haven for poachers and a center for illegal ivory traders. In 1990 alone, an estimated five tons of Zambian ivory was secretly flown to South Africa and Swaziland. By the early 1990s, most of the smuggled ivory was coming out in trucks.[21]

Zambian officials freely admit that corruption was rife, and that security personnel were deeply involved in the ivory trade. Poachers would regularly use sophisticated police and military rifles, such as AK-47s, while anti-poaching patrols, earning just thirty dollars a month, are generally armed with hunting rifles. Zambia's capital, Lusaka, became a base for illegal trade in ivory run by foreigners, including diplomats, from Greece, Italy, North Korea, Senegal, South Africa, and Zaire. Much of the illegal ivory came from elephants in neighboring countries, such as Angola, Botswana, Malawi, Namibia, Zaire, and Zimbabwe. The ivory was carved and processed in Lusaka, and smuggled out via South Africa and Swaziland.[22]

Fortunately, a change in government in Zambia resulted in a concerted effort to protect the elephants. In late 1991, President Kenneth Kaunda's regime was replaced by a new administration determined to clean up the poaching and corruption.

One of the first steps taken by the new government, in January 1992, was to reverse Zambia's position in support of a proposal to down-list elephant populations in southern Africa from CITES' Appendix I to Appendix II, which would have allowed trade in ivory to resume. Indeed, Zambia's National Parks and Wildlife Service had never been consulted on the decision to support the down-listing, and the proposal was riddled with false and misleading information about the country's elephants. For example, the CITES proposal put the elephant population at 37,000, far above what was then the most current survey figure of 20,000 to 25,000. And despite continued heavy poaching in areas outside of South Luangwa National Park, the document misleadingly stated that "Zambia's [elephant] population . . . appears to have stabilized and is increasing in some areas."[23]

But in other areas, anti-poaching actions have been very effective. In the North Luangwa, for example, only 13 elephants were reportedly poached in 1991, compared with 1,000 the previous year.[24] In August 1992, the U.S. Department of Interior reported that although Zambia's national elephant population had declined dramatically, "the greater Luangwa Valley population numbering some 10,000 elephants shows no evidence of significant poaching over the past three years, and its prospects are good if poaching remains contained."[25]

75 Percent of Mozambique's Elephants Shot

In the mid-1970s, Mozambique is thought to have had a healthy and growing elephant population of between 50,000 and 66,500. By 1990, the numbers had been reduced drastically, with perhaps 13,350 remaining in a few remote, inaccessible areas.[26]

Most of the elephant poaching in Mozambique has been carried out by organized, well-armed military units representing four different forces. These include the Frelimo troops of the former pro-Marxist government of Mozambique; the anti-communist rebels, Renamo, armed and backed by South Africa; thousands of soldiers from Zimbabwe, there to back Frelimo and protect the country's outlet to the Indian Ocean; and South African forces, who trained and armed Renamo. In addition, thousands of well-armed local militiamen would shoot elephants and other animals on sight, sometimes for food.

In 1992, the London- and Washington, D.C.-based Environmental Investigation Agency (EIA) issued a report entitled *Under Fire: Elephants in the Front Line*, which pointed out:

> Mozambique's national parks and reserves are located in areas destabilized by the war, abandoned by staff and completely unprotected. Once famed for their beauty and the abundance of wildlife, they have become battlefields and military strongholds . . .
>
> As armed conflict continues to rage in Mozambique, the country's elephants are being methodically wiped out in one area after another. Since 1974, over 50,000 elephants have died. They now exist only in a few scattered strongholds.[27]

And the October 1991 issue of *Africa South* noted in its article "The

Great Wildlife Massacre," "Game parks have been turned into bandit headquarters . . . and poaching seems unstoppable." One report stated that "Frelimo troops regularly wipe out entire herds of game animals including . . . elephants, using helicopter gunships and firing upon herds from the air."[28]

By the late 1980s, Renamo had gained control of most of Mozambique's countryside, killing off the elephants wherever they could be found in these areas. When government troops seized control of a Renamo center at Gorongosa in 1989, they reportedly found a stockpile of some 19,700 elephant tusks.[29]

Several Renamo deserters have told of well-organized ivory poaching and smuggling operations carried out in Mozambique, at the behest of the South African Defence Forces (SADF). In December 1989, a former Renamo platoon leader told an EIA investigator, "my boys used to kill 150 elephants a day, when we received orders from South Africa at the Renamo head office." He said that the SADF "were taking not less than 200 tusks every month from Gorongosa alone," and in August 1985, he supervised the loading of twenty-three tons of ivory onto two cargo planes.[30]

When the 27-year-long civil war finally wound down in 1993, among the big losers were Mozambique's national parks and the country's elephants, which were devastated by the conflict.

Zaire's Elephants: Down by 75 Percent

The U.S. Department of the Interior says that Zaire was once the most important habitat of the African elephant on the continent, but that "elephant populations in Zaire have declined by about 75 percent since 1981, and the ivory harvested from that country was sufficient to supply 30–40 percent of the ivory on the world market during the decade of the 1980s."[31]

The political corruption that has fueled the ivory trade is nothing new for Zaire. In the early 1900s, Joseph Conrad, in his classic novel *Heart of Darkness*, described the nation (then known as the Belgian Congo) as "the vilest scramble for loot that ever disfigured the human conscience and geographical exploration." But even Conrad would have been shocked by the excesses of Zairian President Mobuto Sese Seko, who has become one of the richest men in the world, with a personal fortune estimated at over $5 billion. Some of this gargantuan fortune is known to have come from the sale of ivory.[32]

Poaching of the nation's 63,000 to 90,000 elephants continues, and given the political corruption and instability endemic to the country, the ivory trade ban seems to be the most effective brake on the illegal killing.

Zimbabwe: Poaching, Corruption, and Murder

Zimbabwe has protected and managed its elephant population much better than most of its neighbors have protected or managed theirs. It has attempted to keep poaching under control, and in the course of this effort claimed, in November 1993, to have killed over 160 poachers and captured 89 in recent years. Four wildlife rangers have supposedly been killed in encounters with poachers.[33]

But heavy poaching has nevertheless depleted the elephant (and the rhino) populations of Zimbabwe, especially in such popular tourist areas as Hwange and Mana Pools National Parks. Gonarezhou Park was even closed to tourism in 1991 because of the presence of many armed poachers.[34]

Its relative success notwithstanding, Zimbabwe has at times ignored its poaching problem, preferring to talk about its alleged surplus of elephants. A government report released in late 1991 showed that only 258 elephants were killed from 1964 to September 1991, when in fact the carcasses of 823 elephants that had been killed by poachers were found in Gonarezhou alone in recent years.[35]

There have been numerous reports that soldiers, park rangers, and staff have been involved in the poaching and smuggling of both ivory and rhino horns in and out of Zimbabwe and Mozambique, as well as in the murder of anti-corruption investigators.

The Involvement of the Army

In an extensive 1991 investigation of the situation in Zimbabwe, EIA concluded that the nation was caught up in "institutionalized corruption, murder, and cover-up":

> The Zimbabwe Department of National Parks and Wildlife Management (DNPWM) has repeatedly ignored reports of poaching and complicity within its own ranks. Poaching is out of control in new areas where staff known to be implicated have been posted.[36]

In its 1992 report *Under Fire*, EIA describes and documents the extensive, pervasive corruption:

> The Zimbabwe National Army (ZNA) and Police have been poaching in Zimbabwe and Mozambique. Illegal trade across the Mozambique border has been ignored and people who have tried to stop it, murdered. The Mozambique government has stated that poached ivory

routinely travels illegally from Mozambique through Zimbabwe with ZNA complicity.[37]

The Zimbabwean army has routed its smuggled ivory and other products between Zimbabwe, South Africa, and Mozambique. This smuggling was facilitated by troops from Zimbabwe stationed along Mozambique's border and strategic supply routes during the nation's civil war. An official Mozambique government report states, "Thousands of Zimbabwean soldiers are stationed along the road and railway line from Beira port on the coast. These soldiers are said to poach elephants and other species when the opportunity arises."[38]

Zimbabwe's relative abundance of elephants also brings in poachers from neighboring Zambia, where most of the big-tusked elephants have been killed off. Zambian poachers have been apprehended and even killed in the southern part of Hwange National Park, some 120 miles inside Zimbabwe. Their presence there means that they must have been driven to elephant areas by local collaborators.[39]

Trade in illegal ivory has been surprisingly open, and has been engaged in by one of Zimbabwe's largest ivory dealers and purchasers of raw ivory from the government. In 1991, according to the EIA, this dealer:

> . . . told witnesses that he could easily legalize poached ivory with CITES permits as soon as he received it. He also told an EIA investigator that he could illegally export "two to eight tons" of raw ivory per month. DNPWM staff, as well as a South African dossier, confirm that he is involved in smuggling ivory and rhino horn. . . .

The dealer introduced EIA investigators to his driver, who admitted that he could move illegal ivory: "I can do all loads, any size, . . . connections at the border, that is no problem. . . ."[40]

Wildlife Investigators Killed

In Zimbabwe, it can be extremely dangerous to speak out against official corruption, and several army officers and investigators have been killed under suspicious circumstances after trying to look into or stop ivory smuggling. These killings have received widespread publicity, and have had the effect of suppressing investigations and revelations of poaching. As *The Sunday Correspondent*, a London newspaper, reported on January 21, 1990, "The Zimbabwean army, sent to protect elephants from ivory poachers, is now accused of joining them and murdering opponents."[41]

Perhaps the most highly publicized case is that of 35-year-old ZNA

Captain Edwin Nleya, who in late 1988 reported to the Zimbabwe Defence Ministry evidence of elephant and rhino poaching, smuggling, and cattle rustling by the ZNA in Mozambique and along the Zimbabwe–Mozambique border. Around January 3, 1989, he was reportedly arrested by government security forces and murdered.

As *The Sunday Correspondent* reported, in an article entitled "The Captain Who Knew Too Much":

> There is mounting evidence that Captain Nleya, whose body was discovered on a hillside, was murdered because he knew too much about the army's involvement in elephant and rhino poaching . . . Captain Nleya appears to have stumbled into a poaching conspiracy involving the army.
>
> From interviews with his family and former colleagues in Bulawayo, it is clear that Nleya quarrelled with his superior officers when he told them that sections of the army were involved in the smuggling of poached rhino horn and ivory on a large scale into Mozambique. Shortly before he disappeared, he told one of his brothers he was in danger because he knew too much.[42]

Captain Nleya's brothers have been threatened with arrest; his wife Mercy has received threatening phone calls and strangers have visited the school where she teaches, asking about her. A December 1989 magistrate's inquest concluded that Captain Nleya had been murdered.[43]

Between 1987 and 1990, at least seven other investigators and officials died under suspicious circumstances. These include two friends of Captain Nleya and two National Parks officers investigating ivory smuggling out of Gonarezhou National Park who were killed in a September 1987 ambush. Their scout was abducted and never seen again.[44]

Afterwards, the park was closed to tourists, and the shootings were blamed on Renamo, the guerrilla resistance movement in neighboring Mozambique. Local conservationists claim that wildlife officials, police and army officers, National Parks employees, and even South African military personnel have been heavily involved in poaching operations in Gonarezhou. Closing the park to outsiders and increasing army and police patrols to "protect" it from Renamo allowed the poaching to continue on an even more secret and well-organized basis.[45]

As *The Sunday Correspondent* put it in January 1990, the army proved to be a poor guardian of wildlife:

> In Gonarezhou . . . , the rhino population has been virtually eliminated. Up to 1,000 elephants have been killed over the last two years.

Almost all of the carcasses date back to six months after the army sealed off the park because of Renamo activity.[46]

There have been other suspicious deaths of wildlife investigators. In 1988 and 1989, two Central Intelligence Organization officers looking into the poaching of rhinos and elephants were killed in automobile accidents.[47] And in April 1991, ZNA Lieutenant Shepard Chisango, supervising a military customs post on the border, refused to allow the entry of an army vehicle apparently carrying smuggled goods. He was manhandled and arrested by angry soldiers at the border crossing. After being released, he was again arrested in June. On June 9, 1991, he was found beaten and dead in his cell.[48]

The result of these mysterious deaths, said one local conservationist, has been "a climate of fear prevailing among everyone who knows about what is really going on in the poaching game." The EIA's report concludes, "The coverup of Captain Nleya's murder and other 'accidents' and murders completely undermines claims that Zimbabwe can control poaching."[49]

South Africa: A Central Role in Poaching

South Africa has played a central and unique role in the massive poaching of elephants throughout their range in Africa. South Africa is the intermediary destination for most of the illegal ivory. And in an effort to "destabilize" so-called frontline states opposing its government, South Africa supplied massive amounts of weapons to guerrillas in Angola and Mozambique fighting against Marxist governments. Until these civil wars wound down, these guerrilla groups—Unita in Angola, Renamo in Mozambique—used the guns to kill as many elephants and rhinos as possible in order to finance their covert operations.

South Africa's own elephant population, while relatively well protected from poaching, is small, numbering just 8,000. It is concentrated almost exclusively in the northeast part of the country, in Kruger National Park, which runs along the border with Mozambique.

Poaching has been a fairly manageable problem in South Africa in recent decades, and no significant elephant poaching is known to have taken place between 1983 and 1990. In 1991, poachers—probably refugees from Mozambique—are known to have killed twenty-seven elephants in Kruger and several rhinos in reserves in Natal province. Where poaching (usually of rhinos) has occurred, the government has often made arrests and prosecuted. In February 1988, six senior wildlife rangers were arrested and charged with killing rhinos and smuggling horns over the preceding decade in the Umfolozi Game Reserve in Natal.

In the last half of 1990, seven rhinos were shot in Umfolozi with AK-47s, weapons thought to have been supplied by Mozambicans. And on December 5, 1991, a former senior ranger in Kruger, Ludwig Wagener, was sentenced to five years in jail for allegedly killing four elephants and twenty-nine white rhinos between 1978 and 1988 in the part of the park controlled by the military.[50]

According to Major Pieter Lategan, head of South Africa's Endangered Species Unit, over 140 ivory and rhino horn smugglers were arrested in 1991 alone, but this may have represented only the tip of the iceberg. He said in late 1991 that illegal ivory was coming into South Africa from every country in the region. (The biggest ivory dealer in South Africa is believed to be the family of A.H. Pong in Pretoria, who are said to stockpile tons of ivory in Hong Kong.) From South Africa, much of the ivory and rhino horn was shipped to Taiwan, where the ivory was carved into blocks and sent to Japan.[51]

The U.S. Fish and Wildlife Service recently broke up a South African ivory-smuggling ring in a sting operation. In the summer of 1992, a former South African military officer, Marius Meiring, pleaded guilty in a Connecticut court to illegally smuggling elephant ivory, rhino horns, and guns into the United States. His American partner, John Lukman, served nine months in the Allenwood, Pennsylvania, federal prison. He later charged that several American firms had been dealing in horns from Angola's critically endangered black rhino.[52]

But taking on the South Africa ivory smugglers can also be dangerous. In November 1992, the *Johannesburg Weekly Mail* reported that researcher David Webster was shot and killed after alerting government officials in Mozambique to a network of smugglers dealing in illegal ivory.[53]

On May 10, 1994, a new government, under President Nelson Mandela, took office in South Africa. It remains to be seen if his administration will crack down on the smuggling of ivory from other nations and end his country's role as a leader of the lobby to continue the international trade in ivory.

Angola—Ivory Finances Rebels

As in Mozambique, arms supplied to the Angolan anti-communist rebels, known as Unita and led by Jonas Savimbi, were used to poach elephants in order to help finance the South African program. Most of Angola's elephants, perhaps up to 60,000, were probably killed during the civil war, but reliable estimates of losses and present population levels are not available.

Colonel Jan Breytenbach spent most of his career leading SADF Special

Forces in secret operations in Angola and Namibia, and has publicly revealed how the SADF and Unita worked closely together to massacre elephants and ship out their ivory. He has described numerous cases in which high-ranking officers have quashed attempts to investigate or prosecute instances of ivory smuggling.

As first revealed by the *Johannesburg Sunday Times* in 1989, Breyten-bach described how the joint SADF/Unita operation massacred elephants by the thousands, decimating their populations:

> Elephants were mown down indiscriminately by . . . AK-47 rifles and machine guns. They shot everything, [elephant] bulls, cows, and calves . . . The tens of thousands of elephants became thousands, the thousands hundreds, and the hundreds, tens.[54]

Estimates of remaining elephants in Angola range from 10,000 to 18,000, even up to 50,000.[55] Unita continues to fight on, but the outside forces have withdrawn. With the fighting now greatly reduced, there is the hope that political stability may be achieved in Angola, and with it an effort to protect the nation's remaining elephants.

Malawi

Malawi's elephant population has dropped by more than half, from 4,500 in 1979 to 2,075 in 1992.[56] A government study issued in 1989 found that "poaching is common in all parks, game reserves, and forest reserves," and that poachers from Malawi have also been active in nearby Zambia. Moreover, Malawi has been used extensively as a destination for poached ivory from neighboring states. The nation has objected to the ban on ivory trading, and has been strongly pushing to have elephants downgraded from CITES Appendix I to Appendix II.[57]

Namibia

Namibia has a highly mobile elephant population, with many of the estimated 5,700 animals (as of 1989) migrating back and forth between Angola, Botswana, and Zambia.[58]

Namibia has also served as a conduit for its neighbors' illegal ivory. On September 16, 1989, what newspapers called the world's biggest ivory "bust" took place when police confiscated a truck near Okahandja that was bound for South Africa carrying 972 elephant tusks, reportedly from Angola and Zaire as well as from local elephants.[59]

THE IVORY TRADERS—BURUNDI, JAPAN, AND HONG KONG

Several other nations have played important roles in the uncontrolled poaching of the 1980s, acting as middlemen and merchants for the illegal ivory. Prominent among them are Burundi, Japan, and Hong Kong.

Burundi

The nation of Burundi, located in Central Africa, has the distinction of holding the record for the amount of ivory exported from an African country that has no elephants. Indeed, the nation has played a key role in "laundering" illegal ivory smuggled out of other countries. From 1975 through 1988, at least 2,000 tons of ivory—valued at several hundred million dollars—entered Burundi illegally. From Burundi, the ivory is flown out to Belgium and the United Arab Emirates, and from there it goes to other countries in the Far East. Between 1979 and 1987, Burundi is known to have exported 1,450 tons of elephant tusks.[60]

In recent years, Burundi has tried to sell its ivory stockpile by using South African agents, including a company comanaged by the nephew of South Africa's former Foreign Minister, R.F. "Pik" Botha. In early 1991, Burundi was said to have a stockpile of about eighty-five tons of poached ivory.[61]

Japan

Japan has long been the world's leading importer of ivory, consuming some 100 tons a year, up to 40 percent of the international trade. But the 1989 trade ban caused a drop in the market, with prices falling precipitously and consumer demand dropping by half by late 1990. Japanese ivory merchants are said to be anxiously awaiting the lifting of the ban and the resumption of rising prices for ivory.[62]

Hong Kong

As a major buyer of ivory, Hong Kong has long helped maintain the economic incentive for the killing of thousands of elephants. Before the October 1989 CITES meeting at which the trade ban was agreed upon, Hong Kong was estimated to have a stockpile of some 670 tons of ivory. But six months later, the figure was revised down by a third, to 474 tons, leading many to believe that much of this missing ivory had been smuggled to Japan. Some 40 tons of Hong Kong's ivory stockpile in 1989 was owned by the Rand Company, run by the family of A.H. Pong, a major exporter of ivory from South Africa.[63]

No one really knows how much ivory comes into Hong Kong, since customs officials say they can check only 1 percent of arriving containers. As in Japan, the trade ban has caused a drastic decline in the price of ivory and the industry's viability.

THE TRAGEDY OF A MOTHER AND HER CALF

As awful as the loss of several hundred thousand elephants is, it is witnessing the killing of a single individual that really brings the tragedy in focus. I will never forget HSUS investigator David Wills' story of tracking through the Zimbabwean bush a female elephant, approximately 30 years old, who had a young calf.[64] She had an old wound on her leg, perhaps the consequence of a poacher's snare, that caused her constantly to fall behind the herd, as it was difficult for her to keep pace with the group. Describing this mother's relationship with her young, Wills talks of the constant touching, the low rumbling of voice that would reassure the calf when some sound or movement would startle her.

Wills watched in fascination as the mother would pull a mopani tree down with her trunk and hold it low to the ground so the calf could enjoy the delicate and tender leaves that grow on the tree tops. The love and affection between cow and calf as they bathed in the river and moved through the African countryside was a compelling sight, and it reinforced his appreciation of the complex social and family relationships found among this intelligent and gentle species.

Wills describes the despair and sorrow he experienced when, three days later, he came upon the bullet-ridden carcass of this same mother, dead in the forest. Her face now disfigured where poachers had cut away her ivory, she was still full of unsuckled mother's milk. Her calf was nowhere to be found. The loss of its mother would assure the death of the calf, which would quickly fall prey to lions or hyenas. And all this for a few pieces of white ivory that would become, perhaps, carved figurines to be placed on someone's mantelpiece.

CHAPTER 5

How to Stop the Poaching: Ban the Ivory Trade, or Keep It Going?

... a unilateral ban [on ivory trading] by the United States would undercut African conservation efforts . . . The point is that Africans don't want a ban. They are the people closest to the problem, and we must respect their wishes.

William Reilly
President, World Wildlife Fund,
testifying in opposition to the
Elephant Protection Act
June 1988[1]

As poachers stepped up the pressure on elephants, animal protectionists kept the pressure on governments across the globe to halt the ivory trade, the main cause of the poaching.

On February 16, 1989, The Humane Society of the United States (HSUS) and other organizations, citing new data on the demise of elephants throughout Africa, petitioned the U.S. Department of the Interior to reclassify the African elephant as endangered and ban all ivory imports.[2]

This set in motion a chain of events that culminated, a few months later, in two major actions by the U.S. government: banning commercial ivory imports, and supporting the efforts of wildlife protectionists—which were ultimately successful—to end the worldwide trade in ivory. But this was accomplished only after a major battle between and among various conservation and industry groups that preceded the October 1989 meeting of the Convention on International Trade in Endangered Species of Wild Fauna and Flora (CITES) in Lausanne, Switzerland, where the trade ban was adopted.

OPPOSING THE IVORY BAN

By 1989, the increasingly frequent and ominous reports from Africa of elephants being killed off in area after area were receiving widespread press coverage. This made it difficult for conservation officials and organizations to continue to stall on taking the only action that, it had become apparent, could stem the elephant slaughter—stopping the ivory trade. The HSUS's petition, and its publicity and lobbying activities against the ivory trade, forced the Interior Department and the American conservation community to confront the issue and take a stand one way or the other.

The HSUS was joined by the Animal Welfare Institute, the Animal Protection Institute of America, the International Wildlife Coalition, the Society for Animal Protective Legislation, and other organizations.[3] The HSUS and its allies urged their members to write to then President George Bush, the Secretary of the Interior, and various other government officials urging that action be taken to save the elephants before it was too late.

But some conservation organizations not only refused to endorse a ban on the ivory trade, they actively opposed and spoke out against it. These groups continued to insist that the commerce was good for elephants, because it gave the animals monetary value and thus provided a reason for local people and governments to protect them. Ironically, some of these same groups were regularly conducting publicity and fund-raising campaigns to "save the elephants," while at the same time opposing the only effective action that could save them. The most active was the prestigious and highly respected World Wildlife Fund (WWF).[4]

The opposition of this politically powerful group was particularly damaging to efforts to ban ivory, since it gave governments an excuse for failing to take action. For over a decade, it almost certainly cost the lives of untold numbers of elephants.

WWF: SAVE ELEPHANTS—KEEP THE IVORY TRADE GOING

WWF has done much to educate the public about the plight of Africa's wildlife, and many of its endangered species projects have been extremely valuable. But the group's unwavering commitment to consumptive sustainable use, especially of elephants, succeeded in thwarting the efforts of animal protection organizations such as The HSUS to fully protect elephants. WWF even formed a working relationship with the ivory dealers and insisted that no action be taken to disrupt the trade.

Actually, WWF's opposition to protectionist measures to save the elephant is nothing new, and is consistent with its traditional pro-hunting, pro-commercial use policy on wildlife. This policy is generally not mentioned in its ads, mailings, and fund-raising projects, and would come as a surprise to many if not most of the group's members. But it is a fundamental aspect of WWF's "management" philosophy towards wildlife.

Despite its long-time support for sport and commercial shooting of elephants, and its opposition to an ivory trade ban, WWF has extensively used elephants for fund-raising purposes. At the end of 1988, WWF's British affiliate, the World Wide Fund for Nature, did a four-page-long direct-mail appeal on the plight of the elephant, which raised some $500,000. A subsequent elephant mailing in July 1989 brought in another $335,000.[5]

Meanwhile, WWF's pro-ivory trade policies were encouraging the poaching of elephants throughout Africa and frustrating efforts to stem the slaughter. In June 1988, at Congressional hearings on Representative Anthony Beilenson's Elephant Protection Act, WWF President William Reilly (soon to be appointed by President Bush as Administrator of the U.S. Environmental Protection Agency) testified against the legislation. He argued that banning the importation of ivory into America would be "counterproductive," since "a unilateral ban by the United States would undercut African conservation efforts." "The point," Reilly told the hearing, "is that Africans don't want a ban. They are the people closest to the problem, and we must respect their wishes."[6]

Allan Thornton of the Environmental Investigation Agency (EIA) has been trying for years to stop the poaching of elephants, and has often encountered WWF working against his efforts. Thornton's reaction to WWF's testimony was one of long-suffering frustration: "There it was again, that blind dedication to the 'sustainable use of wildlife' theory: the old intransigent WWF argument that only by selling their ivory could African countries be persuaded to conserve their elephants as valuable assets. It was a theory which in most African countries was being completely disproved by the facts."[7]

Thornton saw, time and again, WWF getting credit and contributions for saving elephants when in fact the group was *opposing* protective measures. In February 1989, a British publication ran a lengthy article on the plight of the elephants, illustrated by EIA's photographs of dead elephants, including one by Thornton himself spread over two pages. But the piece did not even mention EIA, except in a tiny photo credit. "To our dismay," writes Thornton, "the magazine had instead published the name and address of WWF and suggested that donations to help the elephant's cause be sent to them. Even though WWF was still fighting the very idea of a ban on the ivory trade!"[8]

Eventually, in June 1989, WWF reacted to public pressure and came out in favor of a trade ban on ivory. In his book and articles, Bonner attacks WWF not for profiting from the very animals whose interests it was working against, but because, eventually, the group "capitulated" and voted to support the ban, after "public pressure" and the fear of "losing members" overwhelmed its better sense.[9] But whatever the reason WWF switched sides, its call for a trade ban was instrumental in belatedly securing effective action to help elephants. I only wish it had come a decade earlier.

AWF: COMING THROUGH FOR ELEPHANTS

AWF was originally organized in the late 1950s and was incorporated in 1961 as the African Wildlife Leadership Foundation. Its founders were mainly big game hunters interested in the conservation of Africa's wildlife. For many years, AWF has been one of the leaders in promoting and training Africans for leadership positions in conservation activities in Africa, and much of its work has been quite valuable.

AWF has always had a strong pro-hunting, pro-"utilization" orientation, so much so that even by the late 1980s, the group still opposed efforts to ban U.S. importation of and international trade in ivory.[10]

In the middle of May 1988, AWF received widespread publicity when it issued a warning that the African elephant was rapidly disappearing, and called on Americans to help save the species by boycotting ivory. But while the foundation was urging Americans to refuse to buy ivory products, it was at the same time opposing the Elephant Protection Act—legislation that would ban ivory imports into, and sales of ivory in, the United States. A prominent May 15, 1988, article in *The New York Times* headlined "Urgent Call from Wild to Boycott Ivory," explained that:

> . . . the foundation [AWF] did not support an official ban because it might be counter-productive. [An AWF official] explained that a ban might cause resentment among African nations, leading them to resist conservation programs. She said the foundation believed that the best approach was to wage a campaign to persuade Americans to make individual decisions not to buy ivory.[11]

Supporting this position was Dr. David Western, then chairman of the African Elephant and Rhino Specialists Group and director of the international conservation program of the New York Zoological Society (now called the Wildlife Conservation Society or WCS). Western was quoted as saying that "a majority [of conservationists] feel that outright bans would not solve the problem," and that a ban "would exaggerate the problems with wildlife in Africa, because African nations use the revenue from ivory to help finance their conservation programs."[12] (Western was recently appointed Director of the Kenya Wildlife Service, which raises the question of whether Kenya will continue its strong support for the ivory trade ban.)

Fortunately, AWF has in recent years supported the continuation the ivory trade ban, and their support has been crucial in securing and very helpful in maintaining it. Indeed, I must point out in fairness that when AWF did finally come out for the ivory trade ban, its actions were remarkably helpful in winning the ban's passage. In the weeks leading up to, and at, the CITES meeting in Lausanne, AWF played a key role in fighting the good fight, especially its president, Paul Schindler, and vice president Diana McMeekin. At Lausanne, there was hardly a stronger or more effective group working for the trade ban, and AWF deserves much of the credit for its enactment. I hope that we can count on AWF staying the course in supporting the ban over the opposition of some of its African colleagues, several of whom are very influential in the group.

FINALLY—THE U.S. BANS IVORY IMPORTS

As a demonstration of the influence of these African wildlife-oriented organizations, when they did finally call officially for an ivory ban, it was enacted four days later—actually, two days later, if you count only weekdays.[13]

On Thursday, June 1, 1989, WWF and WCS (then called Wildlife Conservation International) called for an immediate end to international trade in ivory. The groups warned that since the CITES meeting in October of that year would consider a trade ban on ivory, "an elephant massacre across Africa is likely before October unless immediate action is taken by all ivory-consuming nations . . . The threat of such a ban will almost certainly fuel a last-ditch effort by poachers and illicit traders to beat the ban."[14]

The following Monday, June 5, President George Bush himself announced that the United States was taking immediate action, saying, "If their population continues to diminish at current rates, the wild elephant will soon be lost from this earth." The President and the Secretary of the Interior said they would "impose a total ban on commercial importation of elephant ivory," while continuing to allow the entry of "legally taken sport-hunted trophies."[15]

On June 8, the European Community also agreed to an import ban, and a week later, Japan severely restricted imports. The next day, Hong Kong, seeing the loss of its leading export markets for ivory, announced a moratorium on raw ivory imports. WWF estimates that these actions resulted in closing down some 70 percent of the world ivory trade.[16]

These decisions by AWF, WWF, and the U.S. government were welcomed by wildlife protectionists, but many expressed dismay that it had taken so long for the government and leading conservation groups to realize what action was needed. As Dr. Susan Lieberman, at that time an elephant specialist at The HSUS, commented, if the proponents of the trade ban had been given some support during the preceding decade, "there would be a lot more elephants alive today."[17] Indeed, the United States had just demonstrated how important its leadership on the issue could be; it is too bad that it took the loss of half of Africa's elephants to prompt the action.

CHAPTER 6

The Poachers' Last Stand at Lausanne

The global demand and the price of ivory has virtually collapsed . . . elephant populations seem to be increasing and perhaps are beginning to recolonize their former range . . . The positive change in population trends is attributed to massive investments in security as well as a reduction in the demand for ivory following the Appendix I listing.

U.S. Department of the Interior
August 1992[1]

It was at the October 1989 meeting of the Convention on Trade in Endangered Species of Wild Fauna and Flora (CITES) in Lausanne, Switzerland, that strong, effective action was at last taken to protect the elephants. Wildlife protection groups finally succeeded in their efforts to have the African elephant placed in CITES' most endangered category, Appendix I. This banned all international commercial trade in elephant products. But the ivory trade ban was enacted only over vociferous opposition, mainly from those who wanted to continue the "sustainable use" of elephants as long as there were any left to kill and profit from.

Animal protectionists lobbying in favor of the Appendix I listing included The Humane Society of the United States (HSUS), the Animal Welfare Institute (AWI), Greenpeace, the Monitor Consortium, the Environmental Investigation Agency (EIA), the International Fund for Animal Welfare, Friends of Animals, and others, as well as the nineteen-member United States delegation headed by Assistant Secretary of Interior Constance Harriman.[2] Some influential pro-management conservation groups also ostensibly supported the proposal, including—belatedly and very reluctantly—the World Wildlife Fund (WWF).

Opposing the Appendix I listing were the ivory industry, the big game hunting lobby, a few African states that were profiting from ivory sales, and several powerful officials of CITES, the World Conservation Union (IUCN), TRAFFIC International, and other conservation agencies and groups. The behind-the-scenes lobbying, intrigue, and back-stabbing that took place at Lausanne would by itself fill a book or two. (An excellent account appears in the book *To Save an Elephant*, by Dave Currey and Allan Thornton of EIA.)[3] But the most interesting, and at times enraging, aspect of the meeting was the way representatives of several conservation groups and of CITES who opposed banning the ivory trade tried to sabotage the proposal without going too public and discrediting themselves.

Indeed, it was a strange alliance of forces that fought, zealously and in vain, to prevent an ivory trade ban from being enacted. Leading the fight were Eugene Lapointe, the French Canadian who had led CITES for the preceding eight years; Rowan Martin, deputy director of research for the Zimbabwe Wildlife Department, who led the Zimbabwean delegation; the delegations from South Africa and Botswana; and representatives of the ivory dealers of Japan and Hong Kong.

At the same time, while publicly championing the trade ban, WWF, along with its affiliate TRAFFIC, worked quietly to undermine the lobbying by wildlife protectionists for such a measure. These groups operated behind the scenes to lobby for the possibility of keeping elephants in some southern African countries such as Botswana, South Africa, and Zimbabwe off of the protected Appendix I list, in exchange for a two-year moratorium on trade. WWF agreed to support the total trade ban only after the proposal was somewhat weakened to facilitate future down-listings of elephant populations, and because of pressure from protectionist groups such as EIA and AWI.[4]

A particularly subtle effort to prevent the trade ban proposal from being accepted was made by Martin Holdgate, then director general of the IUCN. He suggested that some elephant populations be placed on Appendix I and others on Appendix II, where there would be a "voluntary moratorium" on ivory trading for a couple of years for countries that met certain "objective criteria."[5]

All of these "split listings" proposals were largely unrealistic, unworkable, and unenforceable, and would have had the effect of perpetuating the ivory trade and the commercial killing of elephants throughout Africa. But to some of those working for the split listing concept, this was precisely their aim.

ZIMBABWE'S TACTICS BACKFIRE

It is questionable whether the trade ban would have been enacted if its opponents hadn't made some serious errors in judgment and strategy, calling into question their own credibility and integrity and offending many of the delegates.

Some of the most damaging mistakes were made by one of the most active and outspoken of those opposing the ivory trade ban, Zimbabwe's Rowan Martin.

Weeks before Lausanne, at the July 1989 meeting of CITES' African Elephant Working Group in Gabarone, Botswana, discussion focused on a June 1989 report by CITES' Ivory Trade Review Group confirming that the African elephant was in serious trouble, and making it clear that a ban on ivory trading should be enacted. At the meeting, Martin, representing Zimbabwe, alienated so many participants that he undermined his own case for allowing continued trade in ivory. Martin's incredible claims that Zimbabwe's elephants were reproducing at an unprecedented rate—conceiving at seven years old and giving birth at nine—were greeted with open and derisive laughter in the meeting room.

And when Martin complained that Zimbabwe had not been consulted on the study, one of the report's authors, Steve Cobb, pointed out that Martin *had* been invited to participate but had refused, saying "my heart is not big enough to bleed for all the elephants in Africa."[6]

Then, having been twice ridiculed by the scientists at the meeting, Martin turned to a venomous personal attack on Costa Mlay, Tanzania's new wildlife director. Mlay had given an eloquent speech urging an end to the ivory trade, saying, "Every generation will be judged by its moral courage to protect species that are in danger of extinction."

"We have here," taunted Martin, "a crusader who has found a new religion: elephant conservation. The crusader from Tanzania has even found a Bible, which is the Ivory Trade Review Group's report. And he is searching for the Holy Grail, which is a ban on the ivory trade."[7] The personal attack on Mlay was considered to be highly inappropriate for such a meeting, especially coming from a white delegate who continually suggested that the trade ban was an imperial plot by neocolonialist Westerners to deprive Africans of the use of their resources.

Indeed, prior to and at the meeting in Lausanne, the Zimbabwe Wildlife Department took the familiar position in their press releases and position papers that uninformed outsiders were forcing their misguided views on Africans. "We do not like," they said, "the way the West is dictating terms to us when they understand so little about the issues involved . . . Do not listen to the panicked voices of conservationists who have failed."[8]

Ironically, at Lausanne, the first delegation to call for a general ban on the international trafficking in ivory was not that of a Western nation, but that of an African one, Tanzania, headed up by Costa Mlay. Kenya immediately endorsed the proposal, as did the United States and the European Community.[9]

Other arguments against the ivory ban presented by the Zimbabwe delegation were equally absurd and unsupported by the facts, including the often-made prediction that a trade ban would force the industry underground, where it could be neither monitored nor controlled. This ignored the fact that the ivory trade was *already* out of control, with up to 90 percent of the ivory being sold coming from illegally killed elephants.[10]

Zimbabwe's uncompromising, militantly pro-trade position and insulting language proved counterproductive, for it offended many of the delegates. According to Iain Douglas-Hamilton, who has worked for years with officials and conservationists in Zimbabwe studying elephants, "the Zimbabweans seemed happy to write off the rest of the continent north of the Zambezi [River], where five out of every six African elephants still lived." He writes:

> Culling and trading might work in Zimbabwe, but it was not a policy that could be exported to Central Africa or to countries such as Kenya and Tanzania, where men were still dying in the never-ending war against the poachers. Viewed in these terms, such pro-trade attitudes seemed short-sighted and selfish. As one cynical observer put it, "Zimbabwe is determined to fight for its right to trade ivory down to the last Tanzanian elephant."[11]

DID THE IVORY INDUSTRY BUY OFF CITES?

The atmosphere at Lausanne was also fouled by the stench of corruption. It had long been widely known that some government officials, game rangers, and park wardens throughout Africa had been paid off by ivory traffickers to allow the poaching of elephants and trade in their tusks. But now allegations of payoffs and influence-peddling reached right into the CITES Secretariat, its governing body, which was supposed to remain neutral on controversial issues but had been publicly opposing the ivory trade ban.

Many people wonder why the officials at CITES, a treaty set up to protect endangered wildlife, would actually promote commercial trade in such products like ivory. Few people are aware that the ivory industry has actually made large contributions to, and helped to finance, CITES.

Although widespread allegations of bribery of CITES officials have never been proved, it was revealed in 1989 that CITES secretary general Eugene Lapointe had accepted at least $200,000 from the ivory industry to subsidize the organization's budget! The CITES-designated entity monitoring the ivory trade received the $200,000 from ivory traders between 1985 and 1988. The potential conflict of interest here is obvious: The more ivory is traded, the richer the dealers become, and the more money flows into CITES.[12]

Revelations of the corruption of CITES and its cozy relationship with those causing the destruction of elephant herds throughout Africa helped to undermine the treaty's credibility and its effort to prevent the trade ban from being enacted. This was not the only time CITES benefitted financially from the illegal trade in endangered wildlife. The CITES Secretariat on another occasion sold a shipment of illegally smuggled lizard skins that had been confiscated in Guyana to a Japanese dealer for $80,000. After news of this revelation circulated at Lausanne, thirty-eight wildlife-protection groups signed a letter drafted by EIA calling for Lapointe's resignation. He was removed from his position the following year.[13]

Also around the time of the Lausanne meeting, the EIA discovered and revealed that Rowan Martin had been hired by the CITES Secretariat in 1985 to draft its new system for regulating and controlling the ivory trade. The result was a CITES policy to "register" and legalize the huge stockpiles of hundreds of tons of poached ivory in Burundi and Singapore, in order to qualify them for trade under the new CITES regulations.[14] This not only rewarded those dealing in illegal ivory, but encouraged continued poaching of elephants.

Similarly, one of the people CITES has relied on for research and advice on elephants is Ian Parker, a Kenyan hunter, ivory trader, and paid consultant for the ivory industry. He has also served as a paid consultant to CITES, and has been one of the most active and effective opponents of an ivory trade ban.[15]

Parker has always argued that elephants are a luxury that Africa, with its rapidly expanding and increasingly poor and hungry population, simply cannot afford over the long run. Iain Douglas-Hamilton wrote in 1992, "Even now, Ian Parker still maintains that according to 'biological theory,' humans and elephants are competitors and cannot coexist on the same range, the implication being that elephants must disappear as man expands, and the ivory trade cannot be held to blame." Indeed, Parker argued that the ivory traffickers were helping, not harming, Africa by purchasing and creating a market for its ivory.[16]

At a November 1988 meeting of CITES' African Elephant Working Group in Nairobi, Kenya, Allan Thornton of EIA befriended Parker. Thornton recounts in his 1991 book, *To Save an Elephant*, that Parker, not knowing who Thornton was, declared "gleefully" to him at their first meeting, "I loathe conservationists." According to Thornton, Parker then went on to describe how in 1986 he had collected three separate fees for doing the same job. This "job" consisted of "registering" and "legalizing" under CITES a stockpile of ivory in Burundi, for which Parker was to be paid hundreds of thousands of dollars by the government of Burundi, by the trader who owned the ivory, and by the CITES Secretariat.[17] And this was the person that the CITES Secretariat under Eugene Lapointe chose to conduct its official ivory trade study!

But having exercised extraordinary influence over CITES' policies on elephants for years, the ivory industry now faced a confrontation with forces that could not be bought off: the wildlife protectionists.

THE VOTE TO SAVE THE ELEPHANTS

The biggest factor working against the ivory trade was not corruption, or bad manners, or offensive behavior. It was the facts, world opinion, and the glare of the media spotlight on Lausanne.

As *New African* magazine so succinctly put the argument for banning ivory in 1989: "Ban the trade and a fortune in ivory reverts to being a pile of elephant teeth. Keep the trade open, and . . . we are unlikely to have any elephants left to grow teeth."[18] By this time, the plight of Africa's elephants and the Lausanne meeting were making headlines around the world. This made it difficult for the sustained use lobby to cut back-room deals that would keep the ivory trade in business.

Perhaps the most spectacular and successful publicity event was the one so brilliantly orchestrated by then Kenya Wildlife Service (KWS) Director Richard Leakey. The son of the famous Louis Leakey, who first discovered the fossils of human ancestors in Africa, Richard Leaky is an internationally renowned anthropologist who has fought long and hard to save Kenya's elephants. Leakey came up with a unique and dramatic way of calling world attention to the need to stop the ivory trade. And so, on July 18, 1989, Kenyan President Daniel Arap Moi generated massive publicity for the ivory boycott when, before the world's press and cameras, he put the torch to a huge, twelve-ton pile of confiscated elephant tusks worth some $3 million. The event highlighted the plight of the elephants, and was seen on television or read about by an estimated 850 million people around the world, according to Leakey.[19]

All of this publicity and pressure, stirred up and used skillfully in tough, tireless lobbying by the wildlife protectionists, are what persuaded the member nations of CITES to vote overwhelmingly in favor of an Appendix I listing for all of Africa's elephants.

Realizing that action of some sort was inevitable, Zimbabwe tried to head off an ivory trade ban by proposing a so-called "split listing." Under this procedure, most African elephant populations would be placed on Appendix I. But those in Angola, Botswana, Malawi, Mozambique, Namibia, South Africa, Zambia, and Zimbabwe would remain on Appendix II, and thus be subjected to continued international trade in ivory. Given that the latter group included at least three countries whose elephants were being wiped out by massive poaching—Zambia, Mozambique, and Angola—the proposal lacked even the *appearance* of reasonableness, and was defeated by a vote of 70 to 19. However, protectionists were unable to muster the two-thirds vote necessary to have a CITES proposal for an Appendix I listing adopted.

A compromise of sorts was finally reached when Somalia introduced a proposal to place the African elephant on Appendix I, but to allow any range nation to downgrade its elephant population to Appendix II if a panel of experts certified that elephants and ivory exports were being properly managed. The proposal passed with a vote of 76 for, 11 against, and 4 abstaining.[20]

Among the eleven nations voting *against* the proposal to list the elephants on Appendix I were seven African countries that together are home to half of Africa's elephants: Botswana, Cameroon, Congo, Gabon, Mozambique, South Africa, and Zimbabwe.

But most of Africa voted to call a halt to the forces that were draining Africa of its elephants and their ivory, mainly for the benefit of outsiders who cared little if at all about the future of the continent.

THE U.S. CHAMPIONS KILLING ELEPHANTS FOR FUN

While the American delegation played a useful role in securing the CITES Appendix I listing, many of the Lausanne Convention's delegates were amazed to see the United States so vigorously endorse sport hunting of elephants, even as it argued that elephants were seriously endangered and needed strong protection. This was, of course, a demonstration of the U.S. administration's fealty to the big game hunting lobby. Indeed, "sport" hunting of elephants is strongly supported by some powerful conservation groups, such as WWF and AWF, both of which are funded and run in part by hunter-conservationists.

In addition, this policy was supported by then Secretary of State James A. Baker and President George Bush, both of whom are avid hunters. Baker had been effectively lobbied by two of the leading figures in the wildlife protection movement, Christine Stevens of AWI and Craig Van Note, head of the 35-member Monitor Consortium.[21] As a result, Baker was quite helpful in securing U.S. support for the Appendix I listing. According to Van Note, "Baker was a hero. He played a key role in this. He pulled the strings and pushed the buttons to mobilize the powers that be in the international community to get the ban through."

But to delegates unfamiliar with American politics and the clout of the gun lobby, it was a curious and confusing spectacle to see the U.S. condemning killing elephants for profit but promoting killing them for recreation. Delegation leader Constance Harriman, in her opening statement at Lausanne, said that African elephants should be listed as endangered, but that "the United States encourages the African nations to continue to allow sport hunting."[22] The United States specifically proposed that CITES set an annual quota of 750 elephants that could be killed for sport, a move that would have made it easier for nations like the U.S. to allow the import of hunting trophies. The introduction of this proposal puzzled many delegates, and the proposal was voted down. One delegate from Botswana, Mushanana Nchunga, said, "It's strange that the same people who have pushed for an ivory ban are saying it's okay to hunt elephants for sport . . . Okay to decorate the house with tusks, but not for a woman to wear ivory earrings."[23]

The scenario also gave ammunition to the pro-ivory lobby to attack the American position as inconsistent. As Raymond Bonner wrote in *At the Hand of Man*:

> Hypocrisy has never been in short supply in Washington, and it certainly wasn't on this issue. . . . Rowan Martin [of Zimbabwe] . . . pithily summed up the American position this way: "It's OK for elitist white hunters to come out and kill elephants, but it's not OK for local people to make money from them. [24]

For once, Bonner and Martin had a valid point.

In the end, American trophy hunters were bailed out by the Interior Department, which acted under pressure from Representative Jack Fields (R-TX), a leader of the Congressional Sportsmen's Caucus who had also supported the Appendix I listing. Interior ended up issuing regulations allowing the importation into the United States of sport-hunting trophies from South Africa and Zimbabwe, on the grounds that the elephant populations in those countries were healthy and well managed—the same arguments used by these two countries to justify continuing their trade in ivory![25]

THE IVORY TRADE COLLAPSES

When the Appendix I listing went into effect in January 1990, international trade in ivory was banned both into and out of the over 100 member nations of CITES. The effect was immediate and profound—a drastic reduction in both the price of ivory and the poaching of elephants. In Kenya, for example, the illegal killing of elephants dropped by 99 percent in 1990.[26] In East Africa, ivory prices plummeted, dropping from $663 a pound to $22, a decline of 97 percent.[27]

Although ivory that had already been imported into CITES countries could still be sold within those countries, the commodity quickly became unfashionable, and stores found they could not sell their ivory items even at a steep discount.

A 1991 report by EIA found that throughout the world, ivory had lost much of its value:

- Ivory prices have plunged in both Africa and in consuming and trading nations. In Central African Republic, Burundi, Cameroon, Congo, Kenya, Somalia, and Zaire, ivory prices have fallen by 70 percent or more;

- In Japan, prices initially increased just after the ban, but have now fallen significantly. Consumer demand too has dropped dramatically, with retail sales dropping by 50 percent. Many department stores have dropped selling ivory altogether.

- In Hong Kong, most ivory factories have closed down completely. Although many stores advertise huge price reductions, stocks remain unsold. Retail sales have dropped by 70 percent.

- In China, the major carving factories have almost ceased carving ivory. Sales in China have dropped by more than 90 percent.

- In the USA, even with discounts of 40 to 70 percent, there are very few buyers.[28]

Reports from numerous other sources confirmed EIA's findings. In the words of KWS director Richard Leakey, making ivory an unfashionable and illegal commodity to trade in had a dramatic impact:

Huge stockpiles of ivory in Hong Kong and other Far Eastern countries lost their book value. The price of ivory in Kenya and many other African countries plummeted from $140 per pound in April, 1989, to less than $5 a pound in April, 1990. Trafficking in ivory lost its appeal.[29]

In late May 1990, *The New York Times*, based on information gathered during a three-month inspection by wildlife trade expert Esmond Bradley-Martin, reported:

> . . . major ivory carving factories in Asia that produced jewelry, figurines, and tourist trinkets have virtually closed down. . . in Beijing, only 5 of 550 ivory carvers are still employed at the Beijing Ivory Carving Factory, which last year was the biggest in the world. In Hong Kong, one of the largest sellers of ivory, 75 percent of the craftsmen are out of business . . . sales of carved ivory in Hong Kong stores . . . were down by at least half.[30]

In June 1990, *The New York Times* reported that "a year after the federal government banned the importation of ivory from African elephants, the commercial ivory market in the United States has collapsed . . ." Citing a study by WWF and its affiliate TRAFFIC USA, the article noted that "demand for ivory has plummeted, dragging down the price of products still legally available in this country, as well as the price of ivory obtained illegally in Africa." WWF's survey of the fifteen biggest ivory wholesalers in the country found that even after slashing prices 40 to 70 percent, they "still have found few buyers."[31]

The report estimated that the price of raw ivory in Africa had fallen by as much as 90 percent, greatly reducing demand and the incentive to smuggle. All this led elephant expert Dr. Iain Douglas-Hamilton to proclaim, "Where once there was only despair, there's now some hope."[32]

In the turmoil over the collapse of the industry, the ivory dealers even resorted to shooting one another over disputes. Ali Suleiman, one of the major traders in Burundi, was shot to death in Belgium, and another dealer was murdered in his car in South Africa.[33]

POACHING DROPS BY 99 PERCENT

With demand for ivory virtually gone, so was much of the poaching, since there was little reason now for anyone, in many areas, to incur the danger and trouble of illegally hunting elephants for their tusks. It was a simple equation, easy to understand. But for over a decade, some of the world's leading conservation groups and wildlife officials simply refused to grasp the fact that the best way to protect elephants was to remove the economic incentives for killing them. Now the facts were indisputable: Banning the ivory trade meant ending the large-scale poaching of elephants. And the prediction that banning the ivory trade would drive it underground, where it would reel out of control, never came true.

In early 1993, then KWS director Richard Leakey described how the ivory trade ban helped to drastically reduce the illegal killing of elephants:

> Well-armed wildlife protection forces are fully mobile, highly motivated, and operating with the help of an extensive intelligence network. The intense poaching of elephants and rhinos in Kenya has, at least for the moment, become a historical issue. The numbers of elephants killed illegally for ivory has dropped off dramatically: 36 in 1990, 17 in 1991, and 12 by the end of July 1992.[34]

Some poaching did continue, however. Richard Leakey said in May 1990 that elephants were being killed in Tsavo National Park, and that twelve tons of illegal tusks, some from newly killed elephants, had been confiscated in Kenya and Tanzania. But the reason for this continued poaching and smuggling, he said, was the decision by the British government to give Hong Kong a six-month exemption to sell its ivory stockpile, which, at 570 to 670 tons, was the world's largest. Dr. Leakey said that this was no coincidence, "particularly when the people arrested said under interrogation that the ivory would be sent to Hong Kong."[35]

But in March 1994, Leakey estimated that fewer than thirty elephants a year were being poached in Kenya. Poaching in the North Luangwa Valley of Zambia reportedly fell from 1,000 elephants in 1986 to just 12 in 1991.[36]

Iain Douglas-Hamilton said that "for the poachers, the motivation for killing elephants has gone. Formerly, an elephant with ivory was like a paper bag stuffed with money left lying in the bush."[37] Robin Hurt, a big game hunting safari operator in Tanzania, was initially skeptical of the ban's value. But in March 1991, a year and a half after the ban was adopted, he said, "I haven't seen one poached elephant in more than a year," while before the ban, he saw "hundreds of carcasses, everywhere."[38]

In late 1991, EIA issued a briefing paper summarizing the results of the ban on trade in elephant ivory:

- Only 46 elephants were poached in Kenya this year [from all causes], down from 4,000 poached in 1989;
- In Tanzania, no new carcasses were found during the 1991 count in the Selous Game Reserve. Records of fresh poaching are "minimal" elsewhere in Tanzania, the lowest ever recorded;
- Uganda and Somalia have also reported a decline in poaching.[39]

In the August 1992 announcement of its decision to reinforce the earlier moratorium on ivory products, the U.S. Department of Interior observed that as of January 1990, "all legal international trade in elephant products has virtually ceased. The global demand for and the price of ivory have virtually collapsed":

> There is substantial evidence that the illegal offtake of elephants on a continent-wide basis is significantly reduced . . . At present, several elephant populations remain stable and well-protected, and other elephant populations seem to be increasing and are perhaps beginning to recolonize their former range.
>
> Many populations of the elephant are currently stabilizing or perhaps are increasing. The steep rate of decline observed from the 1970's up to the mid- or late-1980's has been halted for most populations . . .
>
> . . . Although some illegal killing continued, elephant poaching seemed to be decreasing in many African countries because of a lack of financial incentives and an increased vigor and effectiveness of government anti-poaching activities . . . . if these trends hold, depleted populations can reasonably be expected to begin recovery . . . The positive change in population trends is attributed to massive investments in security as well as a reduction in the demand for ivory following the Appendix I listing.[40]

Mark and Delia Owens, renowned wildlife researchers and filmmakers who have lived and studied elephants in Zambia's North Luangwa Valley since 1986, wrote in their 1992 book *The Eye of the Elephant*, "The most effective way to save the African elephant is with a continued long-term, complete international moratorium on the sale of all elephant parts, including ivory."[41]

The Owenses, who have been involved in wildlife conservation and research in Africa for over twenty years, received The HSUS's conservationist-humanitarian award at the organization's October 1993 meeting. There they eloquently described their on-the-scene observation of the impact of the ivory trade ban on northeastern Zambia:

> When we arrived in northeastern Zambia's North Luangwa National Park in 1986, poachers were shooting 1,000 elephants a year within the park's borders. As many as 100,000 elephants had been shot in the Luangwa Valley, a 400-mile portion of the Rift Valley. The gentle survivors of this carnage ran at the first sight or scent of humans; standing twenty yards from one would have been unimaginable. Yet in 1993, poachers shot no more than 5 elephants.
>
> One morning we heard gunshots from very nearby, just down the river. We ducked for cover. When the shooting stopped, two male

elephants from our "camp group" lay dead and mutilated, their tusks having been chopped out of their heads.

In our battered truck, we rushed up the escarpment to bring government game guards from the nearest post, so that they could capture the poachers. We found only seven guards to protect a park the size of Delaware! They had only four rifles and a single round of ammunition among them. Understandably, they refused to tackle the poachers, who were armed with AK-47 military rifles.

That was our first glimpse of the evil forces that were destroying North Luangwa. Informants told us that the Zambian army was using its trucks to haul ivory, the police were issuing guns to poachers, and the game warden himself was selling illegal meat from his back door. The game guards were seldom paid their salaries, so instead of protecting the park, they were poaching. Poachers had shot all of the black rhinos and more than 85 percent of the elephants. At that rate, in five years there would be none left.

But when the ban on ivory trade was enacted, the results were dramatic:

Within a few months, the price of ivory in our area of Africa dropped from more than $200 a pound to just $2 a pound. Suddenly there was less incentive than ever to be an ivory poacher; it made economic sense to become a carpenter, a sawyer, a fish seller, or a cobbler.

And the elephants of Zambia, almost completely wiped out, have now begun to recover:

For the first time in twenty years, the elephant population of North Luangwa began to grow. Ninety-three percent of the population had been poached. It will take many years for a recovery, but at least a recovery has begun.[42]

I would like the people who are advocating "sustainable use" of elephants to tell the Owenses—and all the others working in the bush at great personal sacrifice and risk—that lifting the trade ban will be good for elephants and for conservation.

CHAPTER 7

The Move to Lift the Ivory Ban

By implying that the elephant is in less jeopardy in countries that participate in the international ivory trade, . . . the U.S. is encouraging the commercial value of ivory and thus the destruction of elephant herds throughout Africa.

Dr. Ronald Nowak
U.S. Fish and Wildlife Service
elephant and endangered species expert
July 1991[1]

After all that has happened, no matter what the cost, the [ivory] trade must now be kept closed.

Iain Douglas-Hamilton
elephant expert
1992[2]

Before the ivory trade ban, the sustainable use lobby could argue against it from behind a small fig leaf of plausibility. But now, in light of the results of the trade ban—a drastic reduction in poaching, and a beginning of a recovery for Africa's elephants—there can be no dispute about the effectiveness of the ban and the necessity to maintain it—unless, that is, your purpose is to make money off of ivory at whatever cost to the elephants.

ZIMBABWE DEFIES CITES

Five southern African countries—Botswana, Malawi, Namibia, South Africa, and Zimbabwe—have continued to strongly oppose the trade ban on ivory, and to work vigorously to have it lifted. South Africa has its own central coordinating center for marketing ivory, and the other four nations have formed the Southern African Centre for Ivory Marketing (SACIM), ostensibly to "manage elephants and coordinate trade in their products."[3]

In March 1992, these five southern African countries, plus Zambia, asked the Convention on International Trade in Endangered Species of Wild Fauna and Flora (CITES) to down-list their elephant populations from Appendix I to Appendix II, which would permit renewed trade in ivory. The effect of this proposal was to reinvigorate commercial interest in ivory and to stimulate speculative efforts to stockpile ivory on the chance that it might soon be salable and thus valuable again. As a result, poaching again began to increase in Malawi, South Africa, Zambia, Zimbabwe, and elsewhere in Africa.[4]

In 1992, after a change in government, Zambia announced that it would appeal to all CITES nations to continue the ban on trade in elephant parts and products, and that it was withdrawing its reservation to the Appendix I listing.[5]

But Zimbabwe has been particularly adamant about resuming sales of ivory, since it has been stockpiling tusks from culled elephants in the hope that CITES will again legalize such trade. The nation has not only pressured CITES to reopen international trade in ivory, but also in pelts of endangered cheetahs and leopards, and even in horns from its critically endangered and rapidly disappearing rhinos.

Zimbabwe made about $2 million a year selling raw culled ivory during the 1980s (this money went directly into its central treasury), in addition to the private sector sales of carved ivory, which is worth about ten times more than raw ivory. In contrast, Zimbabwe estimated that its "wildlife industry" (mainly tourism) earned $100 million in 1992, over $2 million of which accrued to the government.[6]

Zimbabwe still claims that allowing the renewal of trade in ivory will promote conservation by generating revenue for its parks, despite the undisputed fact that only a tiny fraction of wildlife-generated income is put back into conservation. Of the approximately $83 million that Zimbabwe earned from park tourism in 1993, less than 2 percent was used on wildlife conservation. Moreover, the money earned from selling ivory ($800,000 the last time a sale was held) is insignificant when compared with the revenues from tourism.[7]

Nevertheless, Zimbabwe continues to harshly criticize the trade ban and those who favor it. In an article written in early 1993, Brian Child, senior ecologist for Zimbabwe's CAMPFIRE program (a community-based conservation project), typifies the harsh, nasty rhetoric with which the government attacks those it disagrees with. In rhetoric reminiscent of the anti-Western propaganda of China or the former Soviet Union, Child bitterly condemns proponents of the trade ban, comparing these conservationists to the imperialists who colonized Africa: "Once again . . . imperialism endangers the critical economic link between wildlife and people, this time in the guise of bans on the trade in ivory and other wildlife products. . . . This ideology is being imposed by people ignorant of Africa upon the African people, who cannot afford it. Such imperialism is repugnant. It will knock the final nail into the coffin of African conservation."[8]

Child may indeed have stumbled on the truth, albeit in a perverse way, in linking elephants to imperialism. But haven't the real imperialists and colonial exploiters been the arrogant, elite, wealthy foreigners who (with the help of their local lackeys) have been running the ivory trade, wiping out one of Africa's most valuable "natural resources," and depriving future generations of their irreplaceable natural heritage?

But Zimbabwe is determined to make money off its wildlife, regardless of the cost to the elephants in Africa. And now, having failed to have CITES legalize sale of its ivory, Zimbabwe has been pushing to change the criteria for listing species on Appendix I and threatening to sell ivory in defiance of the trade ban. On December 14, 1993, Zimbabwean Minister of Environment and Tourism Herbert Murerwa officially confirmed this when he announced that Zimbabwe would sell through SACIM its 30,000-ton ivory stockpile, worth an estimated $10 million, even though the sale would violate the CITES ivory ban.[9] If this happens, elephants all over Africa will be joining the continent's ivory stockpile.

Japan has long been the world's biggest consumer of ivory, and the ivory dealers there, with their huge stockpiles, have been eagerly awaiting the lifting of the ban. As the Environmental Investigation Agency (EIA) wrote in 1992:

> There will be considerable interest among the Japanese ivory traders in the possibility of trade re-opening. If it does, there will be a price on the head of every elephant in Africa. The southern African countries say that, between them, they can produce around 25 tons of "legal" ivory annually. Japan's yearly demand is 100 tons. The remaining 75 tons per year will come, as it did before the ban, from elephants poached right across Africa.[10]

A TEXTBOOK FOR THE SUSTAINABLE USE LOBBY

One of the harshest critics of the ivory trade ban and its supporters has been former *New York Times* correspondent Raymond Bonner, author of the 1993 book, *At the Hand of Man: Peril and Hope for Africa's Wildlife,* which was excerpted in the February 7, 1993, *New York Times Magazine.*

Bonner's book contains all the arguments—and then some—made by the sustainable use lobby—big game hunters, the ivory industry, and other "consumptive" interests in governments and the international conservation agencies. It is a virtual textbook of rhetoric for justifying the killing of elephants and other threatened wildlife, and specifically for discrediting the ivory trade ban. These are the themes we will be hearing for years to come in defense of the sport and commercial slaughter of animals.

While Bonner's book appears to have flopped as far as expected sales volume and impact on policy are concerned, the book deserves examination because it so forcefully and persuasively sets forth the sustainable use philosophy—that elephants and other animals have to be used commercially in order to survive as species. And many people who should know better have bought these bogus arguments.

Even the distinguished *New Yorker* magazine, known for its classic articles on the environment (Rachel Carson's *Silent Spring* first appeared in its pages) and its devotion to fact-checking, fell for Bonner's inaccuracies. Bemoaning a pianist's unsuccessful attempt to import a piano with ivory keys, the February 22, 1993 issue of *The New Yorker*'s "The Talk of the Town" section described how a 73-year-old piano had been stripped of its ivory keys and sent back to France, on orders of the U.S. Fish and Wildlife Service:

> This act of butchery against a charming seventy-three-year-old French piano can be understood only in the context of the international hysteria described in last week's *New York Times Magazine,* in an article entitled "Crying Wolf Over Elephants: How the International Wildlife Community Got Stampeded Into Banning Ivory." Its author, Raymond Bonner, described how public opinion, whipped up by alarmist press propaganda and lurid advertising from the wildlife charities, persuaded governments to impose a worldwide ban on trade in ivory in defiance of some of the best expert opinion in the conservation field.

But I don't blame *The New Yorker* for being mixed up after reading Bonner's article—who wouldn't be confused by someone who seems to me to get the facts not just wrong, but backwards, and who thinks Kenya may still have too many elephants?

DOES KENYA HAVE TOO *MANY* ELEPHANTS?

Some of the blunders and misjudgments in Bonner's book are such whoppers they would embarrass most people into quiet retreat. But Bonner grabs hold of his misconceptions and hangs on tight while driving his points home. Indeed, his entire invalid thesis—that commercial trade in ivory is *good* for elephants—is based on even phonier "facts."

For example, Bonner would have us believe that Kenya still has *too many* elephants, and that the presence of any more might prevent the country from being able to feed itself. He writes:

> It is true that Kenya's elephant population has declined sharply, to about 20,000. But given the country's growing human population and its need for land to grow food, that is the maximum number of elephants the country can tolerate . . .

Moreover, citing damage to Ambesoli National Park that was supposedly caused by elephants, Bonner accuses the defenders of the elephants of being the ones distorting the facts:

> The ivory-ban advocates in the yearlong debate prior to the decision at Lausanne conveniently neglected to mention these facts about the situation in southern Africa and about there being too many elephants in Kenya, and they weren't generally known to the public during the ivory-ban crusade.[11]

However, the facts are that Kenya not only does *not* have too many elephants, but it can comfortably support an elephant population over two and a half times larger than Bonner says, according to government estimates.[12]

The massive poaching of elephants in Kenya reduced that country's elephant population by some 90 percent, from 167,000 in 1973 to about 16,000 in 1989, according to no less an authority than the Kenya Wildlife Service. Since the trade ban, the population has begun to recover. In August 1993, the U.S. Fish and Wildlife Service estimated the number of elephants in Kenya at 25,800 (which some consider an inflated number or possibly the result of an improvement in counting methods), and noted that "Kenya can probably support an elephant population *twice* the present population without adversely impacting available habitats or rural Kenya." (Emphasis added.)[13]

In its discussion of the ivory trade, Bonner's book is widely perceived as lacking in objectivity and even accuracy. Some reviewers who have knowledge about Africa and its wildlife dismissed the work's credibility out of hand. In its review, *Time* magazine called the book a "confused rant . . . A myopic, self-righteous take on the politics of ivory [that] sheds little light on Africa's ecological tragedy."[14] Reviewing the book in *The Atlantic Monthly*, Kenneth Brower says that "[Bonner's] ignorance in environmental matters is profound":

> His book is an edifice of *ad hominem* attacks on anyone who favors the ban on ivory . . . Perhaps someone will come forward with good arguments against the ivory ban. If so, I am eager to hear them. They are not to be found in this book. Errors in fact, flaws in logic, and an unmitigated tendentiousness mar Bonner's case throughout.[15]

Brower concludes that Bonner "has fingered the wrong villains, examined the wrong psyches, written the wrong book."

ECONOMIC VALUE AND "ECO-COLONIALISM"

Even Bonner cannot deny the obvious: that Africa's wildlife is in serious trouble. But his solution is not to protect the animals, but rather to continue allowing them to be killed under his newly discovered conservation mantra, "sustainable use":

> If Africa's wildlife is to be saved, it will not be with celebrity appeals, or more firearms for anti-poaching units, or ivory bans. It will require radical policies and changes in attitudes. Westerners who contribute to conservation organizations will have to understand and accept sustainable utilization.[16]

Bonner spends much of the book's 286 pages defending the concept and explaining why killing elephants is good for them.

Bonner even tries his hand at using a catchy slogan to try to explain sustainable utilization. He writes that "a slogan like 'Buy Ivory, Save Elephants' might not bring in major contributions, but it would be honest":

> . . . by giving elephants an economic value, Africans would not only have an incentive to protect them, but money with which to do it. Funds from the sale of ivory could be used for anti-poaching measures and other conservation programs.[17]

But it has long been clear to anyone not hopelessly biased, uninformed, or blind to the facts that just the opposite is true. Most of the money from ivory sales was leaving Africa or was made outside of the continent, and pitifully little of what African governments did make ever went back to conservation. And the most important impact of "giving elephants an economic value"—dead elephants, that is—was to stimulate their massive slaughter. Local people did not benefit from the ivory trade, but were placed in the line of fire. They were not able to protect elephants from poachers. But Bonner is a fine writer and rhetorician, who knows better than to let a sense of balance get in the way of a clever line.

Bonner ends his book on a strange note, suggesting in the final paragraphs of an Epilogue that it is the conservationists, not the poachers and ivory traders, who are imposing their will on Africa. Ignoring the overwhelming support for the trade ban throughout most of Africa, Bonner writes:

> . . . it's too easy to impose bans—and make the Africans pay. Someday the Africans are going to stand up to the rest of the world and do what they decide is best for themselves . . . Africans will not always allow themselves to be dominated by Europe and the United States. They threw off colonialism; one day they will throw off eco-colonialism.[18]

ELEPHANT PRESERVATION: A RACIST, IMPERIALIST PLOT?

Curiously, the idea that elephant protectionists are racists and imperialists recurs over and over again, not just in Bonner's book, but in the rhetoric of the sustainable use lobby from Zimbabwe to Washington. But it is Bonner who has perfected the tactic as a virtual art form.

Bonner seems strangely obsessed by race, leaving the impression in his book that white conservationists are bigots and that their policies are a form of colonialism and imperialism. Bonner seems to resent the role of whites in African conservationism, imputing to them feelings of paternalism, imperialism, and racism, and accusing them of arrogantly imposing their values on helpless Africans. He quotes the resentment of one tribesman towards "whites driving around in cars . . . looking after the wildlife" and he attempts to discredit the World Wildlife Fund (WWF) and the African Wildlife Foundation (AWF) by writing that they were "fathered by patricians who were convinced that whites had to act or the Africans would destroy the game."[19]

Bonner complains that groups like these ignore and show disrespect for blacks, quoting one AWF official as saying that the conservation movement in Africa is "overly white."[20] "Black faces are similarly scarce at WWF, the world's largest conservation organization," Bonner writes, and "its international headquarters are located in Gland, a quintessential Swiss town, small, quiet, neat—and white."[21] Bonner goes on to attack the June 1989 report by the Ivory Trade Review Group—which blamed the decline of Africa's elephants on the ivory trade and was influential in persuading many countries to support a trade ban—because most of the contributors were white.[22]

This racial theme similarly dominates a May 2, 1993, article by Bonner in the *Washington Post*, which contends that the ivory trade ban is misguided because whites promoted it, indeed forced it on the Africans: "The conservation organizations that campaigned and lobbied for the ban were the monopoly of white Westerners—whites ran them; hired whites to staff them; and implemented programs that reflected their values."[23]

Bonner specifically blames the white-dominated international conservation organizations, such as WWF, AWF, and the World Conservation Union (IUCN), for passage of the ivory trade ban in 1989, when in fact these groups fought the idea of a ban for over a decade.

Bonner's book goes on and on in this vein, concluding that "as many Africans see it, white people are making rules to protect animals that white people want to see in parks that white people visit."[24]

Why, one wonders, does Bonner think it is so shameful for whites to be concerned about and involved in saving Africa's wildlife? Many of the groups and individuals he excoriates are working on conservation projects throughout the globe. Should Africa be excluded from attention and help by those who are not the same color as Africans?

IGNORING AFRICAN CONSERVATIONISTS

What is worse, Bonner's racist thesis strikes me as profoundly insulting and demeaning to the very Africans he claims to sympathize with. It implicitly—and unfairly—portrays them as largely passive, inhibited, ignorant, and indifferent to the fate of their nations' wildlife. And most inexcusably, it overlooks or downplays both the leadership role of black Africans in fighting poachers and the ivory trade and the leadership role of whites in promoting the industry. This is especially true in his newspaper and magazine articles and, to a lesser extent, in his book as well.

What about the many brave and dedicated African rangers and wardens in the bush fighting and dying to defend wildlife, daily risking and sometimes giving their lives battling poachers? What about the leadership role of Africans like Costa Mlay, head of Tanzania's wildlife department, who was the first delegate at the 1989 CITES meeting to propose an ivory trade ban? What about the fact that two thirds of the African countries with elephants supported the 1989 trade ban? And when the ban was debated again at the 1992 CITES meeting, not only did all of these nations continue their support, but five African countries that had originally voted against the ban voted in favor of it. (Bonner writes, incorrectly, that these nations "never wavered in their opposition to a ban.")[25] And what about the many African leaders who realize that elephants and other wildlife bring in tourism, which is the mainstay of several African countries' economies, and who work to promote it?

Finally, and perhaps most outrageously, Bonner's thesis ignores the fact that the leaders and main benefactors of the ivory trade, almost without exception, are white Westerners and Asians (mostly ivory merchants in Hong Kong, Japan, and Singapore). The billion-dollar-a-year business, run by outsiders, has destroyed much of Africa's wildlife heritage and future economic potential, while returning only a tiny percentage of the revenues to Africa.

And the major opponents of the ivory trade ban have included not only the formerly apartheid-dominated South Africa, but the effort has been led by whites: Rowan Martin of the Zimbabwe wildlife department; Ian Parker, a wildlife and ivory consultant from Kenya; Chris Huxley, an Englishman who worked for CITES; Anthony Hall-Martin, a government scientist in South Africa. It would be more accurate to say that it is *these* whites who are trying to impose their values on Africans, whose governments have voted overwhelmingly to ban the ivory trade.

THE REAL IMPERIALISTS: THE IVORY TRADERS

Having devoted page after page to castigating Western conservationists as the cutting edge of a new wave of imperialism, Bonner ends his book true to form, offering advice on how Africans can "throw off eco-colonialism": "All we have to do to preserve Africa's wildlife heritage is care about the people as much as we care about the wildlife."[26] The none-too-subtle implication, of course, is that old libel, reiterated at length by Bonner, that wildlife protectionists care more about animals than about people, especially if the people are Africans.

Bonner repeatedly portrays American and Western conservation groups in this light, as "eco-imperialists," imposing their elitist values on poor Africans by denying them desperately needed revenue from ivory sales. But in order to make such a ridiculous assertion, one must ignore a fundamental fact—almost all of the money derived from ivory sales, legal and illegal, was going to smugglers, dealers, governments, and corrupt officials. Very little—if any—ended up going to local villagers or wildlife programs. The overwhelming majority of ivory revenues not only ended up in the pockets of big shots and crooks, it did not even stay in Africa. That is one reason the African states so overwhelmingly supported the trade ban at the 1989 and 1992 CITES meetings.

Dr. John W. Grandy, The HSUS's vice president for wildlife, has eloquently responded to Bonner's thesis, and specifically his characterization of the organization's work as "eco-imperialism." Grandy observes that a world trade in ivory, or rhino horns, or other wildlife parts, will not benefit the people who share the land with the animals, but will harm them:

> The big winners in the ivory trade are the foreign middlemen and a few local operatives, who buy dead wildlife for a pittance and then sell it for a fortune. The big losers are the elephants, who will die and then vanish, and Africans, who will see their rich natural heritage raped, ruined, and abandoned. And once that happens, the tourists who bring their money to Africa to see the elephants will abandon Africa too.
> Then debate over "sustainable use" of elephants will be over, because there will be none left to use, photograph, kill or argue about.[27]

"THE BAN WAS PROBABLY NEEDED"

In the last paragraph of his *Washington Post* excerpt, Raymond Bonner acknowledges what he has argued against throughout the article and his book, admitting that "the [ivory] ban was probably needed in the short term," and did result in a decline in poaching. It was almost as if, having spent years working on his book, he finally realized his conclusions were wrong, and he threw in a disclaimer at the end hoping nobody would notice the contradiction.

But he cannot resist getting in another dig at Westerners, this time through the words of WWF vice president Michael Wright, who, Bonner writes, had argued "strenuously" that a ban on ivory trading was bad for both Africans and conservation:

> . . . the manner in which the ban had been lobbied into existence by western conservation organizations was, in Wright's words, "the worst kind of colonial manipulation." Another conservationist described it as "eco-colonialism."

In his book, Bonner calls this characterization "a fitting epithet for the elephant crusade."[28] He apparently does not notice the huge irony of devoting almost an entire book to attacking the ivory trade ban and the people and philosophy behind it, and then mentioning, at the very end of an excerpted article, that the ban was "probably needed" after all. This admission is indeed a fitting epi*taph* for Bonner's anti-elephant crusade.

CITES 1992: THE TRADE BAN IS MAINTAINED

At the first full CITES meeting since Lausanne, held in February 1992 in Kyoto, Japan, the southern African bloc made the expected effort to have their elephants down-listed from Appendix I to Appendix II of the treaty. But there was little support for the idea, especially since a CITES panel of experts reported that customs procedures in southern Africa would be unable to control smuggling.

Intense lobbying and publicity generated by protectionists fortunately prevented the down-listing effort from ever making any significant headway by means of back-room deals, a not-unusual way for controversial proposals to be passed at such meetings.

The party line of the sustainable use lobby continued to be that familiar old refrain, that the ivory trade ban was forced on the African countries by extreme and ignorant animal protectionists in the developed nations. The "utilization" camp was especially upset that international trade in elephant products other than ivory, such as meat and hides, would not be permitted. Some conservation groups, such as WWF and IUCN, had long been quietly lobbying to lift these restrictions.

Illustrative of the frustration felt by these groups is Ginette Hemley's article in the October 1992 newsletter of TRAFFIC USA, an international agency and affiliate of WWF that monitors and analyzes trade in endangered wildlife. Hemley expresses her disappointment that the just-completed CITES meeting in Kyoto failed to reopen trade in elephant meat and hides, as Zimbabwe and other southern African countries wanted. She explains that "entrenched protectionist positions from influential industrialized nations stymied any debate over the merits of the compromise and prompted quick withdrawal of the proposals."[29]

But the underlying reason the proposal went nowhere is that it had almost no support.

In fact, as the newsletter points out in another article, "a large number of delegations, many African, opposed the proposal, and only the delegation of Switzerland offered its support." This article also lists half a dozen reasons why the proposal to renew commercial trade in some elephant products was soundly rejected by the delegates. One reason cited is that most African countries that still have elephants wanted to maintain the trade ban, which has been "generally effective in reducing illegal hunting."

But some conservation officials still hold out hope the trade ban will be modified. Even Jaques Bernay, Deputy Secretary of CITES, said in November 1993, "If consuming countries can set up rigid controls, a legal ivory trade could be resumed in two to three years," (which would be allowed under the "Somalia amendment" passed in 1989.)[30]

One tactic of sustainable use advocates is to try to discredit the trade ban, citing the fact that with Asian stockpiles of ivory now depleted, poaching is continuing and even on the rise in some areas. But even if the global ivory trade has not been stopped completely, there is no question that poaching of elephants has been *drastically reduced*, to levels just a small fraction of those of previous years. And what little poaching has resumed can be attributed in part to hopeful speculation that CITES will legalize some ivory trading.

The issues of down-listing some nations' elephants to Appendix II (South Africa and Sudan have submitted such proposals) and allowing a resumption of trade in ivory, meat, and/or hides will be discussed, debated, and decided at the next CITES meeting, to be held in Fort Lauderdale, Florida, in November 1994. Wildlife protectionists will be there in force, for the fate of Africa's elephants could well hinge on the decisions made at this meeting.

AMERICA KEEPS THE DOOR OPEN TO IVORY IMPORTS

The U.S. government is also keeping the door open to resuming future trade in ivory. On August 10, 1992, the Interior Department finally acted on The HSUS's 1989 petition, withdrawing Interior's proposal to list some African elephant populations as "endangered," and refusing to upgrade the elephant's status from "threatened" to "endangered."[31] The Department did, however, re-enforce its June 1989 moratorium on the importation of commercial ivory products.

In response to The HSUS's 1989 petition, Interior had published a proposal on March 18, 1991 stating that "most populations of the African elephant . . . appeared endangered . . . the Service determined in the proposed rule that overutilization of the African elephant for commercial purposes was of sufficient threat to warrant reclassification of most populations to endangered."[32]

But now, amazingly, Interior was refusing to acknowledge the elephant's endangered status, and encouraging its future commercial exploitation.

One reason for Interior's latest sellout of the elephants is the attitude and philosophy of the officials responsible for protecting endangered wildlife, especially the author of the 1992 rulemaking, Charles W. Dane, Chief of the Fish and Wildlife Service's Office of Scientific Authority. Dane and his office, which handles foreign endangered wildlife, are widely considered to be exploitation-oriented, indeed dominated by exploitive interests and obsessed with the concept of economic utilization of wildlife.

In its *Federal Register* notice, Interior gave as its reason for changing its mind about upgrading the elephant's protection the fact that over-exploitation seems to be controlled:

> Although elephant populations in 1992 are less than half of those in 1978, a substantial elephant population of 600,000 still exists, and the protection and management of those elephants is superior in 1992 to the conditions that existed in 1978, when the species was classified as threatened, and in 1989, when the Service was petitioned to reclassify. Just as in 1978, an endangered classification would not accurately express the situation of this species.[33]

And just as in 1978, Interior refused to obey the law and give the elephant the endangered status it deserves, despite overwhelming and uncontradicted data, much of which is cited in the department's own notices.

Since a commercial ivory import ban remains in effect, one might ask what difference it makes whether the African elephant is listed as "threatened" or "endangered." The answer is that if it were placed in the "endangered" category, it would be more difficult for sport-hunted elephant trophies to be imported than it is now, requiring a listing in the *Federal Register* of permit applicants.

And continuing the "threatened" listing lets Interior keep the door open to the possibility of allowing commercial ivory imports in the future if African states can adopt credible (on paper, at least) sustainable use programs for elephant management and conservation.

Indeed, Interior hints at just this possibility, noting in its August 10, 1992, rulemaking, in heavily bureaucratic language, that it approves in principle of killing elephants for ivory:

> The Service supports both non-consumptive uses of African elephants as well as certain carefully regulated consumptive uses of African elephants as mechanisms for attaining revenues to enhance elephant and wildlife management throughout the African Continent.[34]

"MAKING A MOCKERY OF THE ENDANGERED SPECIES ACT"

One of the most cogent and perceptive analyses of Interior's policy comes from Dr. Ronald Nowak, a brilliant and courageous U.S. Fish and Wildlife Service scientist and endangered species specialist. A twenty-year veteran of the service, he is extremely knowledgeable about elephants. It was Nowak who authored the Interior Department's 1978 rulemaking placing the African elephant on its "threatened" list.

In 1991, writing as a private citizen, Nowak commented on the response to The HSUS's petition by Interior, which proposed to list most elephants as endangered, but to retain a "threatened" classification for those in several southern African countries, including Botswana, South Africa, and Zimbabwe. His candid and scathing analysis applies even more forcefully to the final 1992 rulemaking, which does not list *any* African elephant populations as endangered.

Nowak begins by pointing out that since Interior listed the African elephant as threatened in 1978, almost two thirds of the animals have been wiped out:

> ...the elephant was classified as threatened in 1978 when its numbers were estimated at 1,500,000. Total numbers are now little more than a third as great, and the numbers in the three countries in which the "threatened" classification would be retained are only a tenth as great. The adverse trends that jeopardized the elephant in the 1970s have increased in intensity. Legally and logically, if the elephant was threatened in 1978, it is "endangered" now.[35]

Nowak is especially critical of Interior's policy of encouraging the maintenance of small, isolated elephant populations in parks, while seemingly allowing or even encouraging the elimination of the rest of Africa's elephants:

> It is almost always possible to look at an "endangered" though wide-ranging species, and pick out some segments that appear to be relatively stable and safe. But even the long-term preservation of these segments would not mean that the over-all species, as a naturally evolving unit and ecological factor, would be secure.
>
> ...Having a few scattered showcase herds of elephants, their numbers constantly having to be culled and their natural movements restricted, will not mean that we have saved the species. Unfortunately, the proposed rule practically sets up countries where such a situation already has developed as models for the rest of Africa to follow.
>
> If Tanzania's numbers are also cut down to 7,800, but are in a seemingly well-protected park, would there then be a reclassification of the group to "threatened?" Is this a worthy objective? Should we be aiming for the maintenance of a few isolated and artificially constricted herds that appear to be stable for the moment, or should our goal be the conservation of naturally functioning populations within the greater ecosystems of Africa?

If the latter is what we wanted, then the correct classification for the entire species *Loxodonta* africana is endangered. While it is unlikely that all elephants will disappear in the near future, we are in immediate danger of losing the species as it was meant to exist—in the form of naturally behaving and evolving populations with a continent-wide ecological role. It is this form that is addressed by the first stated purpose of the Endangered Species Act: to provide a means whereby the ecosystems upon which endangered species and threatened species depend may be conserved.[36]

Nowak refutes the argument that the "sustainable use" of elephants can help conserve the species, observing that the United States' commitment to the concept is "encouraging the destruction of elephant herds throughout Africa":

The United States' proposed rule gives the impression that the elephant is safest in the places where it is commercially utilized and that such exploitation should be an objective throughout Africa. I am concerned that while encouraging the value of ivory might indeed help fund programs that temporarily support the conservation of the relatively small and well-protected groups of elephants surviving in Southern Africa, such encouragement also could spell doom for the far larger and more vulnerable herds in the rest of the continent. There are inadequate or no protective or management mechanisms in most countries, and continuation of the ivory trade in one area, even if legal, will stimulate poaching and rampant illegal movement on an international scale.

We may save the elephants of southern Africa, for the time being, but lose those in Gabon and everywhere else. By implying that the elephant is in less jeopardy in countries that participate in the international ivory trade than it is in countries that do not, the U.S. is encouraging the commercial value of ivory and thus the destruction of elephant herds throughout Africa.

By suggesting that the apparent maintenance of a few small remnant elephant populations is of equal significance, for conservation purposes, to the continent-wide devastation of the entire species and its habitat, the U.S. is helping to insure that there soon will be only small remnants everywhere.[37]

Nowak concludes that the "constantly repeated argument that by giving the elephant (and other wildlife) an economic value we will provide motivation and means for its conservation . . . has never been adequately supported. It was used in the development of the U.S. 1978 elephant regulations with disastrous results." He stresses that there can be no compromise with the ivory trade, writing that Interior must "take the critically necessary step of recognizing that the international ivory trade is an inherent evil," and that any suggestion of permitting this trade will harm wild elephant populations:

> The proposed special regulations would allow the continuation of trade in ivory already in the United States. By allowing any commerce in ivory in our own country, the U.S. government sets a poor example for the world community, especially those African countries that are being asked to forego such commerce . . .
>
> The original elephant classification and regulations published by the Service in 1978 also emphasized the idea that the ivory trade was sustainable, socially acceptable, and of value as a conservation mechanism. This line of thinking contributed to the loss of nearly a million elephants in the period that has since passed. Let us learn from this historical experience and not repeat the same mistakes.

Finally, Nowak acknowledges that Interior's policy is being set in consultation with the trophy-hunting lobby, whose disproportionate influence is damaging the United States' ability to properly enforce the law:

> Right now I am very concerned that one of the motivating factors in maintaining a "threatened" classification in Botswana, South Africa, and Zimbabwe was the desire to facilitate continued potential hunting by American sportsmen. Possibly there was a belief that the more proper course of extending an endangered classification throughout the range of the species would have stopped such hunting and thus brought complaints from influential sportsmen and their associates. Perhaps there also was a belief that, even though the Endangered Species Act provides for permits to import "endangered" species under the circumstances described above, the preparation of such permits in the case of the elephant might become impractical or too controversial.
>
> . . . by keeping the elephant improperly classified, unnecessarily, for the purpose of facilitating sport hunting, the Fish and Wildlife Service would be making a mockery of the Endangered Species Act.[38]

Yet that is precisely what Interior has done—and one of its most highly respected biologists has aptly characterized the action.

"RAMPANT POACHING WOULD RESULT"

The experts agree that a resumption of the ivory trade would cause an ecological disaster, particularly endangering elephants *outside* of the southern African bloc, where poaching and smuggling could not be brought under even a semblance of control.

Richard Leakey, when director of the Kenya Wildlife Service (KWS), strongly opposed lifting the ivory trade ban. He said in 1993:

> I am against the ivory trade being reopened because I do not believe there are adequate controls to prevent it from once again becoming a racket, with demand quickly outstripping legal supplies. Smuggling, corruption, and poor pay are just as much a problem today as they were in 1988, and rampant poaching would result in many African countries.[39]

Unfortunately, Leakey's commitment to protecting Kenya's wildlife and parks has made him enemies, both in and out of government, who launched a "campaign of vilification" against him. In March 1994 he resigned as head of KWS, blaming interests that wanted to allow mining and other commercial exploitation of Kenya's parks.[40]

In 1993, elephant expert Iain Douglas-Hamilton emphasized that any ivory trade in southern Africa would have a negative impact on elephants in other parts of the continent, and that the existence of any ivory market would be a threat to the survival of elephants everywhere. He warns that if the trade ban is lifted, elephants throughout the continent will again come under the gun:

> All over Africa, ivory is still there in stockpiles, hidden in dusty go-downs, buried in the sackful in the bush, locked away in private vaults, waiting to get out . . . in much of Africa, the same grisly crew of crooks, poachers, corrupt officials, and "ivory consultants" is still waiting to exploit a relaxation or abolition of the ban . . . After all that has happened, no matter what the cost, the trade must now be kept closed.[41]

Douglas-Hamilton now preaches what wildlife protectionists have been saying for over a decade and a half:

> If you want to play safe for the elephant, don't buy, sell, or wear ivory. Don't ever allow the ivory trade to flourish again. No human appetite has endangered elephants more than the desire for ivory.[42]

In his widely praised 1992 book, *The Fate of the Elephant*, naturalist Douglas Chadwick predicts what would happen if Zimbabwe carried out its threats to sell ivory despite the CITES trade ban:

> Such a move could undercut the current ban, greatly damage CITES and all species it attempts to protect, revive the ivory poaching

frenzy, put African elephants back in free-fall towards oblivion, and add heavily to pressures upon the already seriously endangered Asian elephant.[43]

Valerius Geist, the widely respected Canadian mammalogist, referring to Raymond Bonner, IUCN, and others, compares advocates of weakening international controls on trade in ivory and other wildlife products to a "sorcerer's apprentice," and warns that uncontrolled forces of wildlife destruction would be unleashed if the ban were lifted:

> The oversimplified arguments for legalizing the ivory trade in South Africa have already gained a credence that is disturbing: the resumption of a limited ivory trade is now being proclaimed by some spokesmen for South African game ranges as "the solution" to nothing less than "sustainable development," generating income for impoverished local communities. But have no doubt, a 'split listing' for the marketing of raw ivory [just by some African nations] would be the thin edge of the wedge, providing a renewed incentive for poaching, and stimulating a dangerous new demand for ivory in growing economies such as China.[44]

Most amazing of all, after writing a book and newspaper articles and making numerous media appearances attacking the ivory trade ban and its supporters, Raymond Bonner now claims—on occasion—that he doesn't want the ban removed. In a May 12, 1993, debate on CBC radio in Toronto with Dr. Ronald Orenstein, project director of the International Wildlife Coalition, Bonner insisted, "I don't advocate lifting the ivory ban. I don't say we should lift it."[45]

Among those most opposed to lifting the trade ban is the new government of Zambia. In a November 1991 interview with EIA, Norbert Mumba, head of the Zambian Species Protection Department, described how disastrous it would be to reopen trade in ivory for southern Africa, saying that it would "greatly affect" his country:

> Where you create the situation that some ivory is legal, other illegal, it just makes it difficult for law enforcement to detect. I won't be able to know whether a necklace or a bangle or an earring has come out of an illegally obtained tusk or a legal one. Legalizing the trade simply creates that loophole . . .
>
> Everyone wants to assume that we can control poaching, which I don't think is the case here, and to a certain extent it's not the case in Zimbabwe . . . it will affect everyone in the region.

When asked if he had a message for CITES, Mumba replied:

To the delegates I would say before we make a big mistake that mankind will live forever to regret, we have to be objective . . . In considering the move from Appendix I to Appendix II, everybody should bear in mind that the population of the African elephant is greatly threatened. Zambia is an example. 100,000 elephants in Luangwa National Park dropping to a level of 20,000 in a period of ten years. If that rate had continued in the next ten, fifteen years, we would be in a situation where it will have been nearly impossible to come across elephants.

Mumba recognizes that "the long-term result of conserving the elephant is by far more than what would come by killing the elephants and selling off their ivory":

From safari tours you can earn ten times over from one elephant than killing it, because it will still be there. Another set of tourists can come and see it tomorrow . . . the tourist trade is so wide you're not only talking in terms of tourists paying to view the elephants, but you have the situation where the airline is also earning and their hotels are earning. It's such a long chain, it by far exceeds straight dealing (of ivory) . . . No doubt about it, elephants are far more valuable alive than dead.[46]

WHAT NEEDS TO BE DONE

The Fish and Wildlife Service's Dr. Ronald Nowak, writing as a private citizen, has proposed a strategy to save Africa's elephants. Saying that the U.S. Department of the Interior's current policy "is not going to do anything for the long-term benefit of African wildlife," he suggests a new approach:

What is needed is a dramatic statement by the United States that will seize the crest of the wave of enthusiasm that built up in support of elephant conservation and set the stage for future programs. Such can only come in the form of an unmitigated declaration that the African elephant is completely endangered and that we support an end to all commerce in ivory, especially including that in our own country. Then and only then will there be a firm basis for the work that will be needed to help Africa's wildlife. Using the universally popular elephant as a flagship, conservationists will have the opportunity to obtain the entirely new dimension of funding and effort that is necessary.

A major push based on the elephant's situation will give us the best chance for meaningful progress. Such a drive can only start from a solid U.S. determination of endangered status for the elephant throughout its range.

"Anything less," he stresses, "will be insufficient, and within another decade there will be recognition of another elephant crisis."[47]

CHAPTER 8

The Debate Over Culling–
Conservation or Commerce?

I'm against it [culling] for moral reasons. I'm opposed to undue cruelty to animals. Elephants know what's happening. They're terrorized by culling. They lead terrorized lives, afterwards. I hate it.

Cynthia Moss
1991[1]

It was easy for armchair ecologists to recommend shooting programs . . . when they had never participated in a cull or studied elephants in the wild.

Oria Douglas-Hamilton
1992[2]

One of the most controversial aspects of elephant "management" is culling, which also goes by the names of cropping, active management, and other euphemisms. Culling is the periodic, planned killing of elephant herds, families, and individuals.

With the loss of between one half and two thirds of Africa's elephants within a decade, you would think it would be difficult for wildlife managers to claim that there are *too many* elephants in some countries. But even though overpopulations of elephants are virtually nonexistent, the lobby that promotes culling is as active as ever, primarily motivated by a desire to cash in on the value of ivory tusks, both those stockpiled in warehouses and those still on live elephants.

Elephants, being very intelligent, will often take refuge from poachers by gathering in parks and other protected areas where they know they will be safe. Sometimes the density of elephants in such areas becomes artificially high, leading to calls for culling. But eliminating such elephants prevents them from repopulating their former ranges when the poaching ceases.

The justification usually given for culling is that it relieves overpopulation of elephants and prevents damage to the environment, especially woodlands. But culling also raises revenues from the sale of ivory and other elephant products, and the meat can be distributed to local people and game farms. There are thus strong financial incentives for wildlife officials to find excuses to cull elephants. And they do.

Using exaggerated and often fabricated data from unscientific elephant counts and population "projections," some African governments, such as those of Botswana and Zimbabwe, are grossly inflating the estimates of their elephant populations in order to justify culling. Since elephants are migratory, these two countries are both including many of the same animals in their elephant "counts."

A five-week-long undercover investigation in 1993 by The Humane Society of the United States (HSUS) and its affiliate Humane Society International (HSI), found that in areas where elephants have been culled and "harvested" on a supposedly sustainable basis, the herds are actually being overkilled and depleted.[3] Based on interviews with numerous scientists, wildlife officials, park rangers, local ecologists, and ivory merchants, the team learned that the government of Zimbabwe has been fabricating and distorting data on elephants in order to justify and maximize their continued commercial slaughter.

HSI's investigation reveals as false Zimbabwe's claims that there are too many elephants in the country, and that thousands have to be killed each year in order to limit destruction of habitat and maintain a maximum diversity of species.

In addition to depleting elephant populations and causing severe distress to surviving elephants, a big problem with culling is that these operations are primarily financed by ivory sales. Thus, in order for culling to work optimally, ivory must have significant value and be subject to international trade. This would require that the current trade ban be lifted or modified, and that the elephant populations be downlisted from the Convention on International Trade in Endangered Species of Wild Fauna and Flora's (CITES) most protected category, Appendix I, to the less protected Appendix II. And once the ivory trade resumes, elephants all over Africa will again be worth more to poachers dead than alive. Therefore, the debate over culling could determine the fate of elephants throughout the continent.

"EVERY DAY THEY LIVE IN FEAR"

Advocates of culling accuse its critics of being too sentimental and emotional about elephants. But it is difficult *not* to become fascinated with and attached to these intelligent, complex, intriguing creatures.

Cynthia Moss, who has lived with and studied the elephants of Kenya's Amboseli National Park since 1972, and authored two books about them, describes in *Echo of the Elephants* how the entire family participates in raising and caring for youngsters:

> Juvenile females are irresistably attracted to small calves and will crowd around a new baby, trying to touch it, pull it closer, or lift it. . . they stand over the calves when they are sleeping, go and get them if they wander away, rescue them from getting caught up in a bush or stuck in a swamp, and rush to their aid at the slightest cry. This behavior allows the mother to feed and rest in peace for much of the time, which is just what a lactating mother needs.[4]

Moss has even observed a female juvenile, "Enid," nurture a crippled calf named "Ely," staying by his side and helping him until he "miraculously" recovered. Afterwards, the bond between the two remained strong; Enid continued to follow Ely around, watched over him when he slept, answered his distress calls, and brought him back when he would wander off.

Even author Raymond Bonner, whose writings generally betray little sympathy for individual elephants, acknowledges that "elephants are sentient animals; they form family relationships, grieve over the death of relatives . . ."[5]

Since one ostensible purpose of culling is to reduce the numbers of elephants, the animals targeted are not mainly adult males but herds of females with their calves and some young males. During a cull, they understand just what is happening to their families and themselves. Since elephants are extremely intelligent, highly social, family-oriented creatures that show a great deal of love and affection for each other, one can hardly imagine the terror caused when the shooting begins.

In their book *Battle for the Elephants*, Iain and Oria Douglas-Hamilton describe a visit by Oria to the "baby pens" holding elephants orphaned by a cull using automatic weapons in Rhodesia (now Zimbabwe):

> Oria visited the 'baby pens' not far from where the symposium was being held. Huddled together in three enclosures were forty small elephants. Survivors of the cull, they were to be sold to zoos and circuses in the USA and other countries. Two very tiny ones were kept apart from the rest in a paddock of their own. One immediately ran

towards Oria, hoping to get some milk; but all she could do was to give him her thumb which he sucked with his soft pink tongue.

Oria wondered how much the shooting of their mothers had affected them. She found it unbearable to think that they would spend the rest of their lives isolated in concrete stables or in cramped enclosures, with nothing more to do but eat what was given to them at regular hours, play with their trunks, and weave back and forth until they died.

"It was easy," Oria felt, "for armchair ecologists to recommend shooting programs for management purposes when they had never participated in a cull or studied elephants in the wild."[6]

The economics of culling haven't changed much since then. According to a 1990 Zimbabwe wildlife department list of animals and products offered for sale that was obtained by The HSUS's investigative team, elephant calves left over from culls are offered to foreign zoos for $2,500 each.[7]

Elephants seem to be traumatized by the shooting of their kin, and when an elephant dies or is killed, other members of the herd are often seen inspecting, fondling, and caressing the body with their trunks. A report on culling by the government of Zimbabwe states that "herds at the time of culling are capable of signalling their distress to other herds considerable distances away." Recent research indicates that these distress calls, often low-frequency rumbles that humans cannot hear, can be heard by elephants several miles away.[8]

The sustainable use lobby likes to portray opponents of culling as elite, urban Westerners, far removed from the reality of the African bush. But some of the strongest opponents of culling are elephant experts and researchers who have studied and lived among elephants for years, even decades.

Because of the elephants' intelligence, sensitivity, and close family and social bonds, and the social impact culling has on them, Richard Leakey, when director of the Kenya Wildlife Service (KWS), often spoke out against culling, saying, "I am against culling on straightforward ethical grounds. There is plenty of evidence that elephants are intelligent, social animals. Can we morally justify culling such creatures? I think not . . . it is possible to form a mental or ethical assumption that elephants warrant different treatment." Leakey also feared that if Kenya began culling, it could hurt the tourism industry, which brings $420 million into Kenya each year.[9]

KWS's Joyce Poole, calling elephant culling "totally barbaric," points out that culling operations using helicopters cause panic among elephants over a wide area, as far as fifteen miles away. "Every day they live in fear of being gunned down from the air," she says. "I have to do everything in my power to avoid culling."[10]

And Cynthia Moss says she is opposed to culling "for moral reasons":

> I'm opposed to undue cruelty to animals. Elephants know what's
> happening. They're terrorized by culling. They lead terrorized lives,
> afterwards. I hate it.[11]

The culling operations referred to above, especially those in Kenya,
have generally been well organized and well planned, and conducted
as best a cull can be. Often, entire herds or families are shot at the same
time so as not to leave traumatized survivors. But often some escape the
slaughter, leaving them without their families, and with an ingrained
fear, and perhaps hatred, of humans.

And killing entire herds is often more the exception than the rule.
What is called culling frequently amounts to people driving around in
Jeeps and Land Rovers, shooting any elephants they see. The lack of
funds and loss of trained and experienced staff has led Zimbabwe to
undertake what it calls "station culls," in which unskilled personnel
drive or walk around shooting whichever elephants they encounter.
Station culls are especially inhumane, and there is doubt that the ivory
gathered is always properly controlled and accounted for.[12]

Richard Leakey has written that while he now knows of no viable
alternative to culling, "no real effort has been made to find alternatives,
[so] it is too soon to say there is none." He adds that "while wildlife
mangers may have to justify culling," the people "will soon say 'no' to
culling":

> It was not so very long ago that people harvested other people as
> slaves. Public opinion eventually said no. During my lifetime, men
> boasted of their heroics in hunting and killing mighty gorillas. Now,
> few can imagine such a thing. Elephants, along with dolphins, whales,
> and other intelligent wildlife, will one day enjoy our respect and
> protection. I hope so, anyway.[13]

Fortunately, there *are* alternatives to culling, which will be discussed
later. One that has long been promoted by The HSUS is immuno-contraception, which has frequently been used successfully in situations
where wildlife managers considered certain animals to be overpopulat-
ing an area.[14]

"LIKE A SLOW TORNADO"

To read the literature of the culling establishment, one would think that
elephants are totally out of place in Africa, or anywhere else for that

matter, destroying whatever areas they inhabit or travel through. The culling lobby's favorite writer, Raymond Bonner, portrays elephants as dangerous, destructive animals that trample and destroy people, villages, crops, and the environment. He writes that "a herd of elephants goes through an area like a slow tornado, snapping off branches and uprooting trees, leaving devastation behind."[15]

Ian Tattersall, a curator at the American Museum of Natural History in New York City, who reviewed Bonner's book for the Sunday *New York Times Book Review*, also paints elephants as dangerous creatures to be controlled and exploited. He writes that the species is "second in potential environmental destructiveness only to *Homo sapiens*, and tends to evoke strong emotional responses among people who have the leisure and means to care, but who don't have to face the inconvenience or downright danger of living with it." He is, of course, referring to opponents of the ivory trade ban, who supposedly do not understand that "judicious culling was a necessary part of any responsible conservation program." However, he says, "that point was lost on these animal-rights advocates who, unlike conservationists, focus misty-eyed on the unrealistic goal of saving every individual animal rather than on preserving species."[16]

Some writers, including those who know little about Africa, or who have a vested interest in promoting the economic exploitation of wildlife, have even hailed Bonner's book as essential reading for anyone who wants to truly understand Africa and its elephants.

An unfortunate example of this is the glowing review the book received in the *Washington Post* by its assistant "Book World" editor Marie Arana-Ward. Echoing Bonner, she describes the results of the ivory trade ban as follows:

> . . . elephants were saved, animals were protected, and the species in danger became the Africans themselves, whose lands and crops began to be overrun as animal populations surged.

Never mind that rampaging elephants are often quickly shot unless they're in a protected area. Arana-Ward goes on to endorse Bonner's "solutions," saying that they are "hard but logical":

> He argues for "sustainable utilization" in the management of animals. Herds should be culled or they will overrun the land. Why not encourage Africans to do this themselves? They can then eat the meat or sell the ivory and the skins at sensible controllable levels.

She concludes that the success of culling programs seems to prove

Bonner's point: "If wildlife is important to Africans economically, there will be a stronger incentive to save it."

She ends her review by calling Bonner's book "a clear-eyed, revelatory account of how international meddling, however well-meaning, has undermined the ecology of the African continent. Bonner makes an impassioned plea for a plan that puts the interests of Africans first." Finally, she writes, the book is "indispensable for environmentalists and Third World Watchers."[17]

Bonner and his acolytes make culling sound so sensible, so logical, so necessary. This is one reason why his book is so dangerous. But as we shall see, in reality culling is usually a dirty, bloody business that can only be justified as a source of income from ivory sales.

Reviewing Bonner's book in the April 1993 issue of *The Atlantic Monthly*, Kenneth Brower says that Bonner's "ignorance in environmental matters is profound." Brower writes:

> Bonner is an advocate of "culling" and of "sustainable utilization," as are, he claims, all conservationists with any sense. He seems to have no inkling of the history of abuses perpetrated in the name of those two concepts. Culling is often just killing. Sustained utilization has seldom been sustainable.[18]

DO ELEPHANTS HARM—OR HELP—THE ENVIRONMENT?

The classic case cited by those who allege that elephants damage the environment is the devastation that befell the woodlands of Kenya's Amboseli National Park. This is brought up repeatedly by Raymond Bonner and other sustained use advocates as an indication of what will happen to many other areas if the elephant numbers are not controlled.

There was indeed damage to Amboseli's trees and other flora. But not everyone agrees that the elephants alone are responsible. Joyce Poole headed the KWS elephant program and has studied elephants for fourteen years. She believes that the periodic die-off of trees in Amboseli is a natural phenomenon, and says, "I don't believe it was the elephants" that caused the damage. Poole does acknowledge, however, that foraging by elephants has prevented the park's trees and "bush" from growing back and "affected the numbers of some other wildlife species," but she also considers elephant culling "totally barbaric."[19]

Moreover, the thinning out of trees has opened up Amboseli to grazing animals. In 1991, elephant researcher and author Cynthia Moss said, "In all the twenty years I've been in Amboseli, I've never seen animals like this year. It's become incredibly rich—there are so many zebra and wildebeest—even though it's no longer a woodland."[20]

And an August 1989 report by Zimbabwe's wildlife department, entitled "Elephant Management in Zimbabwe," makes it clear that even culling may not be effective in maintaining woodlands.

> Even if we reduced elephant numbers overnight to the theoretically calculated densities (which would be impossible), we would be left with the uncertainty that this might not eventually lead to the return of canopy woodlands, or alternatively, that we might not have needed to kill so many elephants . . .
>
> We have information on rates of tree loss at high elephant densities . . . but we have very little data on tree loss after population reduction . . . It is noted that many elephant culls only took place after extensive woodland losses had already occurred . . . In Matusadona, aerial photographs of the highlands show that tree cover continued to decline despite culling 311 elephants.

Indeed, the report discusses at length factors other than elephants that may be responsible for the impacts on vegetation:

> Evidence that elephants alone were responsible for the losses are lacking . . . and the possibility that the losses resulted from interactions between elephants and other ecological factors, e.g., fire and drought, cannot be ignored . . .
>
> In Brachystega woodlands, which were extensively modified by elephants, fire is now a major factor preventing recruitment to the tree layer: recruitment is most unlikely to occur unless the patchwork early burning policy is properly implemented annually, regardless of the density of elephants utilizing the area.[21]

Conservationist Barry Kent MacKay, in his "Nature Trail" column in *The Toronto Star*, points out that "Elephants don't destroy habitat, as Bonner claims; at normal densities they enhance habit for many species, thus supporting genetic diversity."[22]

Travelling elephants even *help* fruit trees and plants to grow because the elephants disperse, through their dung, seeds of various types, some of which cannot germinate without passing through the pachyderms.[23]

Even the pro-culling, pro-sustainable use World Wildlife Fund (WWF) recognizes the elephant's role in promoting, rather than destroying, a diversity of creatures and vegetation:

> Elephants are a "keystone" species, playing an important role in

structuring habitats and preserving biological diversity. By conserving elephants, this diversity and environmental integrity can be preserved on a large scale. If the African elephant were lost, the future of much of Africa's wildlife would be in jeopardy.[24]

Eugene Linden writes in *Time* magazine that advocates of culling should also examine what happens to the forests in the absence of elephants:

> . . . how some trees disappear while others close in, pinching off the network of trails used by other large mammals and reducing the amount of herbaceous vegetation growing on the ground that provides sustenance for lowland gorillas and other creatures.
>
> For millions of years, elephants have opened African forests, fostering conditions beneficial to other large mammals. Bonner, who tends to view elephants solely as a resource for humans to use, never raises the question of whether Africa's ecosystems can survive without this animal that once so dominated the landscape.[25]

Iain Douglas-Hamilton, who understands the environmental changes elephants can cause, calls culling "a lesser evil than the uncontrolled massacres," but admits that he feels "uncomfortable" about it:

> . . . man was pushing these ecosystems and the elephant's way of life ever further away from any natural state, and I was afraid that the temptation of self-perpetuating economic incentives might prove even more irreversible than the habitat changes induced by the elephants.[26]

He also warns that "people abroad do not seem to be aware of the suddenness and speed with which poachers can decimate previously 'overcrowded' elephant sanctuaries. Elephant populations have fallen like ninepins in the last five years . . .".[27] And, of course, they could again.

The destructiveness of elephants, particularly to the environment, has often been grossly exaggerated. But there is no question that elephants *are* potentially dangerous and can be destructive to people and their property, especially to those living near national parks and other protected areas. In Zimbabwe, from 1982 to 1989, some 500 people were killed by elephants, according to the government. In the one-year period ending in July 1991, elephants killed nine people and seriously injured three others in Kenya.[28]

One reason for the large number of human-elephant conflicts in Kenya is that the government has settled people in areas that are traditional elephant migratory routes.[29] And as the nation's human population continues to grow rapidly, the number of conflicts will certainly increase. Indeed, as Africa's population expands from some 560 million today to the expected 3 *billion* by 2050—more than a fivefold increase—there will be even less room left for elephants or any other wildlife, especially large, boisterous mammals.[30]

But for now, there is still plenty of room left for elephants. The argument that inadequate habitat makes elephant culling necessary, if it ever was valid, certainly cannot be made today, following the poaching of perhaps 700,000 elephants in a decade. Even the pro-culling U.S. Department of the Interior, in its August 1992 announcement reaffirming its ban on ivory imports, points out that there is plenty of room for more elephants in Africa:

> . . . habitat destruction, modification, or curtailment does not presently endanger the continental population of the African elephant. Expanded elephant populations could and probably would be tolerated in many African habitats . . .
>
> Kenya can probably support an elephant population twice the present population without adversely impacting available habitats of rural Kenyans.[31]

It is clear that if local people do not share in the benefits from wildlife, they will not tolerate, much less appreciate, animals that sometimes cause damage to crops, property, and lives. As elephant expert Iain Douglas-Hamilton puts it, "Africans will only be willing to share the land with elephants if the benefits from the animals reach the local people."[32]

If efforts are made to protect local people and their crops, and compensate for their losses, elephants can be far more beneficial to them than they are harmful. Indeed, studies have shown that the annual tourist value of elephants in Kenya's Amboseli National Park exceeds $600,000 a year.[33]

A SOUTHERN AFRICAN WILDLIFE SANCTUARY

In areas where elephants have congregated and are causing damage to vegetation, there are alternatives to culling that would be more economically beneficial to local people. One such solution has been offered by Jonathan Gibson, vice chairman of the Chobe Wildlife Trust, a group that works to conserve Chobe National Park in Botswana.

The trust has drafted a Proposed Southern African Wildlife Sanctuary (PSAWS), comprising over 250,000 square kilometers (150,000 square miles) of prime contiguous wildlife areas in Angola, Botswana, Namibia, Zambia, and Zimbabwe.[34] As the trust describes the area involved:

... within the heart of this land lies probably the greatest wildlife resource in Africa, or perhaps even the world ... It is an area containing relatively few people and encompassing already proclaimed national parks, game reserves, and wildlife management areas ... The designated area has been selected, as each of the five countries involved ... has already individually identified and laid aside major portions of the proposed PSAWS for conservation purposes ... This wildlife sanctuary would at once qualify as one of the world's premier wildlife destinations: its sheer size and diversity would place it far above that of East Africa ... [35]

In addition to its enormous tourism potential, one advantage of the sanctuary is that it would permit depleted populations of animals to increase by allowing animals "to move into these areas from heavily pressured zones of high density, as well as by the reintroduction of species to habitats where they previously occurred." The trust notes that "Botswana provides a clear example of the above," and that the sanctuary could eliminate the alleged need to cull elephants:

... elephants have been quick to take advantage of the cessation of hostilities in Namibia and Angola; a large number, presumably from Botswana, have moved into the West Caprivi (Namibia) and will probably ... move into the Angolan sector where wildlife was sharply depleted during the civil war. In this way, the concept of such a large sanctuary can benefit one sector, and resolve problems of excess numbers in another. Within such large and varied ecosystems, nature will find its own balances with a minimal amount of management intervention. [36]

From an economic standpoint, the proposal is quite feasible. Fortunately, besides containing few people, the proposed area is not known to contain soils particularly suitable for farming or any minerals of significant value. The trust concludes that the proposal could be of tremendous benefit not just to the local wildlife but to the people as well:

The concept of PSAWS is no more than a consolidation of existing resources on a regional basis. It does, however, present to its five member states a unique opportunity to, at a stroke, create a huge economic resource, requiring minimal financial and technological input. Yet it could generate sorely-needed foreign exchange and rural opportunities, all on an environmentally friendly and sustainable basis. [37]

There are also proposals to create a so-called megapark comprising South Africa's Kruger National Park and the adjacent area in Mozambique, including the Limpopo Valley.[38] Taking down the elephant-proof fence separating these two areas would remove the rationale for South Africa to hold down its elephant population by culling, while allowing some of the "excess" elephants to move into and repopulate Mozambique, where elephants have largely been eliminated.

Some 95 percent of South Africa's 7,800 elephants live in Kruger, which runs almost the entire length of that country's border with Mozambique. South Africa's elephants were almost wiped out by the year 1900, but protection, breeding, and migration from Portuguese East Africa (now Mozambique) resulted in a population of some 100 elephants by 1926. The population steadily grew, reaching almost 9,000 by 1970.[39] Kruger was fenced in 1974, with the result that many elephants from Mozambique were trapped and cut off from grazing areas and water sources they traditionally visited in the course of their migrations."[40]

If South Africa discontinued its culling of several hundred elephants a year and allowed some of Kruger's elephants to repopulate their natural range next door in Mozambique, it could more than replace the revenue it receives from ivory, hide, and meat sales (about $1.4 million a year in the 1980s) by raising park fees by just one dollar per visitor.[41]

IS CULLING GOOD FOR ELEPHANTS?

Some culling plans and proposals have been so unrealistic it is difficult to see how they could have been taken seriously. One proposal, drafted in late 1991 by the former government of Zambia, even went so far as to recommend culling the severely depleted elephant herds of the Luangwa National Park, where 80 percent of the elephants had already been wiped out. The plan stated, "A sustainable use programme should be introduced in South Luangwa . . . in order to meet the entire running costs of the Park." According to Vernon Bailey, an honorary ranger there for a dozen years, such a policy would be "disastrous":

> It is a very young population [of elephants that] has just recovered from an enormous onslaught that was horrific when you consider the tens of thousands that were slaughtered in a very short space of time.[42]

Even the distinguished, internationally renowned conservationist Peter Scott was persuaded by the advocates of culling. In 1977, writing on behalf of WWF, he discussed the necessity of reducing the elephant population in Zambia's Luangwa Valley by 75 percent—from 100,000 to 25,000! He said, "The idea that 75,000 elephants must be culled will be very difficult for most people to accept. Nevertheless, it seems necessary for WWF to begin at once to explain to its constituency this unhappy paradox of world depletion and local overabundance."[43]

In response, Iain Douglas-Hamilton wrote back to Peter Scott, pointing out that an overpopulation of elephants was *not* the major problem. "The much greater threat," he wrote, was that "man armed with modern weapons, if he should turn against elephants, could rapidly exterminate them." According to Douglas-Hamilton, "A year later, Peter Scott was still mulling over the idea, and in desperation I wrote to him again: . . . We are worried that by the time culling begins in Luangwa, the elephant population may already have been decimated by poachers."[44]

This is, of course, precisely what happened: By 1992, the elephant population of Zambia had been reduced to less than 25,000, with half of these found in the national parks in the Luangwa Valley.[45] The population could certainly have been reduced to close to zero if the proposed culling of the 1970s had been carried out.

The sustainable use lobby has often been able to convince the news media that, in effect, killing elephants is good for them. For example, a front-page story in the July 5, 1992, edition of *The New York Times* was headlined, "Zimbabwe Kills Elephants to Help Save Lives." The article quoted Michael Wright of WWF (he is now president of AWF) as approving of the cull, citing the usual rationales and excuses.

In Kenya, noted wildlife filmmaker Simon Trevor responded that he was "lost for words at the nonsense" quoted from Michael Wright. In a letter to *The Times*, Trevor describes how the culling would harm, not help, the elephant population. He points out that when 20 percent of Tsavo's 45,000 elephants died in a drought, "this began to reduce pressure on vegetation, which has resulted in a very good vegetation cover today."

Trevor also makes clear that "the poaching that followed had nothing to do with resentment from 'peasants' . . . Most of the poaching was carried out by tribes who do not eat game meat. It is well documented that the poaching increase resulted from increased international demand and higher prices for ivory."

Trevor emphasizes that "culling the herd is not going to help. These animals that are surviving must be the ones with the strongest genes. To remove them defies logic . . . I would guess the protein level in the vegetation is so low that reducing numbers of animals will not help those not culled." He adds that "providing game meat [to villagers] is likely to increase poaching by instilling a desire for game meat."[46] Trevor's comments could be applied to culling in general, and indeed the whole concept of sustainable use, since they refute the thesis that elephants and other wildlife benefit from such killing and utilization.

BOTSWANA'S AND ZIMBABWE'S ELEPHANTS—
OVERCROWDED OR OVERCOUNTED?

Today, as in the past, plans to cull elephants are justified on the same bogus grounds—that too many elephants are damaging the environment, or might do so someday.

Since the late 1980s, Botswana and Zimbabwe have been spreading the message that their countries are overcrowded with elephants, indeed overflowing with the pachyderms, and that culling of the herds had to be undertaken for the animals' own good. But the data presented by these two nations is widely thought to be inaccurate and misleading, and in some cases even fabricated.

One way that Botswana and Zimbabwe have been able to exaggerate their elephant populations is by including each other's animals in their counts, in addition to including those from other countries migrating through or seeking refuge in their parks. Thus, culling of herds in these two nations, especially if it is based on inflated numbers, will kill off elephants from severely depleted populations in neighboring countries.

Research by Dr. Ros Reeve of the Environmental Investigation Agency (EIA) demonstrates that Zimbabwe and Botswana have been counting elephants twice, using the same animals in both of the population estimates. Thus, data used by Zimbabwe in 1989 showed that its elephant population had magically increased by 17,000 in the previous two years! Over half of these "new" elephants had been counted in Hwange National Park, where a series of artificial watering points had been created. Hwange sits on the border with Botswana, which had been experiencing a drought for six years, and many of its elephants had been traveling to Hwange for water. According to Reeve:

> Zimbabwe counted elephants in September 1988, when the Botswana elephants were in the park. Four months later, when the elephants had migrated back over the border, Botswana did its count . . . And both countries can say how well managed their populations are, when in fact something quite different is going on.[47]

Also present in Botswana are elephants from the neighboring country of Namibia, which is located along the western coast of southern Africa and whose elephant population is constantly moving back and forth among Angola, Botswana, and Zambia. Namibia also has plans to cull its elephants, which will kill many that its wildlife agency refers to as "seasonal visitors only."[48] This will eliminate elephants from depleted populations in Angola and Zambia, which, if allowed to reproduce, could someday repopulate their former ranges.

Counting highly mobile animals like elephants is a very exacting process, requiring unbiased research methods, good science, and skilled precision in sampling, analysis, and extrapolation. It is doubtful that all or any of these factors were present when Botswana's or Zimbabwe's elephant populations were estimated. But it was impossible to conclusively verify or refute the figures, since Zimbabwe has refused to publish or release its raw data.[49] The only way to accurately count the number of elephants in the region is to do so with independent simultaneous aerial surveys of Angola, Botswana, Namibia, and Zimbabwe, as has long been urged by local conservationists, such as filmmaker Dereck Joubert of Botswana.[50]

Furthermore, these elephant populations are hardly secure from destruction in the future, particularly if political or economic conditions change. As pointed out by the U.S. Fish and Wildlife Service's elephant expert Dr. Ronald Nowak, who concludes (even based on the inflated official figures of Botswana and Zimbabwe plus those of South Africa):

> The loss of elephants in Zambia alone is nearly as great as the number now estimated for the three countries . . . The total number of elephants in Botswana, South Africa, and Zimbabwe, nearly 150,000, may seem large in and of itself, and it is easy to think that the vast biomass represented would be difficult to eliminate. And yet this number is meaningless if one also considers the recent sharp decline of elephants in the rest of Africa, mainly because of killing for the international ivory trade.[51]

HOW MANY ELEPHANTS DOES BOTSWANA HAVE?

No one knows just how many elephants there are in Botswana. Indeed, it varies depending on the time of year. In 1992, the government of Botswana estimated that its elephant population numbered between 49,064 and 68,900, although the latter figure is generally considered to be unrealistically high.[52]

In August 1993, Botswana's wildlife department released the results of its most recent elephant survey, in which it claimed to have counted 70,000 elephants. But according to wildlife experts in the country, including a participant in the census, actual count results were estimated at 40,000 elephants, but later another 30,000 were arbitrarily added on. One knowledgeable source in Botswana, speaking on condition of confidentiality, says of the above survey worker, "He cannot complain officially and keep his job, but he does not accept the count as being remotely representative of the actual figure."[53]

Most of the country's elephants live in and around Chobe National Park, located in northwest Botswana, along the border with Namibia, Angola, and Zambia. Many of Botswana's elephants are refugees from those nations, seeking sanctuary from heavy poaching and civil war. If not killed off by poachers or culling operations, many of these elephants could return to their former ranges and recolonize their homelands when peace returns and conditions stabilize. Conservationist Jonathan Gibson of the Chobe Wildlife Trust has said that "now that hostilities have ceased in Angola, we could see up to half of our elephants moving back in there." But these are the very elephants that could end up being culled.[54]

Most People Oppose the Culling

Parroting the usual rationales for culling, Botswana's utilization lobby has cited habitat destruction to justify its culling plans, but has been unable to come up with firm data to back up its position.

Botswana has failed to conduct studies analyzing the long-term impact elephants that have been having on vegetation, trees, and the environment in general, thus making it impossible to show that culling is necessary or desirable.[55]

Indeed, reported damage to woodlands by elephants in Botswana has been minimal and highly localized. In a 1990 study by the Department of Wildlife and National Parks (DWNP) and the Kalahari Conservation Society, DWNP ecologist Dr. Keith Lindsay expresses skepticism that elephants are causing serious widespread damage to woodlands:

> Ecological systems . . . are naturally dynamic. Change is normal and constancy is rare. A certain amount of damage to vegetation . . . is normal in a naturally functioning ecosystem . . . none of these studies [of elephant-vegetation interaction] has looked at woodland dynamics through time, directly linking changes in mature canopy woodland to the increase in elephant numbers . . . If the elephant-woodland interaction is allowed to continue, experiences from elsewhere in Africa suggest that catastrophe is unlikely.

Lindsay concludes that it is a matter of esthetics rather than of ecological necessity that determines whether or not culling should take place: "In the end, it is human values which define the acceptability of habitat impact by elephants."[56]

Although some financial interests and DWNP have been vigorously promoting the need to cull elephants, there is strong opposition to culling from various quarters within Botswana. For example, a June 1990 meeting in Savuti of local scientists, conservationists, and wildlife managers agreed that there was no need to cull elephants for any ecological or economic reasons. And meetings of tribal people and elders have also expressed opposition to culling.[57]

As Allan Thornton of EIA wrote in 1991:

> Most people in Botswana oppose the proposed elephant kill. There is no economic benefit for them. Tourism provides significant local employment and local people fear the cull would lead to a tourist boycott. Botswanans also do not eat elephant meat. But powerful economic interests, notably shooting teams from Zimbabwe, are lobbying hard to obtain the rights to the ivory, skins, and the culling contracts.[58]

Cattle Crowd Out Wildlife

There are other, less obvious reasons why Botswana wants to reduce its elephant population. Some officials see elephants not only as a good potential source of revenue but also as a nuisance to the expanding, government-subsidized cattle ranching industry, which has devastated wildlife populations in the nation.

Botswana's elephants and other wildlife are under heavy pressure from competition with the growing herds of domestic cattle, which are causing major damage to the nation's ecology. Between 1966 and 1991, the cattle population doubled, to some 2.5 million. Most of the cattle are raised not to feed the local people but for export to Europe in order to generate foreign exchange.[59]

In her book on the turmoil caused by lending to the so-called Third World by the World Bank, the International Monetary Fund, and Western banks and governments, Patricia Adams writes, "Cattle ranching projects in Botswana promoted such intensive grazing that grasslands were destroyed, and traditional pastoral peoples' economies decimated."[60]

Besides the normal problems associated with raising livestock—overgrazing, soil erosion, deforestation, etc.—fences constructed to protect the cattle have wreaked havoc on the local wildlife. Hundreds of thousands of wildebeest, buffalo, antelope, and other creatures have been killed by these fences. Wildebeest have been fenced out of access to water in order to expand the cattle industry, and as a result, the hundreds of thousands of wildebeest that existed in the 1970s fell to less than 40,000 in the early 1990s. And the construction of a 150-mile-long cattle fence in Ngamiland, where there are large numbers of elephants, will decimate the wildlife in that area.[61]

Since most of the cattle are owned by rich and powerful politicians and businessmen, the government has done little to minimize the damage being caused by them.

Botswana does not take kindly to criticism of its policies. In 1986, it deported the well-known wildlife researchers Mark and Delia Owens, who have filmed and been featured in several television wildlife specials. The Owenses' crime was to have pointed out in their book, *Cry of the Kalahari*, how the government's cattle-raising projects were decimating wild animals.[62]

Unlike most other African countries, Botswana has a growing and well-managed economy and could avoid destroying its wildlife if it made a real effort to do so. Indeed, by some measures, it is a remarkably wealthy nation, though many of its rural residents are still mired in poverty, living in mud huts with thatched roofs. Moreover, the Kalahari desert accounts for 70 percent of the nation's land, and is spreading into ranching and farming areas.

The major source of the nation's wealth is the world's richest diamond mine, of which Botswana is co-owner, along with DeBeers Consolidated Mines of South Africa, and which earns the country $1.4 billion a year. These revenues made Botswana's economy the most rapidly expanding of any nation during the last two decades, with gross domestic product (GDP) growing at an average rate of 14.5 percent a year between 1970 and 1980 and at 9.8 percent between 1980 and 1991, according to the World Bank. The nation's $4 billion in foreign reserves are the largest of any non-OPEC nation.[63]

Botswana has also profited from the illegal wildlife trade. It has long been a conduit to South Africa for poached ivory and rhino horns smuggled out of Malawi, Zaire, and Zimbabwe.

It is unfortunate that Botswana shows so little appreciation for the non-consumptive economic value of wild animals. From an economic standpoint, wildlife, if not devastated, can generate enormous tourist revenues. In 1991, 412,000 tourists visited Botswana to view wildlife, spending some $65 million.[64]

Thus, the low priority given to wildlife preservation, apart from humane and conservation considerations, is a misguided and short-sighted policy that will cost Botswana dearly in future years.

Botswana's Trusting Elephants

If Botswana lets its and Zimbabwe's sustainable use advocates persuade it to carry out large-scale culling, it will affect more elephants than those killed off. It could also make many of the remaining elephants less accessible and visible to tourists, diminishing one of the country's major attractions.

In February 1992, an article in *World Magazine* stated:

> Only in Botswana is it possible to approach some of the elephant herds closely to sense their trust, a trust that will be shattered if the marksmen from Zimbabwe are invited in. To live among these wandering giants is to breathe the air of a vanishing freedom. For the moment, Botswana remains their last true kingdom.[65]

My colleague, environmental writer Lewis Regenstein, once told me of camping for a few days in the Okavanga Delta, watching families of elephants come and feed, bathe, and play. Each day, the elephants would come a little closer to the camp's tents. The last day of the trip, the elephants crossed the stream separating them from the camera-toting tourists and began to frolic and feed virtually amidst the tents. It was, he said, an experience none of the visitors would ever forget. But it was one that could not be safely enjoyed if the elephants were avoiding humans and living in fear of being shot by them.[66]

ZIMBABWE'S ELEPHANTS: MULTIPLYING LIKE RABBITS

If Zimbabwe's data are to believed, the country has solved the problem of overkilling of elephants. In an unprecedented and unique demonstration of elephant fertility, the nation can apparently about double its elephant population every five years!

But, alas, Zimbabwe's estimates of its elephant population are simply not credible to knowledgeable observers, and its efforts to convince doubters have literally been laughed at by the experts.

In 1960 (when the nation was known as Rhodesia), there were a reported 32,000 elephants living there. Now Zimbabwe claims to have over 70,000 elephants—despite the culling of 44,000 elephants since 1965, and some poaching of elephants, especially in recent years.[67]

Since 1987, the government's official estimates show an elephant population annually increasing far beyond what is biologically possible:

- in 1988: 42,960
- in 1989: 51,700

- in 1990: 60,000
- in early 1991: 66,439
- in July 1991: 70,000
- in September 1991: 75,000[68]

In fact, these amazing yearly increases in the number of elephants are based on unscientific projections and assumptions. Indeed, Zimbabwe has not conducted an elephant census since 1989, except in Hwange Park. Nor do these exaggerated estimates distinguish between resident elephants and those migrating or seeking refuge from Angola, Botswana, Mozambique, and Zambia. Not surprisingly, Zimbabwe—like Botswana and South Africa—refuses to publish its data and census methods or to subject them to peer review by independent scientists and experts.[69]

And for good reason: their data are literally laughable. At a June 1989 meeting of CITES' African Elephant Working Group, the deputy director of Zimbabwe's wildlife department, Rowan Martin, was openly ridiculed when he presented his figures on his nation's elephant reproduction rate (see page 167). When he asserted that Zimbabwe's elephants were conceiving at seven years old and giving birth at nine, the scientists at the meeting filled the room with laughter.[70] (Under optimum conditions, females do not attain sexual maturity until they are eleven years old, and sometimes not until they are twenty-two; gestation periods average twenty-two months.)[71]

When he was KWS director, Richard Leakey, who basically opposes elephant culling, was one of those who was skeptical of Zimbabwe's claim that the country is overflowing with elephants, and he was not reluctant to accuse the country of inflating its elephant population numbers. Leakey points out that Zimbabwe's claim (made at the March 1992 CITES meeting) that it had a population of 2,000 of the critically endangered black rhino was later shown to have been exaggerated fourfold—there were actually only 500. "If they can't count rhinos, can they count their elephants?," Leakey said in a September 1992 interview. "Besides, they have never allowed us to participate in the count."[72]

MIGRANT ELEPHANTS IN DANGER

It is the migration of elephants into and through Zimbabwe that allows the country to inflate its population estimates for culling purposes and to promote resumption of the international ivory trade, while boasting of its commitment to conservation. Commenting on Zimbabwe's purportedly exploding elephant population, the Ivory Trade Review Group stated in 1989, "Unless elephants have come across the border from Angola or Zambia, these increases cannot be real."[73]

Zimbabwe has finally been forced to recognize that much of its elephant population is migratory, and stated in November 1993, "Zimbabwe and Botswana have recently completed simultaneous counts of their shared elephant population, and are developing a joint management plan for the species in line with IUCN's draft guidelines for sustainable use."[74]

Because of the inflated estimates of Zimbabwe's elephant population, its plans to cull thousands of elephants, based on these figures, could be disastrous—not only for the nation's own elephant herds, but also for those in neighboring countries that migrate through or temporarily reside in Zimbabwe. Thus the government's plan to shoot 5,000 elephants a year puts at risk elephant herds throughout the region, including the severely depleted populations in nearby Angola, Mozambique, and Zambia, as well as those in Botswana. Most of Zimbabwe's elephants live close to, or along the country's borders with, these nations, with elephants regularly moving back and forth over the borders.

One reason elephants from neighboring countries have been attracted to Zimbabwe is that dozens of artificial watering holes have been placed in Hwange and in the Matetsi complex. These watering points were installed close to tourist areas, and they now draw elephants to the area, artificially increasing the density of the elephant population there, especially during the dry season, and often resulting in noticeable damage to nearby vegetation.[75] This, of course, provides a pretext for promoting culling of the elephants.

"TAKING OFF" ELEPHANTS

Elephants in Zimbabwe have long been under heavy pressure from poachers and from culling programs based on inflated population estimates. And there is more to come.

Zimbabwe's Department of National Parks and Wildlife Management (DNPWM) says that the country has about 70,000 to 75,000 elephants, and that their "elephant management goal" is about 43,000 elephants.[76] This means that some 27,000 to 32,000 elephants (not taking reproduction into consideration) will have to be culled, and the culling may have to be continued indefinitely.

In 1991, Zimbabwe announced that it would undertake the largest government-sponsored elephant kill ever—the slaughter of 15,000 elephants. This culling program was based on incredible government estimates that the nation's elephant population had exploded—from

42,960 in 1987 to some 75,000 in late 1991! Experts pointed out at the time that these obviously inflated figures were either outright fabrications or included large numbers of migrating elephants from Angola, Botswana, Mozambique, and Zambia.[77]

Despite the widespread poaching taking place at the time (so heavy that Gonarezhou National Park had to be closed to tourists), in September, 1991, Zimbabwe's first official cull in several years took place in the Chizarira area, where some 250 elephants were shot. The cull was ostensibly undertaken for ecological and management reasons. But the Environmental Investigation Agency learned from local sources that the DNPWM director had ordered that all "trophies" be "of good quality."[78]

In its "rebuttal" of The HSUS's investigative report, Zimbabwe supplied specific figures on its culling program, saying it has significantly reduced its "elephant population reduction exercises" since 1988, "when 2861 were taken off. From 1988 until 1991, only 436 elephants were removed. In 1992, a few hundred were culled during the drought, but over 700 were captured and moved to new areas opened up to elephant as a result of new consumptive wildlife use policies."[79]

However, Zimbabwe also claims that "several thousand elephants should have been taken off" to prevent damage to woodlands "caused by overpopulation," but the Wildlife Department had insufficient funds in its budget to carry out these culls.[80] Note that elephants are never killed—just "taken off," "reduced," "removed," or "culled."

The biggest irony of this situation is that even while launching a sometimes admirable effort to combat poaching, Zimbabwe was at the same time killing elephants as official policy. Maybe the real fight was over who ended up with the ivory.

HSUS'S UNDERCOVER INVESTIGATION

A recent five-week undercover investigation into the situation in Zimbabwe conducted by The HSUS and its affiliate, HSI, reveals that a well-organized cover-up is being carried out to conceal and to mislead the public about the overkilling of much of Zimbabwe's wildlife.

These newly acquired data, gathered during HSI's investigation, clearly show that in areas where elephants and other creatures are to be culled and "harvested" on a supposedly sustainable basis, the herds are actually not capable of sustaining such pressure. Indeed, "sustainable use" practices are being employed as a cover for the planned overhunting of wildlife, including hunting of endangered and threatened species.

In May and June, 1993, HSUS vice president for investigations David Wills travelled with Kathy Milani, a professional filmmaker, to Zimbabwe to assess first-hand the status of elephants and rhinoceroses in that country.

What the HSI team found confirmed their worst fears, and contradicted the official data that Zimbabwe had been giving out for years. Based on numerous interviews with government scientists, park rangers, local ecologists, ivory traders and merchants, and other knowledgeable sources, the team learned that the government has been fabricating and distorting data on elephants in order to justify and maximize their continued commercial slaughter.

HSI's investigation reveals as false Zimbabwe's claim that there are too many elephants in the country, and that thousands have to be killed each year in order to limit destruction of habitat and promote greater biological diversity. In fact, the study, entitled "Zimbabwe: Driving Wildlife to Extinction," determined that there is no ecological need to cull elephants; the motive is primarily financial:

> Zimbabwe's estimates of elephant population sizes are grossly overstated and predetermined to justify government-sanctioned elephant culling operations . . . Elephants have been culled to feed to crocodiles, to sell baby elephants to foreign zoos, and to stockpile ivory and elephant hides for a future legalized trade in the lucrative elephant parts.[81]

According to one ecologist working at Zimbabwe's Hwange National Park, and who spoke at great personal risk to his career and perhaps even to his physical safety, the park's elephant population is less than half what is being estimated. He said that an October 1992 aerial survey by the Zimbabwe Department of National Parks and Wildlife Management (DNPWM) projected a population of 37,000 elephants in the park, over double the actual number. These figures were arrived at, he said, by using methods that intentionally inflate the numbers, including:

> . . . flying over at the heaviest concentration periods, when animals are known to come to water in the cool of the evening . . . between 4:00 and 6:00 p.m., and counting all the elephants who come to drink. And then they extrapolate for the whole damn park. You'll get 37,000 elephants from extrapolation. But the truth is not even half that. It's incredible . . . Hwange could handle four times as many elephants as it currently supports . . .

The ecologist, a trained professional who has participated in elephant surveys, emphasized that "all scientific surveys are suspect in this country because they have a number they want to take [by culling] and the survey has to justify that number."[82]

According to the HSUS/HSI report, great damage is being done by Zimbabwe's pushing to lift the ban on trade in elephant ivory. "It is stockpiling ivory from culled elephants for future sales, hoping they can succeed in convincing CITES to legalize the international ivory trade again . . . Zimbabwe's ivory stockpiles, and its proposals to legalize the trade, are encouraging elephant poaching and stockpiling of ivory by dealers and speculators . . ."[83]

And arguments that money from the sale of ivory will be used to fund conservation programs and parks are undermined by the fact that less than 10 percent of the earnings from tourism, ivory sales, and other income from elephants goes towards wildlife departments and programs.

Other confirmation gathered during the investigation shows how arbitrary, unscientific, and unwarranted are the decisions made to shoot elephants, often against the advice of local rangers. One memo obtained by David Wills summarizes a June 13, 1990, meeting of DNPWM wardens and rangers to discuss a recommended cull of 2,000 elephants in the Zambezi Valley. The memo notes that "the men on the ground" dispute the insistence by the warden that there are "high concentrations of elephant populations." The warden is only person mentioned in the memo to take such a position:

> On population stabilization, reference elephant culling, the Research Branch had recommended offtake of 2,000 elephants while the total population was estimated to be at 12,000.
>
> The men on the ground expressed concern on the high figures estimated by Research because according to the previous numbers, the increase from 1988 has been incredibly high, for example, in 1985 elephants were estimated at 8,000, 2,000 were culled leaving an estimate of 6,000. Again in 1988, 2,250 elephants were taken off. Then in 1989, estimates rose to 12,000.
>
> Officer-in-charge of Marongora said though elephants are migratory using both escarpment and the floor, no big herds have been seen in the area, the biggest herd he had seen was eight animals. He said he feels that animals are within limit. He suggested that ecologists on the ground should be given the chance to do the survey and monitor their areas regularly, and that this will improve communication between the two branches, Research and Management. Ecologist Chidziya confirmed that there was not much damage on the escarpment.

Other wildlife officials at the meeting express concern that elephant numbers in their areas are so low:

Senior Ranger Murandu said that the population of elephants in his area is low and that the hunters have confirmed this . . . In Mana Pools and Chewore, the officers-in-charge said ground cover reveal that population of elephants is low.[84]

On the following day, June 13, 1990, Chief Warden for Resource Management R.J. Ngwarai drafted a memo summarizing the meeting and indicating that culling would proceed despite the lack of any ecological justification:

> The meeting pointed out that within the Zambezi Valley there were no high elephant populations to warrant a cull. It pointed out that there had been no significant vegetation damage since the 1988 elephant reduction exercise.
>
> However, Warden Searle of Matusadona expressed the need to disperse herds of elephants that tend to concentrate on certain areas. He indicated that about 80 elephants could be shot. The house expressed the feeling that staff on the ground should be involved in such small culls.[85]

"ARE THESE PEOPLE NUTS?"

In response to the HSUS/HSI report, which had been widely distributed, Zimbabwe issued a lengthy and detailed "rebuttal" that was most notable for what it *failed* to rebut. While finding some grounds for reasonable disagreement, the report consisted largely of the usual rhetoric of sustainable use, including some demonstrably false assertions. It even disputed The HSUS's reference to "the decline and disappearance of elephant populations across the African continent."

For example, the November 20, 1993, DNPWM publication entitled "Zimbabwe: At the Leading Edge of Conservation," defends the government's policy of "encouraging the sustainable use of wildlife to give it a high financial value," citing elephants as a major success story.

This incredible document dismisses The HSUS's report as an effort to discredit culling and cropping: "Since Zimbabwe is at the leading edge of conservation through sustainable use, it is in the interests of HSUS/HSI to denigrate Zimbabwe's achievements."[86]

Unable to effectively refute the overall accuracy of the HSUS/HSI report, which the government document says "is full of falsehoods and inaccuracies," Zimbabwe laments that "perfectly accurate information is presented in a manner that creates the impression that wildlife management in Zimbabwe has sinister motives."[87]

But what Zimbabwe terms "sinister" motives are in actuality perfectly understandable economic ones—mainly an effort to generate revenue from "consumptive use" of threatened and endangered wildlife whose killing cannot much longer be sustained.

Zimbabwe is well aware that many on-site professionals are skeptical of its elephant counting methods and data, and admits that aerial sampling is often "disputed" and "misunderstood" by them:

> It is commonly found that this methodology is misunderstood by game scouts and many others. As a result, the results are often disputed by those "on the ground."[88]

In its rebuttal, Zimbabwe bitterly attacks the Hwange Park professional ecologist who said that there are fewer than half as many elephants in the park than are being estimated. The rebuttal states that this ecologist "clearly knows nothing about the way Zimbabwe counts its elephants and is completely unqualified to comment . . . Elephants are not counted at water holes in the afternoon. Transacts are flown across the whole park, mostly in the mornings to provide standardized sample counts."[89]

But the park ecologist with whom we spoke was quite knowledgeable and intimately familiar with both the park and the methodologies used to count elephants; he made it clear that it was the DNPWM officials who were not being honest about the situation. Concerning their estimate of 37,000 elephants in Hwange, he stated, "Hwange is 14,000 square kilometers [8,400 square miles]. That's three elephants per square kilometer in the park. Are these people nuts?"[90]

Zimbabwe's DNPWM makes other incredible and demonstrably false statements in its attempt to deny the obvious. For example, it cites as one of HSUS/HSI's falsehoods the reference to "the decline and disappearance of elephant populations across the African continent." Instead, says Zimbabwe, "Elephant populations are not declining across the African continent. Even at the time of the [ivory trade] ban, elephants were stable or increasing in South Africa, Namibia, Botswana, Zimbabwe, and possibly in other countries." This, of course, ignores the involvement of these nations in the legal and illegal trafficking in ivory, an industry that caused the loss of betwen one half and two thirds of Africa's elephants within a decade.

CULLING IS "GOOD BUSINESS"

While culling has traditionally been justified on ecological grounds, Iain Douglas-Hamilton points out that there are other motives as well; it was good business. Consider his account of the results of an elephant cull in Rhodesia (now Zimbabwe):

> Later we were shown the aftermath of a cull—the meat of nearly four hundred elephants drying on low tables in the bush. The park staff did the shooting and wildlife contractors processed and marketed the products.
>
> It was good business. There was no end to the uses which man's ingenuity could devise from the different parts of a dead elephant. Skin from the body, ears and feet was valuable, and could bring in anything up to $200 per elephant. Meat and fat were sold locally. The skin was used for table tops, and the softer belly skins and ears could be used for quality leather goods. Briefcases made of elephant skin fetched $175, and smaller scraps were used for shoes, bags or purses. The elephant feet became foot-stools or umbrella stands, and even the feet of baby elephants were made into pencil holders or cigar containers. The tusks belonged to the National Parks, and were sent to the ivory auctions in Salisbury. Only the bones, trunks and intestines were left in red heaps for the scavengers and flies.[91]

More recently, the dead elephants often went to crocodile farms, to feed the future source of belts, shoes, boots, handbags, and other fashion items. Zimbabwe admits that it still feeds elephant meat to crocodiles, but not as much as it once did. In its response to the HSUS/HSI report, it says:

> The regular feeding of elephants to captive crocodiles ended in 1988, and in any case, the elephants were part of a scientifically derived offtake quota to protect woodlands. Very occasionally, some of the meat from elephant culling is still fed to crocodiles when this is judged to be the most efficient option.[92]

And baby elephants that are spared, after watching their families be slaughtered, are sold to foreign zoos for $2,500 apiece.[93]

Proponents of culling say that the revenues it generates help to fund conservation programs and agencies. However, these funds derived from the sale of ivory and hides do *not* go directly for conservation, but rather into Zimbabwe's central treasury. In a 1991 submission to the U.S. Fish and Wildlife Service, Zimbabwe's DNPWM acknowledged that "all revenues attributable to elephants from the parks and wildlife estates in Zimbabwe were returned to the general treasury."[94]

Thus, the government of Zimbabwe has strong short-term economic incentives to inflate its elephant population data and to push for a resumption of trade in ivory. In the 1980s, the sale of products from culled elephants, mainly ivory, brought in over $13 million. And much of the elephant meat went to local people for consumption. Before the trading ban was enacted, Zimbabwe's Department of National Parks and Wildlife Management compiled a study estimating that elephants, through culled ivory and fees from trophy hunters, could bring in over $4 million a year. As of August 1993, Zimbabwe's stockpile of ivory amounted to nearly thirty-one tons and was "increasing continuously."[95] Even so, it should be remembered, with tourism bringing in almost $100 million a year, the money to be made killing elephants is paltry indeed.

And little of the money raised by wildlife benefits the animals. As in other African nations, the government of Zimbabwe provides to the parks and wildlife department only a tiny percentage of the revenues generated by tourists. In Metabeleland North, in 1990 DNPWM received less than one percent of tourist revenues from Victoria Falls and Hwange National Park.[96]

Moreover, lodging and entrance fees to the parks are kept artificially low. Many of the 200,000 tourists who visit the Rain Forest National Park at Victoria Falls each year spend thousands of dollars to arrive there, and then some $200 per night for a double room at the Victoria Falls Hotel. But DNPWM charges an entry fee of only one dollar. And at Hwange, a three-bedroom chalet goes for just $13 a night. If Zimbabwe raised its $1 to $2 park entrance fees to $10 for foreigners, about what is charged in Botswana, Kenya, Tanzania, and Zaire, the country could raise $5 million.[97]

For these reasons, DNPWM is chronically short of funds, providing a pretext for the government to press for culling programs and renewed trade in ivory to raise the much-needed funds. Indeed, many of Zimbabwe's remaining rhinos were poached during a four- or five-month period in 1993 when the wildlife department ran out of funds and stopped running patrols in remote areas.[98]

Zimbabwe claims that its "wildlife industry, including tourism," earned about $100 million in 1992, of which $2 million accrued to the government. This approach makes the country's wildlife and parks department's budget of $5 million (in 1993) seem more generous. But Zimbabwe acknowledges that it spends only about one half of 1 percent (0.60 percent) of its GDP on protected areas and wildlife, even though they bring in enormous amounts of foreign exchange.[99] (The United States spends even less of its GDP on parks and protected areas, 0.15

percent, but its nature reserves are not nearly as important to its economy.)

Of course, killing elephants on a limited basis can, in the short run, benefit local communities. Zimbabwe's rural development program, called CAMPFIRE, which helps rural villages integrate conservation with development, is vaunted as a model of sustainable use. The project began in 1988 in the Nyaminyami district, where villagers organized a program to sell hunting permits and cull a limited number of animals for their meat and skins. The first year, the program raised about $17,000; today, it produces some half-million dollars a year, with the funds being spent locally on schools, medical clinics, irrigation systems, and armed anti-poaching patrols.[100]

Brian Child, the senior ecologist in Zimbabwe's CAMPFIRE unit, strongly opposes the international trade ban on ivory (which does not apply to domestic sales) and writes with pride that "outside the country's protected areas, which support 66,000 elephants, elephants are exploited for every dollar they will yield, with the proviso that the harvest is sustainable."[101] Child's arguments that "utilization promotes conservation" are typical of those made by the sustainable use lobby, if a bit more overheated. However, the success of a highly localized community-based operation cannot necessarily be transferred to using vulnerable species like elephants in uncontrollable international trade.

Moreover, it is unlikely that CAMPFIRE was ever significantly involved in the ivory trade, but was making money from its elephants through safari hunting activities. Indeed, it can be argued that renewing the ivory trade would put local people in the crossfire, as they would have to protect "their" elephants from ruthless and well-armed poachers.

PART III

How to Save
the World's Wildlife–
Humane Sustainable
Development

Introduction

For that which befalleth the sons of men befalleth beasts . . .
as the one dieth, so dieth the other . . . a man hath no
preeminence above a beast.

Ecclesiastes 3:19

This book has discussed a variety of failed attempts to apply the concept of sustainable use, as well as the increasingly common strategy of attempting to disguise the commercial destruction of wildlife, especially endangered species, by labelling it "sustainable use."

Ironically, much of the destruction of nature and killing of wildlife in recent decades have been financed in part by American taxpayers, through U.S. contributions to such international lending and development agencies as the World Bank and the International Monetary Fund. If a portion of the tens of billions of dollars provided to poor nations each year were earmarked for *true* sustainable use and development, much progress could be made towards helping the people, the economies, and the environments of these countries.

Yes, there really *is* such a thing as true sustainable use, particularly when the interests of individual animals, as well as those of the species, are taken into account. Such humane sustainable use or development can be equally beneficial to communities, wildlife, and the environment. There are, in fact, many successful examples of true sustainable use programs, most of which involve carefully controlled ecotourism activities such as the non-disruptive viewing of whales, parrots, gorillas, elephants, and other wildlife in their natural environments.

But however successful some ecotourism projects can be, in the long run we must accept the reality that most animals will not be saved because they can pay their own way. Indeed, the argument that animals must have economic value in order to survive is the line pushed by those who want to profit from wildlife, the sustainable use lobby—the fur industry, the ivory traders, the big game hunters, and the other promoters of the economic exploitation of wildlife. In the final analysis, humans must learn to appreciate animals for their own sake, for their intrinsic value, if we are to live and survive together on this planet.

This generation of humans holds the fate of wildlife in its hands. Unless we can learn to respect and revere this irreplaceable natural heritage, it will not endure for future generations. Nor, for that matter, will human societies—which, in ways we do not yet fully understand, ultimately depend on the biological communities that sustain them.

Until we decide to protect and preserve the natural environment and the creatures with which we share the earth—even those that do not appear to be immediately useful to us—our planet's future will be in peril—and so will our own.

CHAPTER 9

The World Bank: Subsidizing Destruction as Development

The World Bank has attracted heavy criticism for its role in financing environmentally destructive projects: dams that generate power but flood out communities; agricultural development schemes that cut down pristine rain forests; and mines that produce export revenue but contaminate rivers. . . building dams, highways, power plants and other massive public works projects . . . have—as often as not—enriched elites at the expense of ecosystems and the politically powerless.

Hilary F. French
World Watch magazine
July/August 1994[1]

Many ecologically destructive projects make such little sense economically that no private sector source would finance them. That is where such international lending and development agencies as the World Bank and the International Monetary Fund (IMF) come in. For decades, these organizations have provided the money to pay for countless projects that have wreaked havoc on people, animals, and the environment.

The sums of money involved in funding development projects are staggering, especially those provided by the World Bank. This institution supports economic development projects in over 100 countries, lending some $24 billion annually to fund projects costing $70 billion a year. As of 1993, the bank had $140 billion in outstanding loans on projects costing over $330 billion. In that year, $23.7 billion worth of new loans were made.[2]

American taxpayers have generously financed much of this lending, to the tune of scores of billions of dollars since 1946, and now provide 19 percent of the World Bank's funds. In fiscal year 1994, the United States gave $1.118 billion to the World Bank, plus $151 million to the

Inter-American Development Bank, $75 million to the Asian Development Bank, and $135 million to the African Development Bank.

The World Bank's loans in particular have underwritten the devastation of human societies, wildlife communities, and biological systems around the world. For decades, efforts to reform the bank were for naught.

SUBSIDIZING THE DESTRUCTION OF NATURE

The Humane Society of the United States (HSUS) has long emphasized the need for *humane* sustainable development, which applies a compassionate concern not only to wildlife conservation issues but also to programs involving agriculture and farming, forest protection, and general economic development projects. When the humane aspect of development has been ignored, the result has frequently been disastrous to both people and the environment.

Much of the international development financed by the United States and the world community has resulted in ecologically catastrophic projects that have impoverished local people and devastated the environment. Ironically, U.S. taxpayers, through America's multibillion-dollar contributions to international development agencies, have helped to fund and subsidize much of the damage to rain forests, wildlife, and wilderness of recent years, resulting in the destruction of the homes, livelihoods, and even the lives of local people.

Such organizations as the World Bank, the International Monetary Fund, the U.S. Export-Import Bank, the Inter-American Development Bank, and other international lending and development agencies provide tens of billions of dollars of "development" funds to developing nations for projects that directly impoverish local people. For example, to help generate hard cash for developing nations, these agencies have funded the building of large plantations to produce such export products as tea, sugar, coffee, and cotton. This results in local people losing control of their land, which is turned over to outsiders and converted from farmland that had been used to grow food for the local people into a generator of hard currency that grows crops for export.

These agencies have also lent or spent billions of dollars to subsidize a large amount of the cutting of rain forests and the clearing of land in Central America for cattle ranching and farming. World Bank funding for the notorious Polonoroeste regional development in Brazil helped to increase the amount of deforested area in the state of Rondonia from 1.7 percent in 1978 to 23.7 percent by 1988. However, the quality of the rain forest soil is so poorly suited to agriculture that after a few seasons, it dries up and blows or washes away, turning the land into desert "unfit for man or beast." In South America and Asia, the subsidizing of the construction of large dams and other power projects has caused the inundation of large areas of forest and the displacement of tens of millions of villagers and untold numbers of animals.

Dr. Michael Fox of The HSUS has written:

> . . . to promote humane sustainable agriculture will indirectly help protect wildlife and habitat . . . to a large extent, restoring and protecting wildlife refuges require the development of sustainable agriculture. When indigenous peoples can farm for their own subsistence, they do not need to traffic in wildlife. Humane, sustainable, and socially just agricultural . . . programs in Tanzania and other East African countries will . . . play a major role in protecting the wildlife, natural resources, and people of Africa.[3]

Thus, if U.S. government foreign aid agencies and international lending and development institutions are truly concerned about helping impoverished people and nations, they must stop funding projects that destroy people, wilderness, and wildlife. They should instead begin to adopt humane sustainable development as their guiding principle and fund projects that implement the concept.

FURTHER IMPOVERISHING THE POOR

Perhaps the main result of spending billions of dollars and sacrificing the well-being of millions of people has been to further impoverish, and to inflict greater misery on, developing nations. In her landmark book on the environmental disasters caused by World Bank loans, *Odious Debts*, Patricia Adams describes how "ill-conceived agricultural projects," such as cattle ranching projects that destroy grasslands and the traditional economies of pastoral peoples, are leaving "much of Africa in ecological ruin":

> Tobacco plantations in Africa, also recipients of foreign aid loans, wreaked havoc on tropical soils by draining them of nitrogen, phosphorous, potassium, and other vital nutrients, consuming one acre of forest to cure each acre of tobacco.
>
> In Ethiopia's Awash River Valley, irrigation systems for sugar cane, cotton, and banana plantations destroyed the valley's rich floodplains. . . . To make way for the plantations, 20,000 people were expropriated from their lands, mostly without compensation. Forced to leave, the people and their livestock crowded onto lands held by other tribes near the newly irrigated plantations, forcing them, in turn, to spill onto the lands of their neighbors. Normal migration routes were blocked and tribal warfare intensified as the region's land base eroded. When the rains failed in the

early 1970s and again in the early 1980s, the people, bereft of their former resources, became wards of famine-relief stations. To the Afar people of the Awash River Valley, the misery wrought by this foreign-aid-financed agricultural schemes was so much worse than the droughts and other hardships of the past . . . .[4]

It has long been widely recognized that, instead of alleviating poverty in Africa and other developing countries, the World Bank and IMF have often caused greater economic misery. This has been especially true of their "adjustment" programs, which seek to deal with borrowing countries' excessive debt by instituting harsh domestic austerity programs and increasing export earnings. The result has commonly been a reduction in spending on health, education, and conservation, as well as in wages for low-income workers.

In 1993, Oxfam, the widely respected international relief group, reported that the World Bank's and IMF's programs in Africa "dramatically worsen the plight of the poor." Oxfam pointed out that in Zambia, under the bank's economic programs, consumer prices for poor families doubled in the period of a year and a half, and that the percentage of children suffering from malnutrition has gone up from one in twenty to approximately one in five in the past decade. In much of Africa, per capita spending on public health in 1990 was less than that in the 1970s, and primary school enrollment also has declined.[5]

Thus, the legacy of social and environmental disruption left by these projects has been compounded by this crushing debt load. The countries of sub-Saharan Africa (excluding South Africa) now have a debt of over $180 billion, triple that of 1980, and amounting to 110 percent of the countries' gross national product (GNP) for 1991. Just servicing the huge debt costs $10 billion a year—four times the amount spent on health and education for these countries' 600 million people.

In 1993, IMF and World Bank loans constituted 36 percent of Africa's total foreign debt, accounting for over 10 percent of the export revenues of eight nations, and over a third of those of Uganda and Zambia.[6] Some African nations have had no choice but to try to repay interest and principal on these loans with such readily available "resources" as ivory and timber.

The two largest debtors among the developing nations are Brazil and Mexico, with total debt burdens of $121.1 billion and $113.4 billion, respectively, at the end of 1992. There is thus tremendous pressure on these and other debtor nations to sell off their rain forests and wildlife and convert them into cattle ranching lands in order to raise hard cash from beef exports.[7]

THE IMPACT OF MASSIVE PROJECTS

A quarter of the enormous debt carried by developing nations comes from loans made to build massive hydroelectric dams and thermal-powered electric plants. Patricia Adams writes that such projects "are responsible for much of the destroyed farmland and forests, for induced earthquakes, for the spread of diseases, for the alteration of hydrological regimes, for the erosion of coast lines, and ultimately for the reordering of rivers and land around which millions of people had organized themselves over the centuries."[8]

In Zaire and Rwanda, the World Bank-financed Ruzizi II Regional Hydroelectric Project caused 2,500 local farmers from one of Africa's poorest areas to lose their land, and with almost no compensation.[9]

In India, the World Bank has provided extensive financing for the Sardar Sarovar project. This ecologically devastating development involves the damming of the Narmada River and the creation of a 120-mile-long reservoir. This will inundate the Narmada River Valley and destroy the homes and villages of 90,000 of India's poorest rural inhabitants, mainly tribal people. Another World Bank-financed dam on the Narmada would displace 110,000 more people. The total number of people likely to be displaced in the area has been put at upwards of a quarter of a million. (In March 1993, India announced that it would not ask for future bank funding for the project, which appears to be moving ahead on its own.)[10]

Bruce Rich, in his 1994 book on the World Bank, *Mortgaging the Earth*, points out that "forced displacement of millions of the earth's poorest and most marginalized people is a consequence of its style of development." This, he says, has resulted in:

> ... the creation of a new class of poor, uprooted from every traditional link to the land and the local community . . . the uprooting and depossession of huge rural populations from their less efficient modes of production. . . In the past thirty years, the process has accelerated with almost demonic intensity. In Brazil, the government's planned, concerted efforts to modernize and rationalize agriculture from small holdings producing food for domestic consumption into a capital-intensive, export-oriented machine for earning foreign exchange resulted in the uprooting of 28.4 million people between 1960 and 1980—a number greater than the entire population of Argentina. In India, large-scale development projects have forcibly displaced more than 20 million over the past forty years.

Rich concludes that "although population growth and poverty are often blamed for the growing masses of uprooted people in the developing world, in many countries economic development as it has been practiced is as much the cause of such poverty as a solution."[11]

In September 1989, when the Human Rights Caucus held congressional hearings on the World Bank, its witnesses could not name one project where there had been successful, long-term resettlement and rehabilitation of displaced people. At the time, 1.5 million people were in the process of being displaced by current World Bank projects, and more than that number were threatened by projects then being planned. An internal bank report shows that by the early 1990s, some 2 million people were being dispossessed and impoverished by ongoing bank projects, despite environmental reforms supposedly enacted in 1987.[12]

THE NEW LANGUAGE OF "GREENSPEAK"

In recent years, the World Bank has promised to give more consideration to environmental factors. Bruce Rich, in *Mortgaging the Earth*, characterizes the bank's new rhetoric as "greenspeak, a new Orwellian dialect in which ecological destruction was rebaptized as 'sustainable natural resources management'."[13]

Faced with demands that it reform its lending policies, in 1990 the World Bank created the Global Environmental Facility (GEF) to become the major channel for funding what were said to be environmental protection projects. In theory, GEF was to be jointly sponsored by the United Nations Environment Programme (UNEP) and the United Nations Development Programme (UNDP). But in practice, these agencies were not allowed to be effectively involved in, or in some cases even fully informed about, GEF projects. Nor were private conservation and public interest groups.[14]

An example of how the bank continued to conduct business as usual is GEF's $10 million Congo Wildlands Protection and Management Project. GEF presented the plan in 1991 as a model environmental project, designed to preserve biodiversity in the pristine Nouabele rain forest in the Republic of the Congo.

However, funding for the project was secretly tied to another World Bank loan to the Congo to finance forest exploitation, euphemistically called the Congo Natural Resources Management Project. "The Bank's intention," writes Bruce Rich, "was to use the GEF project to finally jump-start a much larger scheme to increase logging exports . . . The Bank's supposed partner in the GEF was bitterly critical of the GEF project; UNEP condemned the Bank proposal as one that would open up a hitherto intact, isolated rainforest area to logging and encroachment pressures, under the pretense of protecting it."

Indeed, UNEP protested that some highly destructive elements of the project were being concealed from the public and even from donor governments involved in the loan. These elements included the construction of a fifteen-mile-long road into the untouched forest and the opening up of part of the forest to logging. UNEP identified the biggest threat to the Nouabele Reserve and surrounding area as the GEF project itself! As Bruce Rich puts it, "the Congo GEF project is a startling example of the Bank's . . . uncanny ability to present proposals whose underlying thrust is the conversion and partial destruction of ecosystems as unadulterated exercises in environmental protection."[15]

MAKING WILDLIFE FOOT THE BILL

Often, international development policymakers include the commercial exploitation of wildlife in their projects—frequently using the language of sustainability to justify such programs. These policy-makers say that their goals are both the preservation of biodiversity *and* sustainable use, ignoring the inherent contradiction between these concepts.

A good example is GEF's West African Community Conservation and Wildlife Utilization Project. The information document for this project states:

> From the perspective of the environment, the project aims to protect and regenerate the ecosystem and improve biodiversity and environmental stability. It will attempt to reestablish viable wildlife populations and conserve species that would otherwise be in danger of local and global extinction.

But another passage informs us:

> . . . support for traditional subsistence hunting of small mammals and game birds . . . will be an important project component. Nonetheless, it is expected that the most substantial revenues for the communities will come from commercial wildlife operations, including safari hunting, ecotourism, and game cropping.[16]

The GEF-funded Gabon Conservation of Biodiversity through Effective Management of Wildlife Trade Project is a good example of the promotion of wildlife exploitation billed as "sustainable use." The project's description uses all of the politically correct buzzwords of sustainability. Its stated objectives are "to assist in developing and implementing sustainable trade strategies to ensure the long-term survival of wildlife species and the ecosystems they are part of." It also aims "to create a mechanism to sustainably manage wildlife trade in Gabon, and to reinforce government and local community capacity to ensure long-term sustainable management and conservation of biodiversity." Among the expected results of the project is a greater appreciation by the authorities of the value of specific species in trade.[17]

Unfortunately, many of the species targeted for "sustainable use" are endangered or threatened, and cannot withstand such exploitation. A background description of regional biodiversity states that "the region contains a number of wildlife species of economic significance, such as elephants (ivory), crocodiles (food, skins), primates (for pets, food, biomedical research), birds (food, pets), and numerous ungulates and fish locally important as sources of protein." The project intends to increase knowledge of this "resource base" and create the institutional capacity within the Gabonese government to monitor trade and "ensure sustainable use."

The project contains an initiative to assess populations of the African grey parrot and the potential for "sustainable offtake" to be sold in the international pet trade, the very thing that has brought many species of parrots to the verge of extinction. African grey parrots are listed on Appendix II of the Convention on International Trade in Endangered Species of Wild Fauna and Flora (CITES), which means that they may become threatened with extinction if international trade is not strictly controlled.[18] Many other species, such as elephants, that are listed as part of the "resource base" are on CITES' Appendix I, which means that they are threatened with extinction and international commercial trade is banned.

The GEF-funded Amazon Treaty project clearly states that one of its purposes is to supply birds for the pet trade and monkeys for laboratory research. Chapter VI of "Amazonia without Myths," the development policy document of the Commission on Development and Environment for Amazonia, contains a disturbing passage:

> Wildlife management offers interesting possibilities, whether in areas under forestry management or in semi-intensive and intensive management, including the breeding of animals. . . Many denizens of the woods are internationally important, such as primates for medical research and certain birds that are used as mascots [pets]. In the future the region will be able to supply local and world markets with species produced in areas under sustainable management and in animal breeding facilities. The breeding

of wild animals and rational cropping of managed areas should be promoted in this context ... [19]

The United States Agency for International Development (USAID) is also a leading promoter of sustainable use of "natural resources," including wild animals. Since 1986, USAID has funded at least thirty projects that exploit wildlife in some form. Over time, its projects have evolved from the traditional extraction of products, such as rubber or Brazil nuts, by indigenous people to the overt exploitation of wildlife for international trade, ostensibly to increase income opportunities for local people.[20]

One example is the Madagascar Trade in Biodiversity for Environmental Management (TRADEM) project, which openly promotes world trade in wildlife for use as pets and for their skins and other products. The project's proposed identification manual, to be produced for use by customs officials and law enforcement personnel, illustrates the project's extent of concern for conservation. The manual includes a list of "most commonly exported Malagasy animals" that includes at least four species on CITES Appendix I, which are banned from international commercial trade.[21]

Unfortunately, many development policy-makers are grasping at overly simplistic solutions to complex problems and applying them wholesale. The new declarations that sustainable use of natural resources is the solution to poverty (which, in turn, is supposed to help the environment) go virtually unchallenged, because they are couched in terms that seem to uphold the rights of the poor. For example, in World Bank Technical Paper No. 130, "Living with Wildlife: Wildlife Resource Management with Local Participation," the author, Agnes Kiss, writes about the conflict between poor rural people and the environment: "Fortunately, conservationists and development planners are exploring a common solution: developing alternative land uses based on wildlife resources generating food and income for rural communities." This is not a solution for increasingly threatened wildlife and ecosystems, nor is it a solution to the fundamental problems of the poor.[22]

SUBSIDIZING OUR OWN DEMISE

A fundamental shortcoming of so many development projects is that in trying to quantify the worth of nature, they vastly undervalue it. Even conservationists are often guilty of selling nature short. In *Economics and Biodiversity*, Jeffrey McNeely of IUCN notes that the value of conserving natural resources can be "considerable." But as development policy analyst April Adams points out, "the value of natural functions, which result from the complex workings of whole, intact ecosystems, is not considerable, it is *infinite*. All life on this planet, including ours, relies on them. It is impossible to quantify the value of all life on earth. Economic valuation is an inappropriate and inadequate tool for thinking about these issues."[23]

Adams goes on to observe that the natural systems whose destruction we are funding may be essential to our own survival:

> The World Bank's World Development report of 1992, which focuses on development and the environment, goes no further than to blandly state that, "Economic development and sound environmental management are complementary aspects of the same agenda. Without adequate environmental protection, development will be undermined; without development, environmental protection will fail." Saying that "development will be undermined" is a feeble evasion of the fact that life on earth, particularly human life, could be destroyed if environmental degradation continues at its present rate.[24]

HOPE FOR THE FUTURE?

Perhaps the great issue of our time is how to save the major ecological life support systems of the planet, and the fauna and flora that depend on them. In order to achieve this all-important objective, we must transform the developmental lending leader of the world from a promoter of destruction into a force for good.

Indeed, the best vision and strategic plans cannot succeed unless they are supported by adequate financial resources. Therefore, the answer is to channel funding from the World Bank and other international lending institutions into truly humane and environmentally sustainable development.

We must therefore not only continue to oppose projects that harm people, wildlife, and the environment. We must also work equally hard to guide and promote projects that reflect a reverence for life and the dream for a just and humane world.

Fortunately, there is some hope that the World Bank's past mistakes may not necessarily lead to a series of similar disasters in the future. There still exists an immense bureaucratic inertia that continues to turn a blind eye to the habits of the past and revels in the gigantic projects of earlier years, which devastated communities of people and biological treasures. But the beginnings of a transformation in thinking can be seen at the bank.

In the last year and a half, the bank has established the key post of vice president for environmentally sustainable development, and has named a distinguished public official, Ismail Serageldin, to fill the position. He has the responsibility for assuring environmentally sustainable development, bank-wide, over the areas of environment, urban projects, transportation, water, agriculture, social policy, environmental economics, land, and natural habitats, as well as overseeing the bank's GEF operation. Serageldin has won praise from environmentalists by opening up new lines of communication with public interest groups, while working to redirect bank funding and ensure that it meets the standards of true sustainability.

Jan Hartke, the president of EarthKind International and one of the leaders of the global environmental movement, says that "this new, emerging of leadership will not mean that the destructive mindset of the past is over and done with, but clearly progress is being made." He notes:

It is encouraging that a beachhead of hope is being established within these institutions, and that the tenacity of the global environmental movement is finally having a meaningful effect. We now need to build on these accomplishments through constant pressure, steadily applied. In this way, we have hope of effectively responding to the central challenge of our generation: how to reorient our economic system, so that people can attain a decent quality of life without undermining the natural world upon which our civilization itself is based.[25]

CHAPTER 10

Ecotourism: True Sustainable Use

Whale and dolphin watchers now number more than four million per year worldwide . . . Total revenues are at least $318 million.

Erich Hoyt
International Whale Bulletin
1992[1]

There are those who justify the commercial hunting of and trade in animals on the grounds that wildlife must "pay its own way," and have an economic value to local people in order to survive. But it is becoming increasingly clear that if wildlife must be used, the best way to "sustainably utilize" wild animals for profit is through nature-oriented tourism, which is growing rapidly and becoming a major part of the world's largest industry.

There are abundant data demonstrating that live animals, such as whales and elephants, are worth much more in economic terms than dead ones are, and that they can be the basis for a thriving ecotourism industry. Over the long term, such truly sustainable programs can provide a much greater (and theoretically permanent) economic benefit to poor nations and areas than can the killing of wild animals for short-term, temporary profit. Unpersecuted wildlife can, over the long term—indeed for perpetuity—be an invaluable source of income, employment, and economic development through such non-consumptive activities as photographic safaris and scientific study projects and expeditions.

And unlike consumptive use, in which profits are realized not by local people but by middlemen and importers, ecotourism can ensure that revenues are shared by the community that provides services to tourists. Wiping out creatures that can attract tourists and bring in income for the indefinite future, as is now being done in so many areas, is a prime example of killing the proverbial goose that lays the golden egg.

TOURISM: THE WORLD'S LARGEST INDUSTRY

Travel and tourism are the biggest industry in the world, grossing over $3.5 *trillion* a year.[2] And the area of tourism that is growing most rapidly is the nature-based segment, ecotourism, of which wildlife observation and photography are an integral part.[3]

Tourism is now growing by at least 50 percent a decade, and the number of international travellers is projected to grow from 450 million in 1991 to 650 million by the year 2000. By the year 2005, the industry is expected to double in size.[4]

In 1992, the World Travel and Tourism Council (WTTC) reported that worldwide, one in fifteen workers—127 million people—were employed in the travel and tourism industry. The following year, the WTTC estimated that tourism employed 204 million people, almost one in nine workers worldwide. As the 1993 WTTC report points out, in the words of author John Naisbitt, "as a contributor to the global economy, tourism has no equal":

- It has become the world's most important economic activity, generating over 10 percent of the global gross national product.
- It is responsible for 6.9 percent of all government spending, 10.7 percent of all capital investment, and 10.9 percent of all consumer spending.
- It is the number one source of tax revenues, bringing in a whopping $655 billion a year.[5]

According to the World Tourism Organization (WTO), each 1-percent growth in tourism worldwide creates at least a million jobs and adds $10 billion to the world gross national product.[6]

In the United States, the country that is the world's leading industrial power and trader of goods, travel and tourism are now the biggest single sources of foreign exchange income. In 1991, the industry brought in some $51 billion in foreign revenue, $11 billion of which was spent on American airplanes, cruise ships, and other transportation. This compares with $39 billion generated by the sale of agricultural commodities, which was until recently the nation's biggest export industry.[7] Worldwide, tourism earned developing nations some $312 billion in foreign currency, and was topped only by revenues from oil exports.[8]

In his 1994 book, *Global Paradox*, futurist John Naisbitt predicts that tourism will become even more important as a leading economic growth factor in nations across the globe. Naisbitt, the author of the bestseller *Megatrends*, predicts that by the year 2005, 144 million jobs will be created in the tourism industry. Naisbitt believes that the most important factor that is helping to make tourism the world's largest industry is a fundamental shift in attitudes toward travel:

Where once travel was considered a privilege of the moneyed elite, now it is considered a basic human right. In the United States, as well as in other parts of the developed world, families and individuals spend as much on travel as they do on food, clothing, or health care.[9]

THE GROWTH OF ECOTOURISM

Arguably the fastest growing segment of the tourism industry is ecotourism, especially nature-oriented adventure travel.[10] The World Conservation Union (IUCN) defines ecotourism as "environmentally responsible travel and visitation to relatively undisturbed natural areas, in order to enjoy and appreciate nature . . . that promotes conservation, has low visitor impact, and provides for beneficially active socio-economic involvement of local populations."[11]

Although the term "ecotourism" is new, the phenomenon is not. Indeed, the nation's first national parks, Yellowstone and Yosemite, were established in the late 1800s with the support of railroad and steamship companies. They were among the first to recognize and profit from the desire of people to enjoy nature and the outdoors.[12]

Today, nature-oriented tourism is the leading producer of foreign exchange in several countries, including Costa Rica, Ecuador, Nepal, and— until April 1994, when civil war plunged the nation into violence and chaos—Rwanda.[13]

Naisbitt, who is reputed to be the world's leading trend forecaster, says that concern for the environment ranks as the number-one issue of this decade among tourism groups. According to Naisbitt, "concern for the environment is no longer a 'special interest,' it is everyone's interest, and with it has come a strong desire to see the world in all its natural splendor before it isn't there to be seen."[14]

Almost 7 percent of all American tourists—some 8 million people— say they have gone on an "ecotrip," and 35 million Americans say they are interested in taking one.[15] Other sources estimate that every year, between 4 and 6 million Americans take nature-oriented trips abroad.[16] (The discrepancy in numbers between these citations probably results from different definitions of terms.) It is estimated that in 1991, 275 American nature tour operators guided 108,000 travelers, earning revenues of $95 million and profits of $4 million.[17]

There are even more visits to America's national park system every year than there are Americans! The National Park Service reports a total of 274,694,549 recreational visits to its park system in 1992, *not* including visits to National Trails, National Battlefield sites, International Historic Sites, and thirty other affiliated areas. National parks alone recorded a total of almost 59 million visits, and national recreation areas over 50 million.[18]

Even potentially dangerous and uncomfortable adventure-type nature travel has wide appeal. In 1992, some 2 million Americans took white-water rafting trips down class 3 rivers. Travel literature now abounds with offerings for such adventure tours.[19] For example, the "Travel Advisory" page of the May 8, 1994 Sunday *New York Times* travel section contains three articles on unusual nature trips:

- Visits to South Korea's Demilitarized Zone (DMZ), "the remote areas of which are among the most interesting. Wildlife abounds";
- Swimming with wild dolphins in a lagoon in Latin America, as part of a six-day dolphin experience;
- Trips to Ussuriland in Russia's Far East, the home of endangered Siberian tigers and Amur leopards, as well as Asian black bears, Manchurian and roe deer, goral (rare mountain goats), and exotic birds, butterflies, and plants.[20]

Moreover, ecotourists are often preferable to other types of travelers. Nature tourists not only take longer trips, they also spend more money—$264 per day, according to one estimate.[21] One study found that nature travelers in Latin America spent an average of $1,000 more over a two-week period than other tourists. A survey of tour operators reported that 63 percent of tourists would be willing to pay $50 towards conservation in the region visited, and 27 percent would pay $200.[22]

Significantly, nature tourism has the effect of transferring enormous revenues from wealthy industrialized nations to poor developing countries. In 1988, it was estimated that such tourism was generating some $25 billion worth of annual revenues from Northern developed nations to poor Southern countries.[23] Obviously, since 1988, nature- and wildlife-oriented tourism have grown tremendously, as have the revenues produced by such travel.

A cost/benefit analysis of the Virgin Islands National Park in St. John, Virgin Islands, weighed the economic costs of the park (operation and maintenance, taxes on park property) against the benefits (concessionaires' fees, income from tourists, and increased land values). The study concluded that benefits outweigh costs by a ratio of 11.1 to 1.[24]

THE VALUE OF WILDLIFE THROUGH ECOTOURISM

Several economic studies and models have demonstrated the enormous non-consumptive value of wildlife from a tourism and recreational standpoint. A study by the U.S. Department of the Interior, the 1991 National Survey of Fishing, Hunting, and Wildlife-Associated Recreation, showed overwhelming public interest in and support for non-consumptive wildlife-related recreation.[26] The survey revealed that "in 1991, 76.5 million people 16 and older participated in nonconsumptive activities for the primary purpose of feeding, observing or photographing wildlife. They spent $18 billion on these activities." By contrast, only 14.1 million Americans engaged in hunting. Among the study's other findings were the following:

- Nearly 66 million people fed birds and other wildlife around their homes. 55 million observed wildlife near their homes, while 15.6 million visited public parks or natural areas near their homes.
- 30 million people took trips to observe, feed, or photograph wildlife. Of these, 24.7 million observed, fed, or photographed birds, while 22.5 million sought out land mammals. Ten million observed, fed, or photographed fish.
- Expenditures by non-consumptive users include $7.5 billion on trip-related costs, $9.6 billion for equipment, and $1 billion on dues and contributions to wildlife-related organizations and magazines.

In 1982, the U.S. Fish and Wildlife Service released its survey of Americans interested in "non-consumptive wildlife use." It found that some 29 million people took about 310 million nature trips in 1980, including over a million people who made more than 4 million ecologically oriented trips abroad.[27]

Americans, Europeans, and others are travelling the world in search of wildlife-related recreation. Canada's Gulf of St. Lawrence, off the coast of Newfoundland, used to be known for the bloody and brutal seal hunts conducted there every spring, when tens or hundreds of thousands of baby harp seals would be clubbed to death, and sometimes skinned alive, in front of their nursing mothers, for their white pelts. Now, tourism to the area to watch the seals, especially in the Magdalen Islands, provides three times the income that used to be earned from the sale of the seal pelts for many residents.[28] Unfortunately, the large-scale killing of baby seals during the spring hunt continues in nearby areas, mainly off of Newfoundland. According to Michael O'Sullivan, executive director of The Humane Society of Canada, import bans on seal skins by the United States and Western Europe have helped make the hunt uneconomical, but Canadian government subsidies to the sealers have allowed the hunting to continue.[29]

In East Africa, tourism is by far the biggest industry, and is the mainstay of the economy of several countries in the region. According to the Kenya Wildlife Service (KWS), tourism is the country's biggest source of foreign currency, bringing in $424 million from 822,000 tourists in 1991. And it is estimated that in a good year, elephant-viewing alone produces $25 million. This generates substantial employment; some 55,000 people work in the country's wildlife tourism industry.[30]

The economics of ecotourism makes wildlife and its habitat worth a fortune to poor nations. A 1972 study by David Western and Wesley Henry estimated that the wildlife of Kenya's 150-square-mile Amboseli National Park, as a tourist attraction, could generate yearly revenues eighteen times higher than if the park were converted to cattle production.[31] And a 1982 study of Amboseli by Western, then director of the Nairobi Office of the Wildlife Conservation Society and now director of KWS, calculated the value of non-consumptive viewing of the park's wildlife in astronomical terms. He estimated the tourism value of each of the park's lions at $27,000 annually and the total worth of the park's elephants at $610,000 a year. Moreover, Western found that the net value of the park for wildlife viewing was forty dollars per hectare (slightly over sixteen dollars per acre), in contrast to a value of just eighty cents per hectare (thirty-two cents per acre) at most for the park's potential if used for agriculture.[32]

Private landowners also are turning to wildlife to attract tourists, hoping to earn money from land that often cannot support other uses, such as agriculture or cattle raising. South African landowners have enjoyed great success in attracting tourists to wildlife areas, and there are more than 8,000 game ranches, comprising some 64,000 square miles, in the country. In 1992, the Save Conservancy, one of the biggest wildlife reserves on private property, was formed in Zimbabwe when fifteen ranchers took down their common fences. The reserve has become home to several young elephants from nearby Gonarezhou National Park, where drought has reduced the availability of vegetation fed on by the elephant population.[33]

In Rwanda, in central Africa, the growing human population was encroaching on the habitat of the mountain gorillas (made famous by biologist Dian Fossey's book *Gorillas in the Mist*), and the government was under increasing pressure to convert the forests to cropland and cattle pasture. Now, tourists visiting the Parc des Volcans to view the gorillas provide the nation's third biggest source of foreign exchange. No doubt inspired by the movie version of Fossey's book, tourists in small, strictly controlled groups pay $170 an hour to trek to the animals' refuge and see some of the last remaining mountain gorillas, which now number just 600 to 650 in the world.[34] The local villagers thus have a strong economic incentive to protect the gorillas and their forest home.

In addition to the revenues generated by tourism (an estimated $1 million in entrance fees alone), preserving the gorillas' habitat also protects the local forests and watershed, safeguarding the cropland of local farmers. (The civil war that broke out in the spring of 1994, resulting in the killing of perhaps hundreds of thousands of Rwandans, obviously halted the travel of tourists to the country. It has also placed the security of the gorillas in great jeopardy.)

WATCHING WHALES INSTEAD OF KILLING THEM

Whales are a good example of creatures that are worth more—much more—alive than dead. Whale-watching today is an industry that produces hundreds of millions of dollars in annual revenues.

Known for their close family ties, these warm-blooded mammals—the largest creatures ever to inhabit the earth—have captured the imaginations of people around the world. Tourists are willing to travel long distances and spend large amounts of money to observe whales in their natural habitats.

The business of whale-watching began in 1955 in southern California, when boats started taking people out to witness the annual migration of the California gray whales. It soon spread to the coastal areas of New England, Mexico, Canada, Australia, and other areas where cetaceans (whales, dolphins, and porpoises) could be found and observed.

By 1991, whale-watching off California and New England involved some 300,000 people, producing an estimated $3 million in direct revenues, and an additional $1 million abroad. Today, the coasts of some thirty countries plus Antarctica host whale-watching expeditions, conducted aboard cruise liners, fishing boats, sailboats, dinghies, kayaks, rubber inflatables, shore stations, and even helicopters and airplanes (although these can often cause harassment of the whales), and lasting from an hour to several weeks. Whale-watching is even becoming popular in such major whale-hunting nations as Japan, Norway, and Iceland.[35]

In some areas, whales have become part of the local culture, generating sales of artwork, carvings, books, T-shirts, photographs, and other such souvenirs. This has happened on the Hawaiian island of Maui, in whose waters humpback whales, known for their famous "songs," spend December to April mating and nursing their young. The humpbacks can often be viewed from shore, and other cetaceans, such as sperm and pilot whales and spinner and bottlenosed dolphins, can also be seen, some of them year-round.[36]

Commercial whale-watching in Hawaii began at Lahaina on Maui, but has now expanded to the islands of Oahu, Kauai, Molokai, and the big island of Hawaii. The annual value of whale-watching tourism in Hawaii (conservatively assuming 200,000 participants, the 1983 figure) would be at least $5 million a year. If indirect revenues are included, the figure comes to over $17.5 million.[37]

As of 1992, it was conservatively estimated that over 4 million people a year were engaging in whale- and dolphin-watching, directly spending over $75 million on tours. If indirect expenditures such as lodging, food, film, travel, clothing, souvenirs, and entertainment are included, total 1992 revenues exceeded $317 million.[38] Whale-watching continues to grow today. The major factors limiting its expansion are the shortage of whales to view and the harassment of whales (illegal under the Marine Mammal Protection Act) that occurs when too many boats are chasing too few whales at one time.

Erich Hoyt, writing in the *International Whale Bulletin*, published by the Whale and Dolphin Conservation Society, points out that while whale-watching is a non-consumptive use of whales, it must be undertaken carefully so as not to harass the cetaceans or disrupt their lives:

> Tour businesses need to be monitored, additional boat traffic regulated, and the whales protected from harassment caused by aggressive whale- watching. If prospective tour operators examine areas where whale-watching industries have matured and learn from their experiences, whale-watching worldwide can continue to grow with maximum benefits accruing to local communities, companies, scientists, conservation societies, whale watchers, and, ultimately, the whales themselves.

As Hoyt—who compiled much of the above-cited data—points out, whale-watching provides enormous benefits in the areas of education, science, conservation, economics, and recreation:

> Whale-watching can be an important educational activity; both school-children and adults learn about whales, the nature of scientific research, and the importance of marine conservation. Whale-watching in certain parts of the world has helped to encourage support for habitat preservation

for whales and dolphins, and to ensure better management of the ocean's resources.[39]

Whale-watching thus represents a *truly* renewable, ethical, and humane application of "sustainable use." As the World Society for the Protection of Animals pointed out in its statement to the April 1993 meeting of the International Whaling Commission in Kyoto, Japan:

> The underlying principles of sustainable development . . . do not require the direct consumptive exploitation of living marine resources. In fact, the non-consumptive use of living marine resources may be regarded as sustainable utilization. In certain circumstances, such as in the case of whale-watching expeditions, this non-lethal and non-consumptive use provides a more meaningful economic, and more effective short and long term, use of the living marine resource.

NATIONAL FORESTS: WORTH MORE STANDING THAN CUT

Ironically, as nature tourism explodes, the U.S. government is destroying many natural areas and their future recreational potential. This is especially true for national forests. Indeed, from a purely economic standpoint, cutting these forests is one of the least productive uses of them.

For example, a report released in May 1994 by the Wilderness Society shows that tourism and recreation are much better at generating revenue than logging is. This study of southern Appalachian national forests examined 16 million wooded acres in five southeastern states: Georgia, North Carolina, South Carolina, Tennessee, and Virginia.[40] The Wilderness Society determined that the clean water, wildlife habitat, recreational opportunities, and other non-timber resources afforded by the southern Appalachian national forests contribute more to the region's economy than their timber resources do:

- The number of jobs associated with recreation in the region's national forests (9,000) was more than five times the number of jobs associated with timber cut in the forests between 1987 and 1991.
- The gross economic benefits of the recreational opportunities on the Southern Appalachian national forests equal $379 million annually, more than ten times the $32 million in gross annual benefits attributable to the timber program.
- More than half of the U.S. population is within a day's drive of the national forest and park lands of the region. Great Smoky Mountains National Park is the most visited park in the nation.

- According to resource economist Peter Morton, author of the Wilderness Society's report, "the natural beauty and magnetism of the Southern Appalachians' public lands are major reasons for this region's economic growth and transition to a more service-based economy. Unfortunately, the Forest Service is destroying and degrading these valuable natural assets, at taxpayers' expense."
- Non-timber resources and programs in the U.S. Forest Service budget take a back seat to the timber programs, with activities related to the timber-sale preparation and road construction consuming the lion's share of shrinking funds, and recreational activities receiving only a small percentage of the funding. For example, between 1986 and 1991, the Cherokee National Forest devoted 50 percent of its budget to timber sales, but just 16 percent to fish and wildlife and recreation programs.
- Meanwhile, demand for recreation on national forests is expected to explode in the coming years. The Forest Service estimates that recreation throughout the South will increase by 50 percent by the year 2005, and double over current rates by the year 2040.

Peter Kirby, director of the southeast regional office of the Wilderness Society, said, "Many existing wilderness areas in the Southern Appalachians are already overcrowded, and the Forest Service expects demands for their use to increase as the region grows. Yet the agency continues to destroy the wild, roadless character of lands identified as possible future wilderness areas."

CASE STUDIES OF ECOTOURISM

In 1990, the World Wildlife Fund (WWF), with the support of the U.S. Agency for International Development (USAID), published an extensive, 250-page study entitled *Ecotourism: The Potentials and Pitfalls*, which demonstrated how ecological resources can bring in huge amounts of revenue from tourists.

The report analyzes the promise and the perils of ecotourism, summarizing them as follows:

Ecotourism can generate badly needed revenue for local and regional economies, heightened local awareness of the importance of conservation, and new incentives for governments and the dwellers in and around appealing natural areas to preserve them. At the same time, however, the demands placed on ecosystems and natural resources from increased tourism can destroy the very attractions that draw people. Developing ecotourism wisely therefore poses an enormous challenge.

Ecotourism goes on to describe the many ways in which the development of the tourism industry offers the possibility of significant economic expansion at relatively little cost:

> . . . it is a growth industry and therefore highly desirable for the economic development of countries or regions, [and] tourism helps diversify the economy . . . Many conservationists have noted that, since tourism to protected areas tends to occur in peripheral and nonindustrial regions, it may stimulate economic activity and growth in isolated, rural areas.

Noting that "the protected natural areas of Latin America and the Caribbean are becoming increasingly popular vacation destinations with both international and domestic travelers," *Ecotourism* focuses in detail on five countries that were "chosen as representatives of the region's diverse ecological attributes, its climatic zones, and its varied socioeconomic development." The five countries in question are Belize, Costa Rica, Dominica, Ecuador, and Mexico. The study found that almost half of 436 tourists interviewed at airports said that protected natural areas were "the main reason" or "very important" in their decision to visit the area. And over half visited at least one park or preserve during their trips.[41]

Belize

The spectacular marine and coastal areas and the interior wildlands of Belize give the country a variety of nature-oriented tourist attractions, including the world's second-largest barrier reef, which runs 185 miles along Belize's entire coastline. The interior contains a rich variety of birds and other wildlife, many of which are extinct or rare elsewhere, as well as the world's only jaguar sanctuary.

In 1987, 99,266 tourists visited Belize, an increase of 55 percent since 1980. Tourism provided over $47 million in foreign exchange earnings in 1987, and was responsible for the employment of some 9,000 people. WWF airport surveys found that, when asked if parks and protected areas were important in their decision to visit the country, 73 percent of visitors to Belize said they were either "the main reason" (8 percent), "important" (36 percent), or "somewhat important" (29 percent). A majority of the tourists (60 percent) took a boat trip, went bird-watching (57 percent), or took a jungle excursion (56 percent).[42]

In 1991, 223,000 tourists visited Belize, spending some $95 million.[43]

Costa Rica

A small country of just 52,000 square kilometers (31,200 square miles), Costa Rica contains a rich and diverse variety of wildlife, tropical rain forests, coral reefs, mountain ranges, volcanoes, and other natural attractions, many of which enjoy some degree of official protection. Forming a land bridge between North and South America, the country is unique in that it supports varied species from both continents.

In 1986, tourists spent almost $133 million in Costa Rica, representing 16 percent of the nation's total foreign exchange. Tourism is the nation's third largest source of income (after exports of bananas and coffee), and has experienced the biggest growth of all sources of foreign exchange.

Parks and protected areas were important in the decisions of 58 percent of tourists' decisions to visit Costa Rica, and nature-oriented recreation was the activity most commonly participated in. About a third of visitors to Costa Rica participated in wildlife-observing (37 percent), jungle excursions (33 percent), or bird-watching (31 percent). More than half of the tourists visited a natural area, and many spent time at several different parks. Some of the parks receive over 200,000 tourists a year.[44]

Between 1987 and 1990, parks and protected areas enjoyed an 80-percent increase in tourism, and another 25-percent rise took place in 1991, with 60 percent of tourists coming from outside the country. Over half a million people visited Costa Rica in 1991, and they spent a total of $310 million.

In the 1970s, in an effort to preserve its diverse wildlife and forests, and to promote tourism to the country, Costa Rica began setting aside parks and preserves throughout the nation. One of the most beautiful of these sanctuaries is Monteverde, a 27,000-acre biological reserve featuring a highland cloud forest and an amazing variety of spectacular wildlife. Visitors see brightly colored butterflies, whose colors seem to "shimmer and change" in the sunlight, and the rare quetzal bird. The male of this species has an emerald-green body and tail, and a bright-red breast. In order to limit damage and disturbance to the forest, only 100 visitors are permitted in at one time. But surrounding lodges and hotels can accommodate several hundred people, and small businesses catering to tourists have sprung up, including CASEM, a local women's cooperative that sells needlework and homemade souvenirs, grossing over $50,000 annually.

Author Sue Hubbell describes a recent visit to Monteverde, where, finding a group of quetzals feeding on wild avocado, she also spied a related bird, a female elegant trogon, that was "metallic green, with a brownish-orange breast and white- and black-banded tail":

The bird had just captured breakfast: a walking stick of enormous length. Gulping the oddly-shaped insect, a straw with legs, she swallowed hard and intently for several minutes until it had disappeared inside her. Then she tidily wiped her beak on a twig and hopped away.[45]

Visits to the Monteverde private reserve totalled 40,000 in 1991, a jump of 50 percent from 1990.

Dominica

The biggest of the Caribbean's Windward Islands, Dominica, in the Lesser Antilles, is often called "nature island" because it has the most extensive rain forests in the region. Sixty percent of the island is covered with rugged and beautiful mountainous terrain that is teeming with wildlife. The main tourist attractions on the island are two national parks and two forest reserves, and most tourist activities are nature-based.

For 1986, earnings from the 36,400 tourists accounted for a quarter of the country's gross national product, over $10 million. Visitor expenditures are estimated to have increased from almost $3 million in 1980 to over $7 million in 1986. Half of Dominica's tourists said that visiting natural areas was important in their decision to travel there.[46] In 1991, 46,000 tourists visited Dominica, spending some $28 million.[47]

Ecotourism expert Héctor Ceballos-Lascuráin wrote of his travels in Dominica, "I visited the largest boiling lake (of volcanic origin) in the world, appreciated the enormous whale-watching potential of the island (especially sperm whales), and verified the rich birdwatching possibilities there [including] two endemic species of parrots. Government authorities, local communities, and private entrepreneurs are all eager to participate in a well-integrated and fruitful ecotourism scheme."[48]

Ecuador

This nation is full of parks, forests, biological reserves, and wildlife. The primary tourist attractions in Ecuador are the famous Galapagos Islands, with their amazing variety of unique and easily observable animals, such as giant tortoises and iguanas. Tourism more than doubled between 1973 and 1980, to 244,485 visitors, and reached 266,761 in 1986. In 1985, tourism added some $260 million to the economy, making it the second biggest source of foreign exchange after petroleum products.[49] By 1991, 365,000 people a year were visiting Ecuador, and spending $189 million there.[50]

The country's parks and protected areas were the "main reason" given by 52 percent of tourists for visiting Ecuador; another 27 percent said these natural areas were important to their decision to visit the country. Three quarters of the visitors cited natural history as an important motivating factor in their travel decision, and the same percentage toured a natural area, mainly the Galapagos.

According to the Ecotourism Society, travel to the Galapagos Islands has increased from 7,500 tourists in 1975 to 47,000 in 1990. Officials expect that by 1995, tourism to the island will have increased eightfold from 1965.[51]

Ceballos-Lascuráin is helping IUCN to develop an ecotourism plan for the country's mainland, and he believes that "the huge Cuyabeno Wildlife Reserve in the Amazonian region . . . , with its extraordinary biodiversity and singular beauty," could become a more popular ecotourism destination even than the Galapagos Islands:

> An initial success of this project was having contributed, by providing ecotourism arguments, to the achievement of a ban on all oil exploitation and drilling activities in the Reserve. For the first time in the history of this country, oil exploitation has been stopped by providing more sustainable options for future development through ecotourism. A successful ecotourism plan for Cuyabeno will be launched only if the local indigenous communities play an active role in the process, and they seem to be very interested in doing so.[52]

Mexico

Mexico's abundance of plant and animal life is not as well known as its lovely beaches and other tourist attractions, but travel to the country's many parks, reserves, refuges, and natural areas is growing rapidly. In 1987, almost 5.5 million tourists visited Mexico, and tourism has been one of the three major sources of foreign exchange for the last three decades, earning $1.8 billion in 1987. In 1986, over 1.8 million people were employed either directly or indirectly in the industry, and 60 percent of tourists interviewed said that parks and protected areas were important in their decision to visit Mexico.[53] By 1991, the number of tourists visiting Mexico had tripled, to 16.6 million, and tourist receipts were estimated at $4.4 billion.[54]

One of Mexico's prime potential attractions is an area of its highlands where several hundred million monarch butterflies gather for the winter from all over North America. In the 1980s, timber cutting threatened this critical monarch habitat, but conservationists persuaded landowners to preserve the forest, which would be managed for tourism in a cooperative arrangement. These sanctuaries now employ local people to protect them and operate tours of the area. In 1991, some 100,000 tourists visited the two main sanctuaries, reportedly spending millions of pesos on food, lodging, guided trips, and souvenirs.[55]

The extraordinary value of tourism to other Caribbean nations has also been documented. Tourism is now the major industry in each of the thirty states in the region, constituting from 50 to 70 percent of the economy in these nations. In 1992, travel and tourism were providing almost one in six jobs in the region, and it was projected that by 1994, the industry would be responsible for a quarter of the Caribbean states' economy.[56]

EARTHWATCH AND ITS EARTHCORPS

One of the groups most effectively combining ecotourism with conservation through field research is Earthwatch, located in Watertown, Massachusetts. It defines its mission as "to improve human understanding of the planet, the diversity of its inhabitants, and the processes which affect the quality of life on earth" by working "to sustain the world's environment, monitor global change, conserve endangered habitats and species, explore the vast heritage of our peoples, and foster world health and international cooperation."[57]

Earthwatch accomplishes all this by recruiting volunteers to serve in an ecological EarthCorps and work with research scientists on environmental and cultural projects from one end of the globe to the other. The volunteers pay from $800 to $2,500 to take part in expeditions to various parts of the world. In 1993, the organization sponsored some 157 projects in fifty countries, organizing 4,300 volunteers aged sixteen to eighty-five on 780 research teams. Research areas covered included rain forest ecology and conservation; marine studies and ocean ecology; and wildlife preservation.

Some of the major subjects and ecological problems addressed by Earthwatch volunteers are the following:

- Understanding the planet—addressing the fundamental systems that govern the quality of our lives. Expeditions study the legend of Atlantis in Greece; Israeli desert life; volcanoes in Texas, Wyoming, and Russia; villages in the Himalayas; fossils of mammoths and saber-toothed cats in Mexico; and dinosaurs and sharks in Montana.
- Threatened habitats—the need to protect biodiversity and fragile ecosystems. Studies involve island rain forests; wetlands in Czechoslovakia; and saving ocean reefs off the Canary Islands, the Philippines, Maui, the Bahamas, Belize, Tonga, and Fiji.

- Strategies for survival—how plants and animals can deal with human impacts. Expeditions research dolphin intelligence; wild dolphin societies; surveys of whales, dolphins, and sharks in the Bahamas; humpback whales off of Australia and Hawaii; killer whales in Washington's Puget Sound; seals in California; Florida manatees; sea turtles off Costa Rica and St. Croix; monkeys in Sri Lanka and Costa Rica; orangutans in Borneo; kangaroos and wallabies in Australia; elephants in Botswana; loons in the Great Lakes; songbirds in Canada and Hungary; and birds in China, Scotland, and New Zealand.

- Managing the planet—strategies of sustainable living. Studies focus on mountain lions in Idaho; coyotes, cougars, and other predators in San Francisco; elk and wolves in Yellowstone; timber wolves in Minnesota, Isle Royale (Michigan), and Poland; life in Chesapeake Bay; wildlands in Australia; wildlife in Kenya; rivers and rain forests in Chile and Venezuela; llama herding in Bolivia; wild rivers in Estonia; organic farming in Britain; forests in Bohemia and St. Petersburg, Russia; and ecology in Hungary.

- Human impacts—how humankind is threatening and otherwise affecting the planet's biological and cultural diversity. Projects examine the origins of the Apache Indians; hunters of mammoths and mastodons in Utah and in Oxford, England; folk healers and botanists of Mexico; pre-Columbian peoples of Chile; prehistoric Siberian settlements; early hunters and traders of the Pacific Northwest; life in ancient York; Iron Age farming in Hungary; African slave freedom fighters in eighteenth-century Jamaica; sun and wind power in Kenya; herdsmen in Mongolia; village life in the Himalayas; and arts and culture in Vietnam.

Since being established in 1971, Earthwatch has mobilized more than 34,000 EarthCorps volunteers, who have contributed over $22 million and 4 million hours of work, covering some 1,500 projects in 111 countries and 36 states.[58]

THE DANGERS OF ECOTOURISM

Although ecotourism can be enormously beneficial to natural areas, it can be extremely destructive of flora and fauna if not properly regulated. Besides littering and causing air and water pollution, travellers trampling ecologically sensitive areas can do permanent damage. Motorized tourists can be even more harmful. Fragile coral reefs are especially susceptible to damage from snorkelers and scuba divers. And because of inadequate regulation, tours to Antarctica are damaging its delicate environment.

A section of Masai Mara Park in Kenya had to be closed because of the damage being done by minibuses. Six months later, the area had reportedly still had not recovered. Tourists have also wreaked ecological havoc in Kenya's Amboseli Park, helping to create "dustbowls" in dry seasons and huge ruts in wet ones.[59]

Tourists have even caused changes in behavior patterns of wildlife in some areas. In some African parks, cheetahs, which hunt in the daytime, have drastically altered their hunting and feeding habits. Tourist vehicles often scare away cheetahs or the prey they are hunting, making it difficult for the cats to obtain sufficient food for themselves and/or their cubs. As wildlife biologist and ecotourism promoter Barbara Sleeper describes the impact tourism can have on wildlife:

> In heavily visited areas, some animals have become too comfortable around people. Cheetahs hounded by constant observation have become so blasé about people as to commandeer their vehicles for use as observation and resting platforms. Lions and wild dogs will use tourist vehicles for shade. Baboons sit on hoods and peer in windows.

"Unfortunately," she notes, "these behaviors can end up in injury to both animals and people."[60]

Some elements of the sustainable use lobby recognize that tourism has enormous potential to replace consumptive activities like sport and commercial hunting as sources of revenue for poor nations. As a result, attempts to minimize or discredit the value of tourism, and to exaggerate its dangers, are now commonly seen in the literature of the "utilization" camp.

Sustainable use advocate Raymond Bonner apparently prefers that wildlife be shot with a gun rather than a camera. He writes in the *Wall Street Journal* that "from a conservation perspective, it can be argued that hunting should be promoted over tourism." Citing just one report from 1972 that describes tourists harassing lions and interfering with their hunting of food for cubs in a northern Tanzania park, Bonner makes the astonishing assertion that "tourism may even kill more animals than hunters do. It sometimes prevents mothers from feeding their families."

And taking the worst example of the misbehavior and excesses of tourists, he paints the extreme as the typical, accusing tourists of cheating and humiliating natives, and even encouraging begging and prostitution:

> There is another argument for hunting. Tourists assault the dignity and cultures of indigenous people, snapping pictures as if the

person were one of the wild animals, bargaining for jewelry or clothing that the person is wearing and "paying" with a few shillings. The hunter, however, makes only limited contact with local people. Squalid villages with prostitutes and begging children do not spring up near hunters' wilderness camps, as they do near high-rise tourist hotels.

Bonner thus replaces the literary stereotype of the "noble savage" with that of the "noble hunter," who demonstrates his respect for the dignity of the natives by paying to shoot their local wildlife.[61]

An IUCN study by Héctor Ceballos-Lascuráin discusses in a more objective way how the rapidly growing popularity of nature-based tourism can present potential problems as well as opportunities:

It is quite clear that unless this growth receives careful and professional guidance, serious negative consequences—some of which may have terminal effects—could occur . . .

But, he points out, if ecotourism is properly organized, it can offer many social and economic benefits, such as:

. . . generating foreign exchange, creating local employment, stimulating national and local economies, and fostering international peace and increased environmental awareness and education. But appropriate management structure, as well as adequate planning, design, and building guidelines for tourism facilities are required to ensure that tourism enhances rather than detracts from the natural setting. Further, carrying capacity needs to be assessed relative to the management objectives of each area, and appropriate management and physical structures must be designed to keep the number of visitors and the visitation model within the carrying capacity. . . .

Ceballos-Lascuráin warns, however:

If uncontrolled mass tourism is allowed to continue overrunning many areas of natural and cultural significance, irreversible damage will occur in these areas, which are the repositories of biological and cultural diversity in the planet, as well as important sources of income and well being for all countries.

One way he advocates to ensure a "symbiotic relationship between tourism and natural areas" is to use "ecotechniques" to combine an attractive design for physical facilities with a "harmonious interaction with nature." Among the recommended procedures are the use of waste recycling, solar energy, rainwater collection, and local foods and building materials.[62]

The National Audubon Society, which conducts two to three dozen wilderness excursions every year, has developed a code of ethics for nature tourism based on seven guidelines:

1. Wildlife and their habits must not be disturbed.
2. Tourism to natural areas will be sustainable.
3. Waste disposal must have neither environmental nor esthetic impacts.
4. The experience a tourist gains must enrich his or her appreciation of nature, conservation, and the environment.
5. Tours must strengthen the conservation effort and enhance the natural integrity of places visited.
6. Traffic in products that threaten wildlife and plant populations must not occur.
7. The sensibilities of other cultures must be respected.[63]

One ecotourism entrepreneur who has shown that he can do well while doing good is Stanley Selengut, who is described as "an international role model in making environmentalism pay." In 1976, he developed an environmentally sensitive beachfront resort, Maho Bay, on the island of St. John in the U.S. Virgin Islands National Park. In order to disturb as little as possible of the natural ground cover, the 114 rustic tent cabins on Maho Bay were built on stilts and connected by elevated walkways without the use of heavy construction equipment. Waste material is treated and recycled on site in such a way as to enrich the natural vegetation, which provides habitat for insect-controlling birds, frogs, and lizards. The resort is highly successful, attracting 7,000 visitors and bringing in $200,000 a year.

In 1993, Selengut opened another project on St. John called Harmony, a "luxury" resort consisting of three-story cabins built mainly from scrap lumber, discarded tires, and recycled plastic and glass, and run on solar and wind power. Solar power fuels even the ice machines and ovens. In addition to beaches, snorkeling, and scuba diving, both resorts offer lectures and educational material on local wildlife, conservation, and sustainability.[64]

Ecotourism is not without its dangers. But if carefully controlled, it can represent an ideal application of "sustainable utilization" of wildlife that benefits people, animals, and the environment. As Ted T. Cable of

Kansas State University, puts it, "The challenge upon which the future of ecotourism depends is the ability to carry out tours which the clients find rewarding, without degrading the natural or cultural resources upon which it is based."[65]

CHAPTER 11

Appreciating Animals for Their Own Intrinsic Value

> In the past, we have tried to make a distinction between animals which we acknowledge have some value, and others which, having none, can be liquidated when we wish. This standard must be abandoned. Everything that lives has value simply as a living thing, as one of the manifestations of the mystery that is life.
>
> Albert Schweitzer[1]

There is one fundamentally important point that *must* be widely understood and accepted if the world's wildlife is to be saved. In addition to the cold, practical reasons for preserving species, we must learn to appreciate wildlife for its intrinsic value, to respect its innate right to exist, and to have humane concern for the suffering of *individual* animals as well as for the survival of entire species. This is the single most important factor that has been missing from traditional wildlife management and conservation policies—the ethical dimension, a concern for the well-being of the individual animals as well as for the overall species.

A philosophy that ignores this, and cares little or nothing about the suffering of animals, finds itself in a hopelessly contradictory position. It argues, on the one hand, that these are beautiful, interesting, valuable species, that they are of great importance to humanity, and that they must be saved for future generations. But on the other hand, wildlife managers condone, encourage, and even require the killing—for fun, recreation, and profit—of the individual animals. But if we erode respect for individual animals, and kill enough of them, the species itself disappears.

Over the long term, what is now euphemistically called "sustainable use" of wildlife cannot succeed in protecting and preserving viable populations of wild animals. It will instead reduce their numbers and increase the number of species being subjected to commercial trade. The result will be the virtual or actual extinction of many of them, as has happened in the past, and as is happening now with various species throughout Africa and the rest of the world. This is clearly demonstrated by the numerous precedents and studies cited earlier in this book.

In addition to the fact that it simply does not work from a conservation standpoint, the philosophy of sustainable use lacks a moral and ethical underpinning that would give it credibility, integrity, and consistency. It judges animals primarily in economic terms, on their financial worth to humans, ignoring almost completely their feelings, their suffering, and their innate value. It encourages people to kill only a limited number of animals, and to save the rest for their continuing, long-term economic value.

But what if the people in an area can make more from killing off the local animals and using their habitat for farming or mining? Under the concept of sustainable use, what philosophical or ethical principles would effectively prevent this from happening?

If we are to save the world's wildlife, especially that of Africa, we must learn to appreciate animals for their own intrinsic worth. The other rationales we concoct to persuade people to protect wildlife will never be sufficient by themselves to guarantee its ultimate survival.

The bottom line is that wildlife cannot continue to be killed and otherwise used on a large scale for sport and profit without jeopardizing its ultimate survival. If wildlife is to continue to exist, it must be protected and appreciated for its own innate value, and cherished as a precious natural heritage.

As Jan Hartke, the respected president of EarthKind International, once observed:

> In the final analysis, if we are to succeed in saving the beauty, diversity, and life of our planet, people must fall in love with the earth and the animals that call it home. Appeals to utilitarian purposes, while valuable, cannot ultimately succeed without a spiritual dimension that is centered on a deep reverence for life. [2]

It is time for governments, wildlife officials, and conservationists around the world to adopt and promote a new ethic on the conservation of wildlife, one that includes a humane concern for the well-being of individual animals themselves as well as the species.

WILDLIFE MUST BECOME
A SOURCE OF PRIDE AND REVERENCE

Promoting conservation by stimulating humane and ethical attitudes towards animals is based on more than emotional and moral concerns; there are cold, practical ones as well. There is a millennia-long history of human reverence for animals and the natural world.

As the world becomes increasingly overpopulated with people, crowding out and killing off other creatures, wildlife's only real chance for survival is to become a source of human pride and reverence. Most species cannot justify their existence or "pay their own way" through hunting, commercial trade, or tourism. Indeed, promoting reverence and respect for animals is incompatible with regarding them as sources of revenue, to be killed and sold. As author Conger Beasley, Jr., has observed, to people who love and respect animals, the rhetoric of sustainable use is "too crass and utilitarian" to be acceptable; "It reduces animals to quantifiable units and ignores the emotional and mythological dimensions many animals have for the people who live alongside them."[3]

Dr. Richard Mordi, in his 1991 book, *Attitudes Toward Wildlife in Botswana*, discusses how the beliefs and values of local peoples are fundamentally important in determining the success of wildlife conservation efforts in Africa. He strongly condemns the concept of sustainable use:

> In spite of the provision that any commercial utilization of wildlife be sustainable, state classification of wildlife and public perception of animals as a resource to be utilized is ominous. The requirement that wildlife justify its existence economically must be seen as a potential threat to the long-term goals of conservation. Such a philosophy clouds the future of fauna conservation in the country.

Mordi goes on to point out the futility of trying to convince people to conserve wildlife solely as an economic resource:

> It seems as though the future of wildlife will remain precarious until animals are redefined not exclusively as a resource, but as an irreplaceable heritage whose legitimate owner is the future generations of Botswana. Wildlife begins to face a mortal dilemma the moment a generation understands itself to be its sole proprietor, rather than its provisional custodian.[4]

Many Native Americans took into account such true sustainability. Their attitude is demonstrated by the now widely popularized saying, "We do not inherit the earth from our parents. We borrow it from our children." And the six nations of the Iroquois Confederacy and the Sioux Indians based their decision-making processes on considering the effects an action would have on their next seven generations.[5]

The solution, Mordi believes, is to instill in local populations an appreciation for the intrinsic value of wild animals, a goal that has so far proved elusive:

> At the time of writing [1991], no country in sub-Saharan Africa can boast of a large number of indigenous citizens who, in the light of a rapid decline in wildlife populations, feel a personal sense of loss . . . Until middle class indigenous defenders of wildlife emerge, personal involvement in conservation will remain extremely low in the larger public in sub-Sahara Africa.

Mordi lists among "the somber findings" of his study the existence of "a popular perception of wildlife and its habitat as a means to other material ends, particularly at the grass roots level." He concludes that:

> In light of these somber findings, optimism about the future of wildlife in Botswana must be tempered with a sense of uncertainty . . . The widespread perception of animals as a means to other ends in Botswana, unless reversed, is likely to continue to drive more species into extinction.[6]

HUMAN REVERENCE FOR ANIMALS

Through the ages, from the very beginning of recorded history, humans have demonstrated an interest in, and a respect for, the welfare of animals. Such concern has often had a religious basis or manifestation; reverence toward animals has, from the dawn of civilization, characterized human societies throughout the world. Even today, there is deep within our psyches an arcane yet profound understanding that remembers our being part of nature and living alongside the animals. Some scientists believe that humans instinctively yearn for a renewal of this kinship with nature and our fellow creatures.

This "eco-spirituality" is reflected in many of the teachings of the world's major religions, as well as in the spirituality of indigenous peoples, who have traditionally respected and even revered animals as integral parts of their communities and cultures.

THE WORLD'S RELIGIONS TEACH CONSERVATION

It is a little-known fact that *all* of the world's major faiths have, as important parts of their laws and traditions, teachings requiring protection of the environment, respect for nature and wildlife, and kindness to animals.

While it is well known that such tenets are part of some Eastern religions, such as Buddhism and Hinduism, there is also a largely forgotten but remarkably strong tradition of such teachings in Christianity, Judaism, and Islam.

All of these faiths recognize a doctrine of God's love for all creation, and for all of the living creatures of the world. The obligations of humans to respect and protect the natural environment and other life forms appears throughout the sacred writings of the prophets and leaders of the world's great religions.

These tenets of "environmental theology" contained in the world's religions are little known and seldom discussed, much less widely observed or practiced. But the widespread contemporary ignorance of these teachings makes them no less important. Indeed, they are more relevant today than ever, for at a time when the earth faces a potentially fatal ecological crisis, traditional religion shows us a way to preserve our planet and the life forms living and dependent on it.

The Bible's Ecological Message

The early founders and followers of monotheism were filled with a sense of wonder, delight, and awe by the beauty of creation and the seeming wisdom of wild creatures. Indeed, nature and wildlife were sources of inspiration for many of the prophets of the Bible, and one cannot fully understand the scriptures, or their teachings and symbolism, without an appreciation for the natural environment that inspired so much of what appears in them.

The Bible clearly imparts a reverence for life—for God's creation, if you will—which humans were given the responsibility to care for as good stewards. It teaches that if we despoil nature, we are destroying God's handiwork and violating our sacred trust as its caretakers.

There is nothing in the Bible that would justify our modern-day policies and programs that despoil the land, desecrate the environment, and destroy entire species of wildlife. Such actions clearly violate God's commands to humans to "replenish the earth," to conserve natural resources, and to treat animals with kindness, as well as subverting God's instructions to the animals to "be fruitful and multiply" and fill the earth.

In contrast, there are various laws requiring the protection of natural resources to be found in the Mosaic law, including passages mandating the preservation of fruit trees (Deuteronomy 20:19, Genesis 19:23–25); agricultural lands (Leviticus 25:2–4); and wildlife (Deuteronomy 22:6–7, Genesis 9). The Bible often refers to the impressive intelligence of wild creatures, such as in Jeremiah 8:7–8, Proverbs 6:6–8 and 30:24–8, Numbers 22:22–35, and Isaiah 1:3. Numerous other Biblical passages extol the wonders of nature and teach kindness to animals—even including the Ten Commandments, which require that farm animals be allowed to rest on the Sabbath.[7]

Eastern Religions' Reverence for Life

Some Eastern religions are even more emphatic in advocating or requiring respect for animals. Both Hinduism and Buddhism are well known for teaching concern and compassion for all living creatures and for the sanctity of nature and the earth. Such precepts are the cornerstones of these faiths. What is not as widely appreciated is that the Muslim religion, in its laws and traditions, contains extremely strict prohibitions against cruelty to animals and destruction of the natural environment. The Prophet Mohammed taught that animals and natural resources, such as trees, should always be treated with reverence, and that respect for nature is extremely important.[8]

Such principles are, unfortunately, not as widely practiced as they are preached; but there has been some useful application of them. Several groups worldwide are working to apply Buddhist ideals to current problems facing animals and the environment. In October 1985, Buddhist leaders from Thailand and Tibet announced that they were joining forces to try to halt the destruction of the natural environment, calling on Buddhists everywhere to join the campaign. These efforts have been endorsed and supported by the Dalai Lama and other Buddhist leaders worldwide.

Buddhist perspectives have already been effective in influencing the policies of governments and populations of some Asian nations. For example, Sri Lanka has over 17 million people, 70 percent of them Buddhist and 20 percent Hindu. Although the nation is poor and overpopulated, it is still "a country of wildlife, a place where people and wildlife have lived together in a system of mutual tolerance for centuries," according to Dr. Chatsumarn Kabilsingh of Thammasat University in Bangkok, Thailand. Kabilsingh writes:

Buddhist teachings emphasize the importance of coexisting with nature rather than conquering it. Devout Buddhists admire a conserving lifestyle rather than one which is profligate.

The very core of Buddhism evolves around compassion, encouraging a better respect for and tolerance of every human being and living thing sharing the planet.

Wherever Buddhism is influential, studies will usually show some direct benefit for the natural world. In Sri Lanka, predominantly Buddhist, crowded by Western standards, wildlife has not been virtually eliminated as it has been in many parts of the world. The reason, according to researchers, is the country's largely religious and devout population.

Formal protection generally results from government action, but such actions, it is felt, would never have made much effect if they were not readily accepted by the people. Successful conservation there is based on deep philosophical convictions.[9]

In Thailand, Buddhist influence has helped conserve much of the native wildlife. Dr. Kabilsingh observes that the last remaining refuge for the nation's open-billed storks is Wat Phai Lom, a Buddhist temple near Bangkok:

Open-billed storks would be extinct in Thailand but for the fact their last remaining breeding ground is within the sanctuary of this temple.

Ecologists point out it is scientifically important to save this species of bird, whose sole diet is a local, rice-devouring species of snail. Without the storks, the snails would proliferate, then pesticides would be brought in, and an unnecessary, poisonous cycle would go into effect.

Buddhist precepts of personal and social conduct can take much of the credit for saving the open-billed stork in Thailand . . . It is likely that, like the open-billed stork, much of what still survives of the natural world here is linked, in varying degrees, to the influence of Buddhism, the philosophy's focus on awareness, attitudes, and actions which should never harm, and ideally should actively help, all life on earth.[10]

In order to save the rain forests of northeast Thailand, Buddhist monks have even "ordained" trees, clothing them in the sacred orange robs of holy men in an effort to make the cutting of a tree tantamount to the unpardonable sin of killing a monk.[11]

Many of India's most successful and prosperous citizens are adherents of Jainism, a religion so strict in its avoidance of harming living creatures that Jainist monks, when walking outside, wear masks over their mouths and sweep the paths in front of them to avoid inhaling or crushing insects. The Jains have built animal sanctuaries and hospitals throughout the country, where stray and injured camels, cows, water buffalo, pigeons, parrots, and other creatures are cared for.[12]

With some 2 billion Buddhists, Hindus, and Moslems in Africa, Asia, and the Middle East, there is obviously great potential for stimulating a spiritually based appreciation for nature and wildlife in much of the Third World.

Indigenous Peoples' Respect for Animals

Many other religions, including the Baha'i faith and those of Native Americans, Amazon Indian tribes, and other indigenous peoples, stress the sanctity of nature, and the need to conserve wildlife, forests, plants, water, fertile land, and other natural resources.

Native American peoples were shocked by the Europeans' callous and destructive attitude toward what the Native Americans considered kindred creatures and sacred land. The feelings of many of them were expressed eloquently (if apocryphally) in words popularly attributed to Chief Sealth of the Duwamish tribe in Washington state in the mid-1800s. He is purported to have pleaded with the Europeans about to take his land to preserve it and cherish it, saying:

> If I decide to accept your offer to buy our land, I will make one condition. The white man must treat the beasts of this land as his brothers. I am a savage and do not understand any other way . . . What is a man without the beasts? If all the beasts are gone, men would die from great loneliness of spirit, for whatever happens to the beasts also happens to man.[13]

One of our best opportunities to preserve wildlife and wilderness, and to gain the support of local people in this struggle, is to respect, promote, and help support the reverence toward animals and nature of faiths and cultures the world over. We do not have to invent new religions or philosophies in order to save the planet; we just have to return to the roots of our old ones.

THE CONSEQUENCES OF DISRESPECTING NATURE

Although we in the West have lost much of this traditional spiritual appreciation of nature, we are now learning how dangerous it can be to disregard and disrespect the importance of the natural environment.

Some of the world's top scientists have recently alerted us, in "The World Scientists' Warning to Humanity" to the fact that, because of our abuse of nature, the world *really* may be coming to an end:

> We hereby warn all humanity of what lies ahead. A great change in our stewardship of the Earth and the life on it is required if vast human misery is to be avoided, and our global home on this planet is not to be irretrievably mutilated.[14]

This statement was issued on November 18, 1992, by 1,575 of the world's top scientists from sixty-nine different countries, including 99

Nobel Prize winners in the sciences, and representing, in the words of one participant, "the largest group of senior scientists from around the world to ever speak in unison on a single issue." Their warning goes on to observe, "Much of this damage is irreversible on a scale of centuries or permanent . . . If not checked, many of our current practices put at serious risk the future that we wish for human society and the plant and animal kingdoms, and may so alter the living world that it will be unable to sustain life in the manner that we know."[15]

Harvard Professor of Science Edward O. Wilson, perhaps the world's foremost authority on biodiversity, expressed similar views in his May 30, 1993, cover article in *The New York Times Magazine* entitled "Is Humanity Suicidal? We're Flirting with the Extinction of Our Species":

> Many of earth's vital resources are about to be exhausted . . . Natural ecosystems . . . are being irreversibly degraded . . . we are dismantling a support system that is too complex to understand, let alone replace, in the foreseeable future . . . Earth is destined to become an impoverished planet within a century if present trends continue.[16]

As Paul G. Irwin, president of The Humane Society of the United States (HSUS), has written, we are facing a catastrophe of unprecedented proportions that ultimately threatens the well-being and indeed the survival of humans on this planet:

> Today, there are about a dozen critical environmental problems we face, any *one* of which could be devastating to society—and *all* of which are becoming increasingly unmanageable. Unfortunately *none* of the major environmental problems is being adequately addressed, and *all* are getting worse. There is a growing consensus among top scientists and experts that the combination of these problems is leading us to disaster.
>
> . . . the ongoing human destruction of the natural environment is damaging, permanently, irreversibly, and perhaps fatally, the earth's ability to support life.
>
> If we do not act quickly to halt this devastation, and begin to repair what damage we can, humans and most other life forms will not have a long-term future on the planet. Human activity has done more damage to the planet in the last 50 years than in all of the rest of recorded history . . . And if we continue these policies for the next decade or two, we will destroy essential ecological and agricultural systems on which we all depend.[17]

A major problem in our environmental crisis is the massive destruction of wildlife and its habitat. According to the best scientific estimates, each year we condemn to extinction—in vanishing tropical rain forests alone—one species of animal, bird, or plant *every day*.[18]

In destroying and persecuting animals, we do more than harm these creatures; we harm ourselves as well. Cruelty to and abuse of animals do not just reflect the indifference of individuals, corporations, and governments. If tolerated, approved, and permitted to continue, they become the hallmarks of a society—a society whose values are selfish and short-sighted; whose policies are inhumane and unsustainable; and whose inheritance bequeathed to future generations will be empty.

But I believe there is hope for our planet, for our wildlife—and for ourselves.

I see hope that we are beginning to acknowledge that other creatures are, like ourselves, capable of intelligently experiencing pain and misery. We are starting to understand that animals are deserving of some consideration that would spare them, as much as possible, undue abuse and suffering.

Our best hope, I think, lies with those persons who, at least in their better moments, are able to view themselves, and humans in general, as only one part of a very complex and marvelous world, rather than as its master. It lies with those who have chosen to accept the proposition that all life has intrinsic value and is therefore deserving of some of those same considerations we generally reserve for humankind. It lies with those whose vision for a better world is not restricted to a better life for themselves, but includes the welfare of their fellow inhabitants of the globe. And it lies with those who understand that being truly human means being truly humane, and that the wanton and needless destruction of other creatures damages ourselves as human beings.

The most heartening—indeed, amazing—thing is the extraordinary progress we have made, against all odds, over the last two decades in securing protection for so much of our wildlife and its habitat. For this, we can primarily thank the many hard-working, dedicated people in the wildlife protection movement who have persevered, even when it seemed hopeless, against well-funded, well-connected interests, to fight the good fight.

But there is still much to be done, so we will continue this struggle until it is won. And someday, it will be won, because humans will eventually realize that ultimately, we have no choice. If our civilization is to survive, we must protect and save those treasures of nature that make our lives pleasant, prosperous—even possible.

The author of the book of Ecclesiastes, writing thousands of years ago, understood that if wildlife perishes, humans will not long survive:

> For that which befalleth the sons of men befalleth beasts, even one thing befalleth them: as the one dieth, so dieth the other, yea, they have all one breath; so that a man hath no preeminence above a beast.[19]

If humans and wildlife will share the same fate—and our best scientists tell us it is increasingly obvious that we will—we must act quickly and do all that we can to ensure a secure future for ourselves, and for those with whom we share the earth. And we cannot rest until the job is done.

Conclusion

As this book extensively details and documents, a major move is underway, under the euphemism of "sustainable use," to turn much of the world's wildlife into a commercial commodity, to be raised and harvested like a crop and sold for profit, like corn or beans.

But this does *not* have to happen. Animal protection groups in several countries are fighting to secure and maintain protection for wild animals from the changes in conservation policy being proposed and promoted by sustainable use advocates.

The current major fight centers on African elephants, and whether their nascent recovery from a decade of uncontrolled poaching should now be aborted by permitting a resumption of international trade in elephant tusks, skins, or meat.

Battles are also underway over resuming commercial whaling, crippling the Endangered Species Act, and weakening the Convention on International Trade in Endangered Species of Wild Fauna and Flora (CITES).

But the battle is not just over the killing of wildlife for commerce, but also over the principles that will drive our nation, and the world. A civilized world must reject the frivolous destructive use of wildlife, rather embracing wildlife as a treasure and heritage of the earth. What is needed for the new millennium is not a philosophy of death, but rather a philosophy of life — of humane stewardship for all creatures.

Individual citizens as well as organized groups can have an impact on influencing public policy. Anyone interested in protecting wildlife should speak up and speak out on these issues.

You can write to your senators, your congressional representative, and other elected officials, and get your friends and family to do the same. Letters to legislators can make a tremendous difference in how they vote on such issues, and are really the most important weapon we have in fighting the powerful, influential, well-funded lobbyists and special interests that are constantly working to deny protection to wildlife and its habitat.

Since the issues and crises of the day are frequently changing, the best way to get involved and keep up with what is happening is to join one of the preservation-oriented wildlife and animal protection groups. I am particularly proud of the work done by the group that I have had the honor to lead for the past quarter-century, The Humane Society of the United States (HSUS). The HSUS sends out regular bulletins, alerts, fact sheets, magazines, and other material reporting current events, and telling people what they can do about the problems and to whom they should write. The HSUS is located at 2100 L Street NW, Washington, D.C. 20037.

For centuries, humans have exploited other creatures for every imaginable purpose (and some that were pretty unimaginable). We have cruelly plundered and persecuted wild animals to satisfy our own needs and whims, with little regard for the creatures' welfare or, too often, the needs of future generations of humans.

Now, with wildlife throughout the world endangered by a variety of threats, and many species facing extinction, we are finally coming to realize that there is a limit to the exploitation animals can sustain.

Indeed, this generation of humans holds in its hands the fate of the world's wild animals. The decisions we make today will determine the future of wildlife, and perhaps our own future as well.

Notes

Part I: The Myth of Sustainable Use

Introduction

1. Lee M. Talbot, *Principles for Living Resource Conservation*, Marine Mammal Commission, Draft Preliminary Report on Consultations, Washington, D.C., September 1993, p. 6.
2. John G. Robinson,"The Limits to Caring: Sustainable Living and the Loss of Biodiversity," *Conservation Biology*, March 1993, p. 21.
3. Donald Ludwig, Ray Hilborn, and Carl Walters, "Uncertainty, Resource Exploitation, and Conservation: Lessons From History," *Science*, 2 April 1993, pp. 17, 36.
4. Talbot, *Principles for Living Resource Conservation*, p. 5.

Chapter 1
Sustainable Use of Wildlife—Utopian Dream, or Unrealistic Nightmare?

1. Michael Satchell, "Wildlife's Last Chance," *U.S. News & World Report*, 15 November 1993, pp. 69–70.
2. John W. Grandy, The Humane Society of the United States, Washington, D.C., personal communication, 22 June 1994.
3. Paul Irwin, The Humane Society of the United States, Washington, D.C., personal communication, 20 June 1994.

4. Grandy, personal communication.
5. Satchell, "Wildlife's Last Chance."
6. David S. Favre, "Debate Within the CITES Community," *Natural Resources Journal*, Fall 1993, p. 879.
7. William K. Stevens, "Biologists Fear Sustainable Yield Is Unsustainable Idea," *The New York Times*, Science Section, 20 April 1993.
8. World Conservation Union, United Nations Environment Program, and World Wide Fund for Nature, *Caring for the Earth: A Strategy for Sustainable Living* (Gland, Switzerland: United Nations Environment Program, October 1991), p. 10.
9. Steve Edwards, "Sustainable Use: An Alternative to Protecting Species," *Interact*, December 1992.
10. Teresa Telecky, The Humane Society of the United States, Washington, D.C., personal communication, 22 June 1994.
11. Ibid.
12. Favre, "Debate Within the CITES Community," p. 915.
13. Martin Holdgate, "Using Wildlife Sustainably," *People and the Planet*, Vol. 2, No. 3 (1993), p. 27.
14. Allan Thornton and Dave Currey, *To Save an Elephant* (London: Doubleday, 1991), p. 187.
15. Favre, "Debate Within the CITES Community," p. 885.
16. Ibid.
17. Ibid., pp. 885–886, 918.
18. Conger Beasley, Jr., "Live and Let

Die," *Buzzworm: The Environmental Journal*, July/August 1992, pp. 33, 53.

19. Ibid.

20. Stephen Mills, "Species Bought Off Endangered List," *BBC Wildlife*, February 1994.

21. Ibid.

22. Izgrev Topkov, letter to *BBC Wildlife*, 25 February 1994.

23. Ibid.

24. Favre, "Debate Within the CITES Community," p. 904.

25. Izgrev Topkov, letter to *BBC Wildlife*.

26. Ronald Orenstein, letter to *BBC Wildlife*, June 1994.

27. *Caring for the Earth*, p. 1.

28. John. G. Robinson, "The Limits to Caring: Sustainable Living and the Loss of Biodiversity," *Conservation Biology*, March 1993, p. 22.

29. Ibid.

30. Herman E. Daly, "Sustainable Development Is Possible Only if We Forgo Growth," *Earth Island Journal*, Spring 1992, p. 12.

31. *Caring for the Earth*, p. 3.

32. Robinson, "The Limits to Caring," pp. 20–23.

33. Telecky, personal communication.

34. *Caring for the Earth*, p. 4.

35. Ibid., p. 28.

36. Ibid., p. 14.

37. Ibid., pp. 14–15.

38. Robinson, "The Limits to Caring," pp. 20–26.

39. Donald Ludwig, Ray Hilborn, and Carl Walters, "Uncertainty, Resource Exploitation, and Conservation: Lessons From History," *Science*, 2 April 1993, pp. 17, 36.

40. Lee M. Talbot, "Principles for Living Resource Conservation," U.S. Marine Mammal Commission, Draft Preliminary Report on Consultations, Washington, D.C., September 1993.

41. Ibid., p. 6.

42. Ibid., p. 15.

43. Ibid., p. 5.

44. Ibid., p. 27.

45. Ibid., p. 41.

46. Ibid., p. 21–22.

47. Ibid., p. 38.

48. Ibid.

49. John W. Grandy, The Humane Society of the United States, Washington, D.C., personal communication, 25 May 1994.

50. Thomas L. Friedman, "U.S. Puts Sanctions on Taiwan," *The New York Times*, 12 April 1994, pp. C1, C6.

51. Valerius Geist, "Wildlife Conservation as Wealth," *Nature*, 7 April 1994, pp. 491–492.

52. Ibid.

53. Grandy, personal communication, 25 May 1994.

54. Geist, "Wildlife Conservation as Wealth."

55. Ibid.

56. Lewis Regenstein, *The Politics of Extinction*, (New York: Macmillan, 1975), p. x.

57. Ibid.

58. United Press International, "Countries Join in Effort to Save Tigers," 4 March, 1994.

Teresa Telecky, The Humane Society of the United States, statement before the U.S. House of Representatives Merchant Marine and Fisheries Committee on measures to conserve rhinoceroses, 3 November 1993.

Friedman, "U.S. Puts Sanctions on Taiwan."

Thomas L. Friedman, "Taiwan's Wildlife Trade Draws Call for Sanctions," *The New York Times*, 7 April 1994.

59. Telecky, statement before the U.S. House of Representatives Merchant Marine and Fisheries Committee.

Friedman, "U.S. Puts Sanctions on Taiwan."

Friedman, "Taiwan's Wildlife Trade Draws Call for Sanctions."

60. Ian Redmond and Esmond Bradley Martin, "Don't Argue—Save the Rhino," *BBC Wildlife*, November 1992.

Friedman, "Taiwan's Wildlife Trade Draws Call for Sanctions."

61. Friedman, "Taiwan's Wildlife Trade Draws Call for Sanctions."

Friedman, "U.S. Puts Sanctions on Taiwan."

62. Satchell, "Wildlife's Last Chance," p. 69.

Telecky, statement before the U.S. House of Representatives Merchant Marine and Fisheries Committee.

63. Friedman, "U.S. Puts Sanctions on Taiwan."

64. Friedman, "U.S. Puts Sanctions on Taiwan."

Friedman, "Taiwan's Wildlife Trade Draws Call for Sanctions."

65. Satchell, "Wildlife's Last Chance," pp. 70–72.

66. Ibid.

67. Telecky, personal communication.

Beasley, "Live and Let Die," p. 33.

68. Geist, "Wildlife Conservation as Wealth."

Chapter 2
Case Studies of Sustainable Use

1. Dr. Charles Munn, Wildlife Conservation International, letter to Congressman Gerry Studds, 7 May 1991.

"Flight to Extinction: The Wild-Caught Bird Trade," Animal Welfare Institute and the Environmental Investigation Agency, Washington, D.C., 1992, p. 13.

2. Lee M. Talbot, "Principles for Living Resource Conservation," The Marine Mammal Commission, Draft Preliminary Report on Consultations, Washington, D.C., September 1993.

3. Dereck Joubert, *Report on the Hunting Concession Areas (Linyati/Selinda/James' Camp)*, report to the Director of Wildlife, members of the Tawana Land Board, and the Office of the President of Botswana, 1993.

"Filmmaker Claims Northern Botswana's Wildlife Is in Serious Decline; Blames Overhunting," *African Wildlife*, September-October 1993.

4. "Facts About the Wild Bird Trade,"

"U.S. Bird Importation Facts," "Please Help Us Stop This Cruelty," and "The Pet Trade in Wild-Caught Birds," The Humane Society of the United States, Washington, D.C., undated.

"Flight to Extinction," p. 4.

Animal Welfare Institute Quarterly, Summer 1992, Fall 1992.

5. Ibid.

6. "The Pet Trade in Wild-Caught Birds."

7. Teresa Telecky, The Humane Society of the United States, Washington, D.C., personal communication, 30 June 1994.

8. Ibid.

9. Steven R. Beissinger and Enrique H. Bucher, "Can Parrots Be Conserved Through Sustainable Harvesting?" *BioScience*, March 1992, p. 164.

10. "Flight to Extinction," p. 24.

11. Ibid., p. 5.

12. Telecky, personal communication.

13. Ibid.

14. "Flight to Extinction," p. 23.

15. "Spix's Macaw: The Last Wild Bird," *Birds International*, Vol. 3, No. 1.

Telecky, personal communication.

16. Bruce Babbitt, "An Environmental Agenda for the 1990's," *HSUS News*, Spring 1993, pp. 18–20.

17. *Humane Society of the United States et al. v. Bruce Babbitt et. al.*, U.S. District Court for the District of Columbia, 29 March 1994.

HSUS News, Spring 1994, p. 3.

18. "U.S. District Court Finds for HSUS in Wild Bird Lawsuit," The Humane Society of the United States, Washington, D.C., 4 April 1994.

19. "Wild Bird Act Under Attack," Society for Animal Protective Legislation, 1 June 1994.

20. Telecky, personal communication.

21. Beissinger and Bucher, "Can Parrots Be Conserved Through Sustainable Harvesting?" pp. 164–172.

22. Ibid.

23. Ibid.

24. Ibid.

25. Ibid.

26. Telecky, personal communication.

27. "Flight to Extinction," pp. 4, 12.

28. Ibid., p. 13.

29. David S. Favre, "Debate Within the CITES Community," *Natural Resources Journal*, Fall 1993, pp. 913–915.

Charles A. Munn, "Macaws," *National Geographic*, January 1994.

30. Ibid.

31. Charles H. Janson, "A Walk on the Wild Side," *Wildlife Conservation*, March/April 1994, p. 42.

32. Ibid., p. 36.

33. Ibid., p. 43.

34. Erich Hoyt, "Whale Watching Around the World," *International Whale Bulletin*, Summer 1992, pp. 1–8.

35. John Barbour, *International Wildlife*, cited in Lewis Regenstein, *The Politics of Extinction* (New York: MacMillan, 1975), p. 62.

36. Regenstein, *The Politics of Extinction*, p. 62.

37. The Associated Press, "Whaling Dispute Puts U.S. in Middle," *Washington Post*, 18 May 1994, p. A4.

Linda Kanamine, "Whaling Panel Faces 30-Foot 10-Ton Topic," *USA Today*, 23 May 1994.

38. Regenstein, *The Politics of Extinction* pp. 63–65.

Richard Ellis, *The Book of Whales* (New York: Knopf, 1980), pp. 50–58, 59–70.

39. *Report of the Scientific Committee*, International Whaling Commission, Puerto Vallarta, Mexico, 23 May 1994, p. 11.

40. Regenstein, *The Politics of Extinction* pp. 63–64.

Ellis, *The Book of Whales*, pp. 50–58, 59–70.

41. Ibid.

42. Ibid.

43. Ronald M. Nowak, comments submitted to the U.S. Fish and Wildlife Service on proposed rule to revise classification of the African elephant, 10 July 1991.

44. *Hunting Methods for Minke Whales in Norway, Report From the 1993 Scientific and Traditional Catch*, The Norwegian College of Veterinary Medicine, Oslo, Norway, May 1994.

45. Linda Kanamine, "Whaling Panel Faces 30-Foot 10-Ton Topic."

46. Animal Welfare Institute, "Blood and Gore," *The Washington Times*, 17 May 1994, p. A-5.

47. Birger Hofsten, vice president of Raufoss A/S, letter to The Humane Society of the United States, 26 April 1994.

Patricia Forkan, "HSUS Declares Boycott Victory," news release, The Humane Society of the United States, Washington, D.C., 30 September 1993.

48. Hofsten, letter to The Humane Society of the United States.

Forkan, "HSUS Declares Boycott Victory."

Patricia Forkan, personal communication, 30 June 1994.

49. "Resolution on Special Permit Catches by Japan in the North Pacific," Agenda Item 14, International Whaling Commission, 25 May 1994.

50. Patricia Forkan, personal communication, 6 July 1994.

Dave Currey, "The IWC: Broken Promises Threaten Whales and Dolphins," *The Animal Welfare Institute Quarterly*, Summer 1991, pp. 1, 6–7.

51. Currey, "The IWC: Broken Promises Threaten Whales and Dolphins," p. 7.

52. James Baker, statement on RMP/RMS resolution, International Whaling Commission, Puerto Vallarta, Mexico, 1 June 1994.

53. *Animal Welfare Institute Quarterly*.

54. The Associated Press, "Whaling Dispute Puts U.S. in Middle."

Linda Kanamine, "Whaling Panel Faces 30-Foot 10-Ton Topic."

55. Memorandum of conversation following the meeting between Vice President Gore of the U.S. and Prime Minister Brundtland of Norway, Washington, D.C., 5 October 1993.

56. Ibid.

57. Linda Kanamine, "Whaling Panel Faces 30-Foot 10-Ton Topic."

The Associated Press, "Whaling Dispute Puts U.S. in Middle."

58. Animal Welfare Institute, "Blood and Gore."

Animal Welfare Institute et al., "Vice President Gore Supports Norwegian Whaling," news release, 17 May 1994.

59. Ibid.

60. Alexey V. Yablokov, "Validity of Whaling Data," *Nature*, 13 January 1994.

61. Animal Welfare Institute, "Blood and Gore."

62. "Development of Molecular Genetic Methods for the Identification of Whale Products," paper submitted by the delegation of New Zealand to the International Whaling Commission, Puerto Vallarta, Mexico, May 1994.

63. Patricia Forkan, personal communication, 1 July 1994.

64. Forkan, personal communication.

"Whaling Around Antarctica Is Banned by World Body," *The New York Times*, 27 May 1994, p. 2.

65. Forkan, personal communication.

66. Scott Bronstein, "Sea's Bounty Reduced by Alarming Amounts," *The Atlanta Journal & Constitution*, 24 July 1993.

67. Michael D. Lemonick, "Too Few Fish in the Sea," *Time*, 4 April 1994, pp. 70–71.

Tom Knudson, "The Cod Shortage," *Wall Street Journal*, 22 March 1994, pp. A1, A5.

68. Timothy Egan, "U.S. Fishing Fleet Traveling Coastal Water Without Fish," *The New York Times*, 7 March 1994, pp. A1, A10.

69. Bronstein, "Sea's Bounty Reduced by Alarming Amounts."

Knudson, "The Cod Shortage."

Lemonick, "Too Few Fish in the Sea."

70. Knudson, "The Cod Shortage."

71. Ibid.

72. Knudson, "The Cod Shortage."

Living Oceans News, Winter 1993, p. 4.

73. *Living Oceans News*, Winter 1993.

74. Ibid.

75. Ginette Hemley, "CITES 1992: Endangered Treaty?" TRAFFIC USA, August 1992.

Conger Beasley, Jr. "Live and Let Die," *Buzzworm: The Environmental Journal*, July/August 1992, p. 53.

76. Hemley, "CITES 1992: Endangered Treaty?"

77. *Living Oceans News*, Winter 1993.

78. *Living Oceans News*, Winter 1993.

Bronstein, "Sea's Bounty Reduced by Alarming Amounts."

79. Bronstein, "Sea's Bounty Reduced by Alarming Amounts."

Lemonick, "Too Few Fish in the Sea."

"California Sharks Facing New Threat," *The Atlanta Journal & Constitution*, 16 April 1994.

80. Bronstein, "Sea's Bounty Reduced by Alarming Amounts."

81. "They Might as Well Use Dynamite," *The New York Times*, 12 April 1994.

82. Bronstein, "Sea's Bounty Reduced by Alarming Amounts."

83. Ibid.

84. Egan, "U.S. Fishing Fleet Traveling Coastal Water Without Fish."

85. Ibid.

86. Bronstein, "Sea's Bounty Reduced by Alarming Amounts."

"They Might as Well Use Dynamite."

"Our Living Oceans," National Marine Fisheries Service, Report on the Status of U.S. Living Marine Resources, 1992, Washington, D.C., December 1992, p. 29.

87. Ibid.

88. Ibid.

89. John Robbins, *Diet for a New America* (Walpole, N.H.: Stillpoint, 1987).

90. *Living Oceans News*," Winter 1993.

91. Michael H. Glantz and Lucy E. Feingold, eds., *Summary Report of the Climate Variability, Climate Change, and Fisheries Project*, National Center for Atmospheric Research, Boulder, Colorado, September, 1980, pp. 17–21.

92. *Ibid.*, pp. 22–23.

93. *Ibid.*, pp. 95–98.

94. William K Stevens, "Biologists Fear

Sustainable Yield Is Unsustainable Idea," *The New York Times*, Science Section, 20 April 1993.

Donald Ludwig, Ray Hilborn, and Carl Walters, "Uncertainty, Resource Exploitation and Conservation: Lessons From History," *Science*, 2 April 1993, pp. 17, 36.
95. John G. Robinson, "The Limits to Caring: Sustainable Living and the Loss of Biodiversity," *Conservation Biology*, March 1993, p. 25.
96. Ludwig et al., "Uncertainty, Resource Exploitation and Conservation."
97. Stevens, "Biologists Fear Sustainable Yield Is Unsustainable Idea."
98. Lee M. Talbot, "Principles for Living Resource Conservation," The Marine Mammal Commission, Draft Preliminary Report on Consultations, Washington, D.C., September 1993, pp. 8–9.
99. Ibid., pp. 9–11.
100. Ibid.
101. Paul W. Cook, Jr., "Commercial Fisheries Evade Conservation," letter to *The New York Times*, 30 March 1994.
102. John W. Grandy, The Humane Society of the United States, Washington, D.C., personal communication, 12 June 1994.
103. "1985 Waterfowl Breeding Surveys Find Duck Numbers the Lowest in 30 Years," U.S. Fish and Wildlife Service, Washington, D.C., 23 July 1985.
104. "Waterfowl: Status and Fall Flight Forecast, 1993," U.S. Fish and Wildlife Service, Washington, D.C., 25 July 1993, pp. 16–18, 24–25.

J.A. Dubovsky, et al., "Trends in Duck Breeding Populations, 1955–93," Office of Migratory Bird Management, U.S. Fish and Wildlife Services, 2 July 1993, pp. 1, 10–11.
105. U.S. Fish and Wildlife Service, *Draft Environmental Impact Statement on the Federal Aid to the States for Fish and Wildlife Restoration*, Washington, D.C., 1978.
106. Douglas H. Chadwick, *The Fate of the Elephant* (San Francisco: Sierra Club Books, 1992).

107. Douglas Chadwick, personal communication to Lewis Regenstein, 1976.
108. Ibid.
109. Ted Kerasote, *Bloodties* (New York: Random House, 1993).

Ted Williams, "Open Season on Endangered Species," *Audubon*, January 1991.
110. "Endangered Species Permit," *Federal Register*, 12 December 1978, p. 58121.
111. Richard M. Parsons, "Safari Club Gearing Up for IUCN's Debates," *Safari Times*, December 1993, p. 13.
112. Kerasote, *Bloodties*.

Williams, "Open Season on Endangered Species."
113. Parsons, "Safari Club Gearing Up for IUCN's Debates."
114. Richard M. Parsons, "SCI Testifies at House Hearings on Rhinos," *Safari Times*, December 1993, p. 3.
115. Raymond Bonner, "A Conservationist Argument for Hunting," *Wall Street Journal*, 14 May 1993.
116. William I. Morrill, "The Tourist Safari Hunter's Role in Conservation," *Safari Journal*, February 1994, p. 122.
117. Ibid., p. 123.
118. "Hunting Lobby Takes Aim at Marine Mammal Protection Act," *Wildlife Watch*, April 1994, pp. 1, 8.
119. John H. Cushman, Jr., "Revising of Law Protecting Dolphins Divides Conservationists," *The New York Times*, 14 March 1994, p. A10.
120. Wayne Pacelle, personal communication, 10 June 1994.
121. Telecky, personal communication, 21 June 1994.
122. Bill Keller, "$100,000 to Kill a Doddering Rhino?" *The New York Times*, 27 December 1992.
123. Caroline Alexander, "The Brigadier's Shooting Party," *The New York Times*, 13 November 1993, p. 23.
124. Ibid.
125. Allan Thornton and Dave Currey, *To Save an Elephant* (London: Doubleday, 1991), pp. 87–88.
126. Dereck Joubert, *Report on the Hunting*

Concession Areas (Linyati/Selinda/James' Camp).

"Filmmaker Claims Northern Botswana's Wildlife Is in Serious Decline; Blames Overhunting."

127. Ibid.
128. Ibid.
129. Ibid.
130. Ibid.
131. Ibid.
132. Ibid.
133. Ibid.
134. Ibid.
135. Ibid.
136. Ibid.

Section II: The Fight to Save the Elephants

Introduction

1. Ronald M. Nowak, comments submitted to the U.S. Fish and Wildlife Service on proposed rule to revise classification of the African elephant, 10 July 1991.
2. Ibid.

U.S. Fish and Wildlife Service, "Retention of Threatened Status for the Continental Population of. the African Elephant," *Federal Register*, 10 August 1992, p. 35481.
3. Conger Beasley, Jr., "Live and Let Die," *Buzzworm: The Environmental Journal*, July/August 1992, p. 53.

Chapter 3
America's Chance to Save Africa's Elephants

1. U.S. Fish and Wildlife Service, "Listing of the African Elephant as a Threatened Species," *Federal Register*, 12 May 1978, p. 20502.
2. Ronald M. Nowak, comments submitted to the U.S. Fish and Wildlife Service on proposed rule to revise classification of the African elephant, 10 July 1991.
3. Ibid.

U.S. Fish and Wildlife Service, "Reten-

tion of Threatened Status for the Continental Population of the African Elephant," *Federal Register*, 10 August 1992, p. 35481.
4. Iain and Oria Douglas-Hamilton, *Battle for the Elephants* (New York: Viking Penguin, 1992), p. 338.
5. U.S. Fish and Wildlife Service, "Listing of the African Elephant as a Threatened Species."

Fund for Animals, "African Elephant Threatened With Extinction," news release, Washington, D.C., 18 August 1977.
6. Fund for Animals, "African Elephant Threatened With Extinction."
7. *Federal Register*, 16 January 1978.
8. Ibid.

U.S. Fish and Wildlife Service, "Listing of the African Elephant as a Threatened Species," p. 20501.

Fund For Animals, "Survival of African Elephant Jeopardized," news release, Washington, D.C., 1 May 1978.
9. U.S. Fish and Wildlife Service, "Listing of the African Elephant as a Threatened Species," pp. 20500–20501.
10. Ibid.
11. Douglas-Hamilton, *Battle for the Elephants*, pp. 13–14.
12. U.S. Fish and Wildlife Service, "Listing of the African Elephant as a Threatened Species," p. 20501.

Raymond Bonner, "Crying Wolf Over Elephants," *The New York Times Magazine*, 7 February 1993, p. 30.
13. U.S. Fish and Wildlife Service, "Listing of the African Elephant as a Threatened Species," p. 20502.
14. Ibid.
15. Fund For Animals, "Survival of African Elephant Jeopardized."
16. Lewis Regenstein, personal communication, 12 May 1994.
17. Bonner, "Crying Wolf Over Elephants."
18. U.S. Fish and Wildlife Service, "Retention of Threatened Status for the Continental Population of the African Elephant.-

19. Confidential source, personal communication, 1988.

20. Nowak, comments submitted to the U.S. Fish and Wildlife Service on proposed rule to revise classification of the African elephant.

21. U.S. Fish and Wildlife Service, "Retention of Threatened Status for the Continental Population of the African Elephant," p. 35473.

Chapter 4
The Poaching Explosion of the 1980s

1. U.S. Fish and Wildlife Service, "Retention of Threatened Status for the Continental Population of the African Elephant," *Federal Register*, 10 August 1992, p. 35481.

2. Ibid.

Ronald M. Nowak, comments submitted to the U.S. Fish and Wildlife Service on proposed rule to revise classification of the African elephant, 10 July 1991.

William Conway, "What Happens to Elephants Goes Far Beyond Elephants," *Wildlife Conservation*, March/April 1993, p. 2.

Edward R. Ricciuti, "The Elephant Wars," *Wildlife Conservation*, March/April 1993, p. 16.

3. Conway, "What Happens to Elephants Goes Far Beyond Elephants."

4. Ibid.

Nowak, comments submitted to the U.S. Fish and Wildlife Service on proposed rule to revise classification of the African elephant.

Ricciuti, "The Elephant Wars."

5. Iain and Oria Douglas-Hamilton, *Battle for the Elephants* (New York: Viking Penguin, 1992), p. 338.

6. Riccuiti, "The Elephant Wars.".

7. U.S. Fish and Wildlife Service, "Retention of Threatened Status for the Continental Population of the African Elephant," p. 35479, 35480.

Environmental Investigation Agency, *Under Fire: Elephants in the Front Line,*

Washington, D.C., April 1992, pp. 9, 12–14, 40.

8. Nowak, comments submitted to the U.S. Fish and Wildlife Service on proposed rule to revise classification of the African elephant.

9. U.S. Fish and Wildlife Service, "Retention of Threatened Status for the Continental Population of the African Elephant," p. 35474.

10. Ibid., pp. 35477, 35480–35481.

11. Nowak, comments submitted to the U.S. Fish and Wildlife Service on proposed rule to revise classification of the African elephant.

12. U.S. Fish and Wildlife Service, "Retention of Threatened Status for the Continental Population of the African Elephant," p. 35481.

13. Ricciuti, "The Elephant Wars," p. 16.

14. Ibid.

15. Richard Leakey, "Elephants Today and Tomorrow," *Wildlife Conservation*, March/April 1993, p. 58.

16. Ibid.

17. Raymond Bonner, *At the Hand of Man* (New York: Knopf, 1993), p. 51.

18. Environmental Investigation Agency, *Under Fire*, pp. 9, 12–14.

19. Ibid.

U.S. Fish and Wildlife Service, "Retention of Threatened Status for the Continental Population of the African Elephant," p. 35480.

20. Environmental Investigation Agency, *Under Fire*.

21. Ibid., pp. 10, 14–15.

22. Ibid.

23. Ibid., p. 9.

24. Ibid., p. 13.

25. U.S. Fish and Wildlife Service, "Retention of Threatened Status for the Continental Population of the African Elephant," p. 35483.

26. Ibid., p. 35479.

Environmental Investigation Agency, *Under Fire*, p. 40.

27. Ibid., pp. 32, 40–41.

28. Ibid.

"The Great Wildlife Massacre," *Africa South*, October 1991.

29. Environmental Investigation Agency, *Under Fire*, pp. 32, 40–41.

30. Ibid.

31. U.S. Fish and Wildlife Service, "Retention of Threatened Status for the Continental Population of the African Elephant," pp. 35479–33482.

32. Deborah Scroggins, "Young's Talks With Ruler of Zaire," *Atlanta Constitution*, 7 April 1994, p. A10.

"Zaire Drifts Into Anarchy," *The New York Times*, 24 May 1994, p. A6.

33. Department of National Parks and Wildlife Management of Zimbabwe, "Zimbabwe: At the Leading Edge of Conservation," 20 November 1993, p. 5.

34. Environmental Investigation Agency, *Under Fire*, p. 20.

35. Ibid.

36. Ibid., p. 16.

37. Ibid.

38. Ibid., p. 17.

39. Ibid., pp. 12–13.

40. Ibid.

41. Ibid., pp. 18–19.

"Nleya's Enquiry: 3 Suspects Die Mysteriously," *Sunday Times* (South Africa), 17 November 1991.

"Zimbabwe Smugglers Kill Another Officer," *New African*, November 1991.

"Mystery Surrounds Soldier's Death," *The Sunday Mail* (Zimbabwe), 18 August 1991.

Julian Borger, "The Captain Who Knew Too Much," *The Sunday Correspondent* (London), 21 January 1990.

42. Borger, "The Captain Who Knew Too Much."

43. Environmental Investigation Agency, *Under Fire*, p. 18.

44. Ibid., pp. 19–20.

45. Ibid.

46. Borger, "The Captain Who Knew Too Much."

47. Environmental Investigation Agency, *Under Fire*, pp. 18–19.

48. Ibid.

49. Environmental Investigation Agency, "Zimbabwe—The Captain Nleye Case," *The Animal Welfare Institute Quarterly*, Washington, D.C., Winter 1992, p. 3.

50. Environmental Investigation Agency, *Under Fire* pp. 33–37.

Clyde Johnson, "Rhino Skeletons: Ranger in Court," *The Star* (South Africa), 8 August 1990.

"Secrets of Renamo's Ivory Trade Uncovered," *The Independent* (South Africa), 8 June 1991.

"War Veteran Links SADF to Unita Ivory Slaughter," *Sunday Times* (South Africa), 18 November 1989.

51. Environmental Investigation Agency, *Under Fire*, pp. 37–39.

52. Jim Motavalli, "Vendetta," *The Animals' Agenda*, May–June 1993, p. 23.

53. Ibid.

54. Ibid.

Environmental Investigation Agency, *Under Fire*, p. 33.

55. U.S. Fish and Wildlife Service, "Retention of Threatened Status for the Continental Population of the African Elephant," p. 35479.

56. Ibid..

Environmental Investigation Agency, *Under Fire*, pp. 48–49.

57. Ibid.

58. Ibid.

U.S. Fish and Wildlife Service, "Retention of Threatened Status for the Continental Population of the African Elephant."

59. Environmental Investigation Agency, *Under Fire*.

60. Ibid., pp. 51, 54.

Bonner, *At the Hand of Man*, p. 95.

61. Environmental Investigation Agency, *Under Fire*.

62. Ibid., p. 53.

63. Ibid., p. 52.

64. David K. Wills, personal communication, October 1993.

Chapter 5
How to Stop the Poaching

1. Allan Thornton and Dave Currey, *To Save an Elephant* (London: Doubleday, 1991), p. 37.
2. U.S. Fish and Wildlife Service, "Proposed Endangered Status for Certain Populations of the African Elephant," *Federal Register*, 18 March 1991, pp. 11392–11393.
3. Ibid.
4. Thornton and Currey, *To Save an Elephant*.
5. Raymond Bonner, "Crying Wolf Over Elephants," *The New York Times Magazine*, 7 February 1993, p. 30.
6. Thornton and Currey, *To Save an Elephant*.
7. Ibid.
8. Ibid., p. 116.
9. Bonner, "Crying Wolf Over Elephants."
10. Ibid., p. 17.
11. Philip Shabecoff, "Urgent Call From Wild to Boycott Ivory," *The New York Times*, 15 May 1988.
12. Ibid.
13. "Ivory Imports Banned to Aid Elephant," *The New York Times*, 7 June 1989, p. 15.
14. Ibid.
15. U.S. Department of the Interior, "United States Imposes Immediate Ban on Elephant Ivory Imports," news release, Washington, D.C., 6 June 1989.
16. "U.S., the E.C., and Japan Halt Ivory Imports."
17. Philip Shabecoff, "New Lobby Is Helping Wildlife of Africa," *The New York Times*, 9 June 1989, p. 14.

Chapter 6
The Poachers' Last Stand at Lausanne

1. U.S. Fish and Wildlife Service, "Retention of Threatened Status for the Continental Population of the African Elephant," *Federal Register*, 10 August 1992, p. 35484.
2. Allan Thornton and Dave Currey, *To Save an Elephant* (London: Doubleday, 1991, pp. 184–203.
Teresa Telecky, personal communication, 15 April 1994.
3. Thornton and Currey, *To Save an Elephant*, pp. 184–203.
4. Ibid., pp. 70, 195–97.
Telecky, personal communication, 15 April 1994.
5. Thornton and Currey, *To Save an Elephant*, p. 187.
6. Ibid., p. 114.
7. Ibid., pp. 164–65.
Iain & Oria Douglas-Hamilton, *Battle for the Elephants* (New York: Viking Penguin, 1992), p. 339.
8. Douglas-Hamilton, *Battle for the Elephants*, p. 338.
9. Ibid., p. 339.
10. Ibid., p. 338.
11. Ibid.
12. Ibid., p. 336.
Thornton and Currey, *To Save an Elephant*, p. 171.
Ted Gup, "Train of Shame," *Time*, 16 October 1989, p. 72.
13. Thornton and Currey, *To Save an Elephant*, p. 191.
14. Ibid., p. 173.
15. Ibid., p. 69.
Douglas-Hamilton, *Battle for the Elephants*, p. 342.
Raymond Bonner, *At the Hand of Man* (New York: Knopf, 1993), pp. 51, 101–104, 115.
16. Thornton and Currey, *To Save an Elephant*, p. 165.
Douglas-Hamilton, *Battle for the Elephants*, p. 342.
17. Thornton and Currey, *To Save an Elephant*, pp. 70–74, 173.
18. Douglas-Hamilton, *Battle for the Elephants*, p. 335.
19. Edward R. Ricciuti, "The Elephant Wars," *Wildlife Conservation*, March/April 1993, p. 18.

Richard E. Leakey, "Elephants Today and Tomorrow," *Wildlife Conservation*, March/April 1993, p. 58.

20. Douglas-Hamilton, *Battle for the Elephants*, pp. 339–342.

Thornton and Currey, *To Save an Elephant*, pp. 198–203.

Bonner, *At the Hand of Man*, p. 157.

21. Christine Stevens, personal communication, 22 April 1994.

Craig Van Note, personal communication, 27 April 1994.

22. Bonner, *At the Hand of Man*, p. 269.

23. The Associated Press, "Nations Reject U.S. Plan to Allow Tusk Imports," in *The Atlanta Constitution*, October 1989.

24. Bonner, *At the Hand of Man*, p. 270.

25. Ibid.

26. Ibid., p. 157.

Leakey, "Elephants Today and Tomorrow," p. 59.

Jane Perlez, "Ban on Ivory Trading Is Reported to Force Cutbacks at Factories," *The New York Times*, 22 May 1990.

Environmental Investigation Agency, "Elephant Poaching Down After CITES Ban," Washington, D.C., 1991.

27. Perlez, "Ban on Ivory Trading Is Reported to Force Cutbacks at Factories."

Ricciuti, "The Elephant Wars," p. 18.

28. Environmental Investigation Agency, "Elephant Poaching Down After CITES Ban."

29. Leakey, "Elephants Today and Tomorrow," p. 59.

30. Perlez, "Ban on Ivory Trading Is Reported to Force Cutbacks at Factories."

31. "Ban on Ivory Has Killed Demand in U.S., Study Finds," *The New York Times*, June 1990.

32. Ibid.

33. Thornton & Currey, *To Save an Elephant* p. 177.

Douglas-Hamilton, *Battle for the Elephants*, p. 342.

34. Leakey, "Elephants Today and Tomorrow," p. 59.

35. Perlez, "Ban on Ivory Trading Is Reported to Force Cutbacks at Factories."

36. Gary Streiker, Cable News Network, 9 March 1994.

Ronald Orenstein, "Elephants on the Edge," *The World and I*, 1992.

37. Douglas-Hamilton, *Battle for the Elephants*, p. 344.

38. Bonner, *At the Hand of Man*, p. 157.

39. Environmental Investigation Agency, "Elephant Poaching Down After CITES Ban."

40. U.S. Fish and Wildlife Service, "Retention of Threatened Status for the Continental Population of the African Elephant," pp. 35474, 35481–82, 35484.

41. Orenstein, "Elephants on the Edge."

42. Mark Owens and Delia Owens, "Saving Elephants," *HSUS News*, Spring 1994, pp. 22–27.

Chapter 7
The Move to Lift the Ivory Ban

1. Ronald M. Nowak, comments submitted to the U.S. Fish and Wildlife Service on proposed rule to revise classification of the African elephant, 10 July 1991.

2. Iaian and Oria Douglas-Hamilton, *Battle for the Elephants* (New York: Viking Penguin, 1992), pp. 344–345.

3. Department of National Parks and Wildlife Management of Zimbabwe, "Zimbabwe: At the Leading Edge of Conservation," 20 November 1993, p. 2.

4. Environmental Investigation Agency, "Elephant Poaching Down After CITES Ban," Washington, D.C., 1991.

5. "Ivory Trade Advocates Lose as Zambia Calls for Appendix I for African Elephants," *AWI Quarterly*, Winter 1992, p. 1.

6. Allan Thornton, "Bogus Elephant Claims of South Africa and Zimbabwe," *AWI Quarterly*, Fall 1991, pp. 10–11.

Department of National Parks and Wildlife Management of Zimbabwe, "Zimbabwe: At the Leading Edge of Conservation," p. 10.

Raymond Bonner, *At the Hand of Man* (New York: Knopf, 1993), p. 107.

7. Department of National Parks and Wildlife Management of Zimbabwe, "Zimbabwe: At the Leading Edge of Conservation."

Humane Society of the United States and Humane Society International, "Zimbabwe: Driving Wildlife to Extinction," Washington, D.C., 7 October 1993, p. 7.

8. Brian Child, "The Elephant as a Natural Resource," *Wildlife Conservation*, March/April 1993, pp. 60–61.

9. Reuters, "Zimbabwe to Sell Ivory Stockpile," in *The Washington Times*, 16 December 1993.

10. Environmental Investigation Agency, *Under Fire: Elephants in the Front Line*, Washington, D.C., April 1992, p. 54.

11. Raymond Bonner, "Crying Wolf Over Elephants," *The New York Times Magazine*, 7 February 1993, p. 53.

12. U.S. Fish and Wildlife Service, "Retention of Threatened Status for the Continental Population of the African Elephant," *Federal Register*, 10 August 1992, p. 35477.

13. Ibid.

14. Eugene Linden, "Blaming the Victim," *Time*, 7 June 1993.

15. Kenneth Brower, "Tusk, Tusk," *The Atlantic Monthly*, April 1993, pp. 122–127.

16. Bonner, *At the Hand of Man*, p. 278.

17. Bonner, "Crying Wolf Over Elephants," p. 36.

18. Bonner, *At the Hand of Man*, p. 286.

19. Marie Arana-Ward, "Trouble in Paradise," *Book World, The Washington Post*, 18 April 1993.

Bonner, *At the Hand of Man*, p. 44.

20. Ibid., p. 82.

Raymond Bonner, "Why No Ebony in the Ivory Ban?" *Washington Post*, 2 May 1993.

21. Bonner, *At the Hand of Man*, p. 81.

22. Bonner, "Why No Ebony in the Ivory Ban"

23. Ibid.

24. Ibid.

25. Bonner, "Crying Wolf Over Elephants," p. 30.

26. Bonner, *At the Hand of Man*, p. 286.

27. John W. Grandy, letter to the *Washington Post*, 4 May 1993.

28. Bonner, "Why No Ebony in the Ivory Ban?"

Bonner, *At the Hand of Man*, p. 157.

29. Barry Kent Mackay, "Traffic Is Out of Line," *The Toronto Star* (Canada), 25 October 1992.

30. Michael Satchell, "Wildlife's Last Chance," *U.S. News & World Report*, 15 November 1993, p. 70.

31. U.S. Fish and Wildlife Service, "Retention of Threatened Status for the Continental Population of the African Elephant," p. 35474.

32. Ibid.

33. Ibid.

34. Ibid., p. 35476.

35. Nowak, comments submitted to the U.S. Fish and Wildlife Service on proposed rule to revise classification of the African elephant.

36. Ibid.

37. Ibid.

38. Ibid.

39. Richard E. Leakey, "Elephants Today and Tomorrow," *Wildlife Conservation*, March/April 1993, p. 89.

40. Pauline Jelinek, "Renowned Paleontologist Richard Leakey Resigns," The Associated Press, Nairobi, 23 March 1994.

Donatella Lorch, "Noted Kenya Conservationist Resigning in a Political Storm," *The New York Times*, 15 January 1994.

41. Douglas-Hamilton, *Battle for the Elephants*, pp. 344–345.

Ricciuti, "The Elephant Wars," *Wildlife Conservation*, March/April 1993, p. 32.

42. Iain Douglas-Hamilton, "You Can Help Elephants," *Wildlife Conservation* March/April 1993, pp. 74–75.

43. Douglas H. Chadwick, *The Fate of the Elephant* (San Francisco: Sierra Club Books, 1992), p. 467.

44. Valerius Geist, "Wildlife Conservation as Wealth," *Nature*, 7 April 1994, p. 492.

45. Debate between Raymond Bonner and Ronald Orenstein, Morningside, CBC Radio transcript, 12 May 1993.

46. Environmental Investigation Agency, *Under Fire*, p. 8.

47. Nowak, comments submitted to the U.S. Fish and Wildlife Service on proposed rule to revise classification of the African elephant.

Chapter 8
The Debate Over Culling

1. Raymond Bonner, *At the Hand of Man*, (New York: Knopf, 1993), p. 107.

2. Iain and Oria Douglas-Hamilton, *Battle for the Elephants*, (New York: Viking Penguin, 1992), pp. 121–22.

3. The Humane Society of the United States and Humane Society International, "Zimbabwe: Driving Wildlife to Extinction," Washington, D.C., 7 October 1993.

4. Cynthia Moss, *Echo of the Elephants: the Story of an Elephant Family*, (New York: William Morrow, 1992), pp. 83, 86.

5. Bonner, *At the Hand of Man*, p. 284.

6. Douglas-Hamilton, *Battle for the Elephants*, pp. 121–22.

7. The Humane Society of the United States and Humane Society International, "Zimbabwe: Driving Wildlife to Extinction," Appendix I.

8. Edward R. Ricciuti, "The Elephant Wars," *Wildlife Conservation*, March/April 1993, p. 28.

9. Richard E. Leakey, "Elephants Today and Tomorrow," *Wildlife Conservation*, March/April 1993, p. 28, 89.

10. Ricciuti, "The Elephant Wars," p. 29.

11. Bonner, *At the Hand of Man*, p. 107.

12. *Weekly Mail*, 4–10 September 1992.

13. Leakey, "Elephants Today and Tomorrow," p. 89.

14. Allen T. Rutberg, "An Introduction to Wildlife Immuno-Contraception," Humane Society of the United States, Washington, D.C., December 1993.

15. Raymond Bonner, "Crying Wolf Over Elephants," *The New York Times Magazine*, 7 February 1993, p. 52.

16. Ian Tattersall, "The Elephant Wars," *The New York Times Book Review*, 2 May 1993.

17. Marie Arana-Ward, "Trouble in Paradise," *Book World, Washington Post*, 18 April 1993.

18. Kenneth Brower, "Tusk, Tusk," *The Atlantic Monthly*, 3 April 1993, p. 124.

19. Ricciuti, "The Elephant Wars," pp. 24, 28.

20. Bonner, *At the Hand of Man*, pp. 224–225.

21. Environmental Investigation Agency, *Under Fire: Elephants in the Front Line*, Washington, D.C., April 1992, p. 27.

22. Barry Kent Mackay, "Expose on African Ivory Ban a Shameful Distortion," *The Toronto Star*, February 1993.

23. Neil Cumberlidge, "Elephants," in *The Environmental Encyclopedia* (Chicago: Gale Research, Inc., 1994), p. 263.

24. "Don't Buy Ivory," *Focus*, Summer 1989, p. 5.

25. Eugene Linden, "Blaming the Victim," *Time*, 7 June 1993.

26. Douglas-Hamilton, *Battle for the Elephants*, pp. 118, 123.

27. Ibid.

28. John Waithaka, "The Elephant Menace," *Wildlife Conservation*, March/April 1993, pp. 62–63.

29. Ibid.

30. William Conway, "What Happens to Elephants Goes Far Beyond Elephants," *Wildlife Conservation*, March/April 1993, p. 2.

31. U.S. Fish and Wildlife Service, "Retention of Threatened Status for the Continental Population of the African Elephant," *Federal Register*, 10 August 1992, p. 35477.

32. Iain Douglas-Hamilton, "You Can

Help Elephants," *Wildlife Conservation*, March/April 1993, pp. 74–75.

33. Elizabeth Boo, *Ecotourism: The Potentials and Pitfalls*, Vol. I, (Washington, D.C.: The World Wildlife Fund, August 1992), p. 16.

34. Jonathan Gibson, *Proposal for a Southern African Wildlife Sanctuary in the Wetlands Associated With the Source of the Zambezi System*, Chobe Wildlife Trust, Kasane, Botswana.

35. Ibid.

36. Ibid.

37. Ibid.

38. Ibid.

Ronald M. Nowak, comments submitted to the U.S. Fish and Wildlife Service on proposed rule to revise classification of the African elephant, 10 July 1991.

U.S. Fish and Wildlife Service, "Retention of Threatened Status for the Continental Population of the African Elephant," p. 35479.

39. Ibid.

Ricciuti, "The Elephant Wars," pp. 26.

Environmental Investigation Agency, *Under Fire*, p. 36.

40. Ibid.

41. Ibid.

42. Ibid., p. 9.

43. Douglas-Hamilton, *Battle for the Elephants*, p. 117.

44. Ibid.

45. U.S. Fish and Wildlife Service, "Retention of Threatened Status for the Continental Population of the African Elephant," pp. 35480, 35483.

46. Simon Trevor, "Killing Elephants Won't Help Zimbabwe," "Letters," *The New York Times*, 1 August 1992.

47. Allan Thornton and Dave Currey, *To Save an Elephant*, (London: Doubleday, 1991), pp. 162, 174.

48. Environmental Investigation Agency, *Under Fire*, pp. 42–43, 46–47.

49. Thornton and Currey, *To Save an Elephant*, p. 161.

50. Nowak, comments submitted to the U.S. Fish and Wildlife Service on proposed rule to revise classification of the African elephant.

51. Ibid.

52. Environmental Investigation Agency, *Under Fire*, pp. 42–43.

53. Confidential source, personal communication, 1993.

54. Gibson, *Proposal for a Southern African Wildlife Sanctuary in the Wetlands Associated With the Source of the Zambezi System*.

Environmental Investigation Agency, *Under Fire*, pp. 42–43.

55. Thornton and Currey, *To Save an Elephant*, p. 161.

56. Environmental Investigation Agency, *Under Fire*, pp. 43–44.

57. Ibid.

58. Allan Thornton, "Bogus Elephant Claims of South Africa and Zimbabwe," *AWI Quarterly*, Fall 1991, pp. 10–11.

59. Environmental Investigation Agency, *Under Fire* pp. 44–45.

60. Patricia Adams, *Odious Debts* (London: Probe International, Earthscan, 1991), p. 21.

61. Nowak, comments submitted to the U.S. Fish and Wildlife Service on proposed rule to revise classification of the African elephant.

62. Ronald Orenstein, "Elephants on the Edge," *The World and I*, 1992.

63. Constance Mitchell Ford, "Botswana, a Diamond in the Rough," *Wall Street Journal*, 2 March 1994.

64. World Tourism Organization, *Yearbook of Tourism Statistics*, 1993.

65. "Last Sanctuary for the Elephant," *World Magazine*, February 1992.

Environmental Investigation Agency, *Under Fire*, p. 42.

66. Lewis Regenstein, personal communication, 22 April 1994.

67. Ricciuti, "The Elephant Wars," p. 16.

68. Thornton, "Bogus Elephant Claims of South Africa and Zimbabwe."

Environmental Investigation Agency, *Under Fire* p. 25.

69. Ibid.
    Ricciuti, "The Elephant Wars," p. 26.
70. Thornton and Currey, *To Save an Elephant*, p. 164.
71. Ronald M. Nowak, "African Elephant," in *Walker's Mammals of the World* (Baltimore: The Johns Hopkins University Press, 1991), p. 1284.
72. Ricciuti, "The Elephant Wars," p. 26.
73. Department of National Parks and Wildlife Management of Zimbabwe, "Zimbabwe: At the Leading Edge of Conservation," 20 November 1993, p. 2.
74. Thornton, "Bogus Elephant Claims of South Africa and Zimbabwe."
75. Ibid.
76. U.S. Fish and Wildlife Service, "Retention of Threatened Status for the Continental Population of the African Elephant," pp. 35480, 35483.
77. Thornton, "Bogus Elephant Claims of South Africa and Zimbabwe."
78. Environmental Investigation Agency, *Under Fire*, p. 21.
79. Department of National Parks and Wildlife Management of Zimbabwe, "Zimbabwe: At the Leading Edge of Conservation," p. 4.
80. Ibid.
81. The Humane Society of the United States and Humane Society International, "Zimbabwe: Driving Wildlife to Extinction," p. 6.
82. Ibid.
83. Ibid., p. 8.
84. C. Tshuma for Warden Giyayi, minutes of the management meeting held on the 13th of June 1990, at Marongora Conference Room, Department of National Parks and Wildlife Management, Marongora, Zimbabwe, as published in The Humane Society of the United States and Humane Society International, "Zimbabwe: Driving Wildlife to Extinction."
85. R.J. Ngwarai, "Meeting of Mashonaland West Heads of Station on Management Programme for Zambezi Val-
ley: 12 [sic] June 1990 at Marongora," as published in The Humane Society of the United States and Humane Society International, "Zimbabwe: Driving Wildlife to Extinction."
86. Department of National Parks and Wildlife Management of Zimbabwe, "Zimbabwe: At the Leading Edge of Conservation," p. 1.
87. Ibid.
88. Ibid., p. 8.
89. Ibid., pp. 8–9.
90. The Humane Society of the United States and Humane Society International, "Zimbabwe: Driving Wildlife to Extinction," p. 6.
91. Douglas-Hamilton, *Battle for the Elephants*, p. 122.
92. Department of National Parks and Wildlife Management of Zimbabwe, "Zimbabwe: At the Leading Edge of Conservation," p. 9.
93. The Humane Society of the United States and Humane Society International, "Zimbabwe: Driving Wildlife to Extinction," p. 5, Annexes I and III.
94. Thornton, "Bogus Elephant Claims of South Africa and Zimbabwe."
95. Department of National Parks and Wildlife Management of Zimbabwe, "Zimbabwe: At the Leading Edge of Conservation," p. 10.
    Ricciuti, "The Elephant Wars," pp. 26, 30.
96. Environmental Investigation Agency, *Under Fire*, pp. 16, 22.
97. Ibid.
    Ian Redmond and Esmond Bradley Martin, "Don't Argue—Save the Rhino," *BBC Wildlife*, November 1992.
98. Department of National Parks and Wildlife Management of Zimbabwe, "Zimbabwe: At the Leading Edge of Conservation," p. 5.
99. Ibid., pp. 6, 10.
100. Michael Satchell, "Wildlife's Last Chance," *U.S. News & World Report*, 15 November 1993, p. 75.
101. Brian Child, "The Elephant as a Natu-

ral Resource," *Wildlife Conservation,*
March/April 1993, pp. 60–61.

**Part III: How to Save the World's
Wildlife—Humane Sustainable
Development**

Chapter 9
*The World Bank: Subsidizing
Destruction as Development*

1. Hilary F. French, "The World Bank:
Now Fifty, But How Fit?" *World Watch,*
July/August 1994.
2. Ibid.
   Bruce Rich, *Mortgaging the Earth,* (Boston: Beacon Press, 1994), pp. 7–8.
3. Michael Fox, personal communication, June 1993.
4. Patricia Adams, *Odious Debts,* (London: Probe International, Earthscan,
1991), pp. 21–22.
5. Rich, *Mortgaging the Earth,* pp. 186–87.
6. Ibid., p. 310.
   John Darnton, "In Decolonized, Destitute Africa, Bankers Are the New Overlords," *The New York Times,* 20 June
1994, pp. A1, A7.
7. Kenneth N. Gilpin, "Brazil Reaches
an Agreement With Big Banks on Debt,"
The New York Times, 17 April 1994.
8. Adams, *Odious Debts,* p. 21.
9. Rich, *Mortgaging the Earth,* p. 150.
10. Ibid., pp. 150–51, 302.
11. Ibid., pp. 155–56.
12. French, "The World Bank: Now
Fifty, But How Fit?" p. 15.
13. Rich, *Mortgaging the Earth,* p. 153.
14. Ibid., pp. 155, 175.
15. Ibid., pp. 178–180.
16. April Adams, "Sustainable Use of
Wildlife and the International Development Donor Organizations," June 1994.
17. Ibid.
18. Ibid.
19. Ibid.
20. Ibid.
21. Ibid.
22. Ibid.

23. Ibid.
24. Ibid.
25. Jan Hartke, personal communication, 15 July 1994.

Chapter 10
Ecotourism: True Sustainable Use

1. Erich Hoyt, "Whale Watching
Around the World," *International Whale
Bulletin,* Summer 1992, pp. 1–8.
2. World Travel and Tourism Council,
Travel and Tourism, 1993.
   "Travel & Tourism Is Top Employer,"
Travel Weekly, 6 April 1992.
   John Naisbitt, *Global Paradox* (New
York: William Morrow, 1994), pp. 103–
104.
   Héctor Ceballos-Lascuráin, "Overview on Ecotourism Around the World:
IUCN's Ecotourism Program," IUCN
Workshop 3: Sustainable Use of Natural
Resources, IUCN General Assembly,
January 1994, p. 30.
3. Ibid.
   The Ecotourism Society, "Ecotourism
Statistical Fact Sheet," North Bennington, Vermont, 1994.
4. Ceballos-Lascuráin, "Overview on
Ecotourism Around the World."
   Yearbook of Tourism Statistics, (Madrid:
World Tourism Organization, 1992.)
5. Naisbitt, *Global Paradox.*
   World Travel and Tourism Council,
Travel and Tourism.
6. Ceballos-Lascuráin, "Overview on
Ecotourism Around the World."
   World Tourism Organization, *Yearbook of Tourism Statistics.*
7. Naisbitt, *Global Paradox,* pp. 105, 131.
8. Ibid.
9. Ibid.
   Ernest Holsendolph, "Several Findings in New Naisbitt Book," *The Atlanta
Constitution,* 15 April 1994.
10. Ceballos-Lascuráin, *Yearbook of Tourism Statistics.*
11. Ibid.
12. Ted T. Cable, "Ecotourism" in *The*

Environmental Encyclopedia (Chicago: Gale Research, Inc., 1994), p. 256.

13. Naisbitt, *Global Paradox*, p. 130.

14. Ibid., p. 140.

15. The Ecotourism Society, "Ecotourism Statistical Fact Sheet."

Philip Burgess, "Market Approach to Conservation," *Rocky Mountain News* (Denver), 11 August 1992, p. 29.

16. Ibid.

17. Ibid.

18. "Table 1, Recreation Visits . . . in the National Park System," *Statistical Abstract*, 1992, National Park Service, Washington, D.C., p. 21.

19. Naisbitt, *Global Paradox*, p. 125.

20. "Travel Advisory," *The New York Times*, 8 May 1994, Travel Section, p. 3.

21. The Ecotourism Society, "Ecotourism Statistical Fact Sheet."

22. Ibid.

23. Ibid.

24. Elizabeth Boo, *Ecotourism: The Potentials and Pitfalls*, Vol. 1 (Washington, D.C.: World Wildlife Fund, 1990), pp. 16–17.

25. Ibid.

26. U.S. Department of the Interior, "Most Americans Enjoy Wildlife-Related Recreation," news release, Washington, D.C., 14 September 1992.

27. Ibid.

28. Philip Burgess, "Market Approach to Conservation."

Michael O'Sullivan, "Seals and the Economics of Despair," *Toronto Star*, 23 May 1994.

29. Michael O'Sullivan, personal communication, May 1994.

30. The Ecotourism Society, "Ecotourism Statistical Fact Sheet."

Edward R. Ricciuti, "The Elephant Wars," *Wildlife Conservation*, March/April 1993, p. 33.

Iain Douglas-Hamilton, "You Can Help Elephants," *Wildlife Conservation*, March/April 1993, p. 75.

31. Boo, *Ecotourism: The Potentials and Pitfalls*, Vol. 1, p. 16.

32. Ibid.

33. Edward Ricciuti, "The Elephant Wars," p. 34.

34. Boo, *Ecotourism: The Potentials and Pitfalls*, Vol. 1, p. xiv.

Philip Burgess, "Market Approach to Conservation."

35. Erich Hoyt, "Whale Watching Around the World."

36. Ibid.

37. Ibid.

38. Ibid.

39. Ibid.

40. The Wilderness Society, "Recreation Contributes More to Southern Appalachian Economy Than Timber'" plus "Fact Sheets," Washington, D.C., 25 May 1994.

41. Boo, *Ecotourism: The Potentials and Pitfalls*, Vol. 1, pp. xi, xviii.

42. Ibid., Volume 2, pp. 2–3.

43. World Tourism Organization, *Yearbook of Tourism Statistics*, 1993.

44. Boo, *Ecotourism: The Potentials and Pitfalls*, Vol. 1, pp. xvi–xvii.

The Ecotourism Society, "Ecotourism Statistical Fact Sheet."

45. Sue Hubbell, "In Search of Blue Butterflies," *The Sophisticated Traveler, The New York Times Magazine*, Part II, 15 May 1994.

46. Elizabeth Boo, *Ecotourism: The Potentials and Pitfalls*, Vol. 2, pp. 53, 56, 58–59, 62–63.

47. Ceballos-Lascuráin, "Overview on Ecotourism Around the World," p. 32.

48. Ibid.

49. Boo, *Ecotourism: The Potentials and Pitfalls*, Vol. 1, p. xvi; Vol. 2, pp. 77, 83.

50. World Tourism Organization, *Yearbook of Tourism Statistics*.

51. The Ecotourism Society, "Ecotourism Statistical Fact Sheet."

Naisbitt, *Global Paradox*, p. 128.

52. Ceballos-Lascuráin, "Overview on Ecotourism Around the World," p. 32.

53. Elizabeth Boo, , *Ecotourism: The Potentials and Pitfalls*, Vol. 2, pp. 107–108, 110, 112, 115.

54. World Tourism Organization, *Yearbook of Tourism Statistics*.

55. D. Matthews, "Mountain Monarchs," *Wildlife Conservation*, September/October 1992, pp. 27–29.

David Favre, "Debate Within the CITES Community," *Natural Resources Journal*, Fall 1993, p. 914.

56. John Naisbitt, *Global Paradox*, p. 132.

57. Brochures and material from Earthwatch, Watertown, Massachusetts, 1993.

Lewis Regenstein, "Earthwatch," in *The Environmental Encyclopedia* (Chicago: Gale Research, Inc., 1994), pp. 242–243.

58. Ibid.

59. Raymond Bonner, *At the Hand of Man*, (New York: Knopf, 1993), p. 244.

60. Barbara Sleeper, "How to Watch Wildlife", and "Ecotourism: Charting New Paths," *Animals*, March/April 1992.

61. Raymond Bonner, "A Conservationist Argument for Hunting," *Wall Street Journal*, 14 May 1993.

62. Ceballos-Lascuráin, *Overview on Ecotourism Around the World*, pp. 29–31.

63. Michael Ray Taylor, "Go, but Go Softly," *Wildlife Conservation*, March/April 1994, pp. 15–16.

64. Ibid., pp. 17–19.

65. Ted T. Cable, "Ecotourism."

Chapter 11
Appreciating Animals for Their Own Intrinsic Value

1. Ann Cottrell Free, ed., *Animals, Nature, and Albert Schweitzer*, (Washington, D.C.: Flying Fox Press, 1988).

2. Jan Hartke, Washington, D.C., personal communication, 6 July 1994.

3. Conger Beasley, Jr., "Live and Let Die," *Buzzworm*, July/August 1992, p. 53.

4. A. Richard Mordi, *Attitudes Toward Wildlife in Botswana*, (New York: Garland Publishing, 1991).

5. Ibid.

6. Ibid.

7. Lewis Regenstein, *Replenish the Earth: The Teachings of the World's Religions on Protecting Animals and Nature*, (New York: Crossroad, 1991), pp. 19–44.

8. Ibid., pp. 221–260.

9. Ibid., pp. 243–244.

Chatsumarn Kabilsingh, "How Buddhism Can Help Protect Nature," *Tree of Life: Buddhism and Protection of Nature* (Buddhist Perception of Nature, Hong Kong, 1987), p. 7.

10. Ibid.

11. Ibid.

12. Lewis Regenstein, *Replenish the Earth*, pp. 229–32.

13. Ibid., p. 102.

"This Earth Is Sacred," *Environmental Action Magazine*, 11 November 1972, p. 7.

14. "The World Scientists' Warning to Humanity," 18 November 1992; as cited in Lewis G. Regenstein, *Cleaning Up America the Poisoned*, (Washington, D.C.: Acropolis Books, 1993), p. 12.

15. Ibid.

16. Edward O. Wilson, "Is Humanity Suicidal?" *The New York Times Magazine*, 30 May 1993.

17. Paul G. Irwin, Foreword to Lewis G. Regenstein, *Cleaning Up America the Poisoned*, pp. 7–8.

18. Wilson, "Is Humanity Suicidal?"

Walter H. Corson, ed., *The Global Ecology Handbook*, The Global Tomorrow Coalition (Boston: Beacon Press, 1990).

Council on Environmental Quality, *The Global Environment and Basic Human Needs*, Washington, D.C., 1978.

19. Ecclesiastes 3:19.

Index

Active management. *See* Culling.
Adams, April, 192
Adams, Patricia, 165, 185, 187
Africa South, 99
African Development Bank, 184
African Elephant and Rhino Specialists Group, 112
African Elephant Working Group, 117, 120, 168
African Wildlife Foundation (AWF), 93, 112, 113, 135, 136
African Wildlife Leadership Foundation. *See* African Wildlife Foundation.
Air Afrique, 41
Alexander, Caroline, 76
Alexander the Great, 40
Ali, Brigadier Mohamed Abdul Rahim Al Ali, 76
"Amazonia Without Myths," 190
Amboseli National Park, 133, 151, 155, 158, 200, 211
American Association of Zoological Parks and Aquariums. *See* American Museum of Natural History.
American Federation of Aviculture, 43

American Hunters' Educational and Legal Protection Fund, 91
American Ivory Importers Association, 91
American Ornithologists' Union, 46
American Zoo and Aquarium Association, 91
Anchovy, Peruvian, 62
Andrus, Cecil, 92
Angola, elephant poaching in, 105–106
Animal Protection Institute of America, 110
Animal Welfare Institute, 42, 46, 53, 110, 115, 116
Arana-Ward, Marie, 154, 155
Asian Development Bank, 184
At the Hand of Man: Peril and Hope for Africa's Wildlife (Bonner), 122, 133–134, 135–138
Atlantic Monthly, 134, 155
AWF. *See* African Wildlife Foundation.

Babbitt, Bruce, 42
Baker, James, 52
Baker, James A., 121

Battle for the Elephants (Douglas-Hamilton), 91, 151–152
BBC. *See* British Broadcasting Company.
Bears, wildlife farming of, 37
Beasley, Conger, Jr., 20, 217
Beilenson, Anthony, 91, 111
Beissinger, Steven R., 44
Belize, ecotourism in, 205
Bernay, Jaques, 139
Bible, ecological teachings in, 219–220
Big Cypress National Preserve, 67
Biodiversity. *See* Diversity, biological.
BioScience, 44
Bonner, Raymond, 71, 75, 122, 132 133–138, 146, 151, 154, 155, 211
Botha, R.F. "Pik," 107
Botswana, elephants in, 162, 163–167
Bradley-Martin, Esmond, 124
Breeding. *See* Farming, wildlife.
Breytenbach, Jan, 105, 106
British Broadcasting Company (BBC), 20
Brower, Kenneth, 134, 155
Brown, Ron, 65
Brundtland, Gro Harlem, 25, 53
Brundtland Commission. *See* World Commission on Environment and Development.
Bucher, Enrique H., 44
Buddhism, environmental theology of, 219, 220–221
Buffalo, population studies of, 79
Burundi, ivory trade in, 107, 123
Bush, George, 110, 113, 121

Cable, Ted T., 213
Cabot, John, 58
Cameroon, ivory trade in, 123

CAMPFIRE, 130, 177
"Captain Who Knew Too Much, The," 103
"Caring for the Earth: A Strategy for Sustainable Living," 7, 14, 25, 26–27, 28–29
Carson, Rachel, 132
Carter, Jimmy, 90
Ceballos-Lascuráin, Héctor, 207, 212
Central African Republic, ivory trade in, 123
Central Intelligence Organization (Zimbabwe), 104
Chadwick, Douglas, 68–69, 145
Cherny, Ernst, 54
Child, Brian, 130, 177
China
    ivory trade in, 123
    trade violations of, 36
    wildlife farming in, 37
Chisango, Shepard, 104
Chobe bushbuck, population studies of, 80
Chobe National Park, 78, 158
Chobe Wildlife Trust, 158, 159, 164
Christianity, environmental theology of, 219
CITES. *See* Convention on International Trade in Endangered Species of Wild Fauna and Flora.
Clark, Colin, 32
Clinton, Bill, 36, 53, 57, 73
Cobb, Steve, 117
Cockatoo, Moluccan. *See* Parrots.
Commission on Development and Environment for Amazonia, 190
Congo, ivory trade in, 123
Congo Wildlands Protection and Management Program, 188

Congressional Sportsmen's Caucus, 72
Conrad, Joseph, 100
Conservation Biology, 7, 28, 62
Convention on International Trade in Endangered Species of Wild Fauna and Flora (CITES), 1, 11, 14, 18, 19, 20, 21, 22, 23, 27, 35, 36, 37, 40, 41, 42, 43, 46, 58, 70, 71, 86, 107, 109, 113, 115–118, 118–120, 120–121, 130, 131, 136, 137, 139, 140, 172, 190, 227
Costa Rica, ecotourism in, 206–207
Cropping. *See* Culling.
Cry of the Kalahari (Owens), 166
"Crying Wolf Over Elephants: How the International Wildlife Community Got Stampeded Into Banning Ivory" (Bonner), 132, 133, 134
Culling, 149–177
Cusick, Steve, 62

Dalai Lama, 220
Daly, Herman E., 25
Dane, Charles W., 140
Day, Michael, 37
DeBeers Consolidated Mines of South Africa, 166
Defenders of Wildlife (DOW), 42, 43
Department of National Parks and Wildlife Management (DNPWM) (Zimbabwe), 101, 169, 170, 171, 173, 174
Department of Wildlife and National Parks (DWNP) (Botswana), 164, 165, 175, 176
Diversity, biological, 26–29
DNPWM. *See* Department of

National Parks and Wildlife Management.
Dominica, ecotourism in, 207
Douglas-Hamilton, Iain, 89, 91, 118, 119, 124, 125, 145, 157, 161, 174
Douglas-Hamilton, Oria, 89, 129, 149
DOW. *See* Defenders of Wildlife.
DWNP. *See* Department of Wildlife and National Parks.

EarthKind International, 193, 216
Earthwatch, 209–210
Ecclesiastes, 181, 225
Echo of the Elephants (Moss), 151
Eco-imperialism. *See* Imperialism, ecological.
Economics and Biodiversity (McNeely), 191
Ecotourism, 195–225
Ecotourism Society, 208
Ecotourism: The Potentials and Pitfalls, 204–205
Ecuador, ecotourism in, 207–208
Egan, Timothy, 57, 61
EIA. *See* Environmental Investigation Agency.
"Elephant Management in Zimbabwe," 156
Elephant Protection Act, 109, 111, 112
Elephants
  culling of, 160–161
  the environment and, 155–158
  ivory trade's threat to, 96–106
  overcrowding and overcounting of, 162–163
  poaching of, 105–106
  population of, in individual countries. See under individual countries.

preservation of, 134
U.S. role in saving, 89–94
Encephalopathy, spongiform,
    38
Endangered species, 19–23.
Endangered Species Act. *See* U.S.
    Endangered Species Act.
Endangered Wildlife Trust, 91
Environmental Investigation
    Agency (EIA), 42, 46, 99, 101,
    111, 115, 116, 125, 131, 162

Farming, wildlife, 37
Fate of the Elephant, The (Chad-
    wick), 68, 145
Federal Register, 92, 95, 141
Fields, Jack, 72, 122
Fish Forever, 60
Fisheries, ocean, destruction of,
    56–65
Fishermen's Protective Act, 36
Forests, national, 203–204
Forkan, Patricia, 55, 56
Fossey, Dian, 200
Fox, Michael, Dr., 185
Frelimo, 99
French, Hilary F., 183
Friedman, Thomas L., 33
Friends of Animals, 115
Fund for Amimals, 90
FAO. *See* United Nations Food
    and Agriculture Organiza-
    tion.

Gabon Conservation of Biodiver-
    sity through Effective
    Management of Wildlife
    Project, 189
Galapagos Islands, 207, 208
GEF. *See* Global Environment
    Facility.
Geist, Valerius, 34–35, 38, 146
General Motors, 51

Gibson, Jonathan, 158
Global Environmental Facility
    (GEF), 188, 189
Global Paradox (Naisbitt), 196
Gonarezhou National Park, 101,
    103, 170
Gore, Al, 17, 53, 54
Gorillas in the Mist (Fossey), 200
Grandy, John, Dr., 33, 138
Great Smoky Mountains Na-
    tional Park, 203
"Great Wildlife Massacre, The,"
    100
Greenpeace, 115
"Greenwashing," 16

Hall-Martin, Anthony, 137
Harriman, Constance, 115, 122
Hartke, Jan, 193, 216
Harvard University, 73
Heart of Darkness (Conrad), 100
Henry, Wesley, 200
Herbst, Robert, 92
Hilborn, Ray, 29, 63
Hilgard, E. W., 29
Hinduism, environmental theol-
    ogy of, 219, 220–221
Holdgate, Martin, Dr., 18, 116
Hong Kong, ivory trade in, 107–
    108, 114, 123
House Subcommittee on Environ-
    mental and Natural Resources,
    70
Hoyt, Erich, 195, 202
HSI. *See* Humane Society Interna-
    tional.
HSUS. *See* Humane Society of
    the United States, The.
Hubbell, Sue, 206
Human Rights Caucus, 188
Humane Society International
    (HSI), 150, 171, 172
Humane Society of the United

States, The (HSUS), 10, 36, 42, 43, 51, 109, 114, 115, 150, 153, 170–173, 184, 223, 228
Humane Society, The (Canada), 200
Hunting, safari. *See* Hunting, sport.
Hunting, sport, 65–66
  affect on evolution, 68
  in Africa, 66, 73–81
  in America, 66,–67, 72–73
  in Canada, 72–73
  promotion of, 69–72
Hunting, tourist. *See* Hunting, sport.
Hurt, Robin, 125
Huxley, Chris, 137
Hwange National Park, 98, 101, 162, 168
Hyenas, population studies of, 79

ICCAT. *See* International Commission for the Conservation of Atlantic Tunas.
IMF. *See* International Monetary Fund.
Imperialism, ecological, 137–138
Inter-American Development Bank, 184
Interior Department. *See* U.S. Department of the Interior.
International Commission for the Conservation of Atlantic Tunas (ICCAT), 59
International Fund for Animal Welfare, 115
International Monetary Fund (IMF), 165, 183, 184, 186
International Whale Bulletin, 195, 202
International Union for the Conservation of Nature and Natural Resources (IUCN), 14, 15, 18, 19, 24, 27, 35, 93, 139, 146
International Whaling Commission (IWC), 2, 16, 50, 52
International Wildlife Coalition, 22, 110, 146
Irwin, Paul G., 10, 223
"Is Humanity Suicidal? We're Flirting with the Extinction of Our Species" (Wilson), 223
Islam, environmental theology of, 219, 220–221
IUCN. *See* International Union for the Conservation of Nature and Natural Resources; World Conservation Union.
IUCN/SSC Specialist Group on Sustainable Use of Wild Species, 19
Ivory trade
  AFW's opposition to, 112–113
  collapse of, 123
  controversy over banning, 90–94
  results of ban on, 124–127
  results of resumption of, 144–147
  threat to elephants from, 96–106
  WWF's opposition to, 110–112
  See also under individual countries.
Ivory Trade Review Group, 117, 135, 169
IWC. *See* International Whaling Commission.

Jainism, environmental theology of, 221
Jankowsky, Joel, 54
Janson, Charles H., 47
Japan
  illegal whaling practices of, 51
  ivory trade in, 107, 114, 123, 131
jinbu, 37

Johannesburg Sunday Times, 106
Johannesburg Weekly Mail, 105
Jordan, Vernon, 54
Joubert, Beverly, 78
Joubert, Dereck, 39, 78, 79–81, 163
Judaism, environmental theology of, 219

Kabilsingh, Chatsumarn, Dr., 220
Kalahari Conservation Society, 164
Kalt, Joseph P., 73
Kansas State University, 214
Keller, Bill, 74
Kenya
    culling of elephants in, 153
    elephant poaching in, 97, 125
    elephant population in, 133
    ivory trade in, 123
Kenya Wildlife Service (KWS), 97, 113, 120, 145, 152, 155, 200
Kenyatta, Jomo, 97
Kiss, Agnes, 191
Kruger National Park, 104
KWS. *See* Kenya Wildlife Service.

Lapointe, Eugene, 116, 119
Larkin, P., 63
Lategan, Pieter, 105
Lausanne (Switzerland), CITES meeting in, 115–118, 133
Leakey, Louis, 120
Leakey, Richard, 97, 120, 123, 124, 125, 145, 152, 153, 168
Lechwe, population studies of, 80
Lieberman, Susan, Dr., 114
Limits of Growth, The, 24
Linden, Eugene, 157
Lindsay, Keith, Dr., 164
Lions, population studies of, 79–80
Linyanti Concessions, 78
"Living with Wildlife: Wildlife

Resources Management with Local Participation" (Kiss), 191
Loliondo Game Controlled Area, 76
Luangwa National Park, 147, 160
Luangwa Valley, 97
Ludwig, Donald, 29, 63
Lukman, John, 105

Macaw, Spix's. *See* Parrots.
MacKay, Barry Kent, 156
McMeekin, Diana, 113
McNeely, Jeffery, 191
Mad cow disease. *See* Encephalopathy, spongiform.
Madagascar Trade in Biodiversity for Environmental Management, 191
Malawi, elephant poaching in, 106
Mana Pools National Parks, 101
Management, intensive, 14. *See also* Sustainable use.
Management, sustainable natural resources, 14. *See also* Sustainable use.
Mandela, Nelson, 105
Manu National Park and Biosphere Reserve, 47
Marine Mammal Protection Act, 52–53, 72, 73
Marlenee, Ron, 70
Martin, Rowan, 116, 137, 168
Maximum sustainable yield (MSY), 16, 63. *See also* Sustainable use.
Megatrends (Naisbitt), 196
Meiring, Marius, 105
"Memorandum of Conservation," 53
Mexico, ecotourism in, 208–209
Milani, Kathy, 170

Mitchell, George J., 65
Mlay, Costa, 117, 136
Mobuto Sese Seko, 100
Mohammed, 220
Moi, Daniel arap, 120
Monitor Consortium, 115
Montana Fish and Game Department, 68
Mordi, Richard, Dr., 217
Moremi Wildlife Reserve, 78
Morrill, William J., Dr., 71–72
Mortgaging the Earth (Rich), 187–188
Morton, Peter, 204
Moss, Cynthia, 149, 151, 153, 155
Mozambique, elephant poaching in, 99–100
MSY. *See* Maximum sustainable yield.
Mumba, Norbert, 146, 147
Munn, Charles A., Dr., 39, 46
Murerwa, Herbert, 131

Naisbitt, John, 196, 197
Namibia, elephant poaching in, 106
National Audubon Society, 59, 62, 213
National Geographic, 68
National Marine Fisheries Service (NMFS), 31, 56, 58
National Rifle Association, 91
National Wildlife Federation, 91
Nature, 34, 54
New African, 120
New York Times, The, 14, 57, 61, 73, 74, 112, 123, 124, 161, 198
New York Times Book Review,The 154
New York Times Magazine, The, 132, 223

New York Zoological Society. *See* Wildlife Conservation Society.
New Yorker, The, 132
Ngina, Mama, 97
Ngwarai, R.J., 173
Nkonga, Caleb, 98
Nleya, Edwin, 103
NMFS. *See* National Marine Fisheries Service.
Norway, illegal whaling practices of, 51, 53
Nowak, Ronald, Dr., 50, 85, 92, 93, 96, 129, 141, 142, 143, 144, 147

Odious Debts (Adams), 185–186
"$100,000 to Kill a Doddering Rhino? Africa Thinks About Making Wildlife Pay for its Survival" (Keller), 74–75
Orenstein, Ronald Dr., 22, 146
O'Sullivan, Michael, 199
"Our Common Future" (Brundtland Commission), 25
Overfishing. *See* Fisheries, ocean, destruction of.
Owens, Delia, 126, 166
Owens, Mark, 126, 166
Oxfam, 186

Pacelle, Wayne, 73
Parakeet, gray-cheeked. *See* Parrots.
Parker, Ian, 119, 120, 137
Parrots, history of sustainable use of, 40–48
Pelly Amendment. *See* Fisherman's Protective Act.
Pet Industry Joint Advisory Council (PIJAC), 42
PIJAC. *See* Pet Industry Joint Advisory Council.

Pilanesburg National Park,
    173
Poaching, elephant, 124–127
Polar bears, trophy hunting of,
    72–73
Pong, A.H., 105, 108
Poole, Joyce, 152, 155
President's Council on Environ-
    mental Quality, 90
"Principles for Living Resource
    Conservation" (Talbot), 31–33,
    63, 64–65
"Principles of Effective Manage-
    ment" (Hilborn, Ludwig,
    Waters), 30–33
Proposed Southern African Wild-
    life Sanctuary (PSAWS), 158,
    159
PSAWS. *See* Proposed Southern
    African Wildlife Sanctuary.

Quayle, Dan, 70

Rand Company, 108
Raufoss A/S, 51
Reeve, Ros, Dr., 162
Regenstein, Lewis, 93, 167
Reilly, William, 109
Religions, Eastern, environ-
    mental theology of, 220–221
Religions, indigenous, environ-
    mental theology of, 222
Renamo, 99, 100, 103, 104
Revised Management Procedure
    (RMP). *See* Revised Manage-
    ment Scheme.
Revised Management Scheme
    (RMS), 52, 53
Rhinos. *See* Rhinoceroses.
Rhinoceroses
    poaching of, 104–105
    sport hunting of, 35–37, 70–71,
    73–76

Rich, Bruce, 187, 189
Robinson, John G., 7, 28, 62
Roman Empire, 96
Ruzizi II Regional Hydroelectric
    Project, 187

SACIM. *See* Southern African
    Centre for Ivory Marketing.
SADF. *See* South African Defence
    Forces.
Safari Club International (SCI),
    69, 70, 71, 72, 91
Safari Journal, 71
Sardine, Pacific, 62
Savimbi, Jonas, 105
Savuti Channel, 79
Schaefer, Dick, 60
Schindler, Paul, 113
Schreiner, Keith, 92
Schweitzer, Albert, 215
SCI. *See* Safari Club International.
Science, 29, 63
Scott, Peter, 160, 161
Searle, Warden, 173
Selengut, Stanley, 213
Serageldin, Ismail, 193
Serengeti National Park, 76
Shepherd, David, 91
Silent Spring (Carson), 132
Sleeper, Barbara, 211
Society for Animal Protective
    Legislation, 110
Somalia
    elephant poaching in, 125
    ivory trade in, 123
South Africa, elephant and rhino
    poaching in, 104–105
South African Defence Forces
    (SADF), 100, 105, 106
South Atlantic Fishery Manage-
    ment Council, 60
South Korea, trade violations of,
    36

Southern African Centre for Ivory Marketing, (SACIM), 130, 131
Stevens, Christine, 53, 122
Stevens, William K., 14
Stewart, Ian, 52
Strauss, Robert, 54
Suleiman, Ali, 124
Sunday Correspondent, The, 102, 103
Sustainable development, 14. *See also* Sustainable use.
Sustainable economy, 14. *See also* Sustainable use.
Sustainable growth, 14. *See also* Sustainable use.
Sustainable living, 14. *See also* Sustainable use.
Sustainable society, 14. *See also* Sustainable use.
Sustainable use, 1–3, 7–11, 19–23, 26–29
  case studies of, 39–81
  commercial trade and, 33–37
  conservation debate over, 11–13
  consumptive, 9
  difficulties involved in practicing, 30–33
  distrusting claims of, 29–30
  as a euphemism for killing, 13–16
  fallacy of, 16–17
  of forests, 31
  history of, 23–26
  non-consumptive, 9
  urban preservationists and, 17–19
Sustainable Use Committee. *See* IUCN/SSC Specialist Group on Sustainable Use of Wild Species.
Sustainable utilization, 14. *See also* Sustainable use.

Sustained yield, 14. *See also* Sustainable use.
Taiwan, trade violations of, 36
Talbot, Lee M., Dr., 31, 63
Tanzania, elephant poaching in, 125
Tattersall, Ian, 154
Telecky, Teresa, Dr., 15, 36
Thammasat University (Bangkok), 220
Theology, environmental, 219
Thornton, Allan, 77, 111, 120, 165
Tiger Trust, 37
Tigers
  farming of, 37
  hunting of, 37
Time, 134, 157
To Save an Elephant (Thornton and Currey), 77, 116, 120
Topkov, Izgrev, 21
Toronto Star, The, 156
Tourism, 196–197
TRADEM. *See* Madagascar Trade in Biodiversity for Environmental Management, 191
TRAFFIC, 15, 59, 116, 124, 139
Trevor, Simon, 161
Tsavo National Park, 125

Uganda, elephant poaching in, 125
Umfolozi Game Reserve, 104
UNEP. *See* United Nations Environment Programme.
"Under Fire: Elephants in the Front Line," 99, 101
Unita, 104, 105, 106
United Nations Conference on the Human Environment, 24
United Nations Environment Programme (UNEP), 17, 24, 188, 189
United Nations Food and Agri-

culture Organization (FAO), 53

United States, ivory trade in, 113–114, 121–122, 123, 140–141

University of British Columbia, 29

University of Calgary, 34

University of Cordoba (Argentina), 44

University of Washington, 29

"Urgent Call from Wild to Boycott Ivory," 112

U.S. Agency for International Development, 191, 204

U.S. Department of Commerce, 53

U.S. Department of State, 31

U.S. Department of the Interior, 35, 49, 67, 70, 71, 90, 92, 93, 94, 96, 99, 100, 109, 110, 115, 122, 126, 140, 141, 142, 147, 199

U.S. Endangered Species Act, 1, 70, 90, 93, 141–144, 227

U.S. Export-Import Bank, 184

U.S. Fish and Wildlife Service, 31, 43, 50, 70, 85, 96, 105, 132, 133, 141, 199

"U.S. Fishing Fleet Traveling Coastal Water Without Fish" (Egan), 57

U.S. Forest Service, 204

U.S. House of Representatives, 53

U.S. Marine Mammal Commission, 7

U.S. Marine Mammal Protection Act, 1, 55

U.S. News & World Report, 9, 12

U.S. Senate, 53

U.S. Wild Bird Conservation Act, 43

USAID. *See* U.S. Agency for International Development.

"Using Wildlife Sustainably" (Holdgate), 18–19

Van Note, Craig, 122

Virgin Islands National Park, 198

Wagener, Ludwig, 105

Wall Street Journal, 57, 71, 211

Walters, Carl, 29, 63

Washington Post, The, 136, 138, 154

WCI. *See* Wildlife Conservation International

WCS. *See* Wildlife Conservation Society.

Webster, David, 105

West African Community Conservation and Wildlife Utilization Project, 189

Western, David, Dr., 112, 200

Whale and Dolphin Conservation Society, 202

Whales, history of sustainable use of, 48–56

Whale-watching, 201–203

Whaling, illegal, 51, 53

Wildlife Conservation International (WCI), 39, 46, 47

Wildlife Conservation Society (WCS), 7, 62, 112, 113

Wildlife Watch, 78

Wills, David, 108, 170, 172

Wilson, Edward O., 223

Wise use, 14. *See also* Sustainable use.

World Bank, 11, 25, 165, 183–193

World Commission on Environment and Development, 25

"World Conservation Strategy, The," 24

World Conservation Union (IUCN), 14, 91, 116, 136, 197

World Magazine, 167

"World Scientists' Warning to Humanity," 222

World Travel and Tourism Council (WTTC), 196

World Watch magazine, 183

World Wide Fund for Nature, 111. *See also* World Wildlife Fund.

World Wildlife Fund (WWF), 15, 24, 93, 109, 110–112, 113, 115, 116, 124, 135, 136, 139, 156, 161, 204

Wright, Michael, 161

WTTC. *See* World Travel and Tourism Council.

Yablokov, Alexey V., 54

Yale University, 44

Yellowstone National Park, 197

Yosemite National Park, 197

Young, Don, 72

Zaire
 elephant poaching in, 100
 ivory trade in, 123

Zambia, elephant poaching in, 97–99, 125, 126, 127

Zambian Species Protection Department, 146

Zebra, population studies of, 79

Zimbabwe
 culling of elephants in, 150, 152, 153
 elephant poaching in, 101–104
 elephant population in, 162–163, 167–170
 position on lifting ivory ban, 129–131
 role at CITES meeting in Lausanne, 116–118

"Zimbabwe: At the Leading Edge of Conservation," 173

"Zimbabwe: Driving Wildlife to Extinction," 171

"Zimbabwe Kills Elephants to Help Save Lives," 101

Zimbabwe National Army (ZNA), 101–102

Zimbabwe Wildlife Department, 116

ZNA. *See* Zimbabwe National Army.